Refounding Environmental Ethics

Refounding Environmental Ethics

Pragmatism, Principle, and Practice

Ben A. Minteer

TEMPLE UNIVERSITY PRESS
Philadelphia

TEMPLE UNIVERSITY PRESS
Philadelphia, Pennsylvania 19122
www.temple.edu/tempress

Published 2012

Library of Congress Cataloging-in-Publication Data

Minteer, Ben A., 1969–
Refounding environmental ethics : pragmatism, principle, and practice / Ben A. Minteer.
p. cm.
Includes bibliographical references (p.) and index.
ISBN 978-1-4399-0083-3 (cloth : alk. paper)
ISBN 978-1-4399-0084-0 (pbk. : alk. paper)
1. Environmental ethics. 2. Environmental responsibility. 3. Pragmatism. 4. Environmentalism—Philosophy. I. Title.

GE42.M56 2012
179'.1—dc23 2011016211

⊗ The paper used in this publication meets the requirements of the American National Standard for Information Sciences—Permanence of Paper for Printed Library Materials, ANSI Z39.48-1992

Printed in the United States of America

2 4 6 8 9 7 5 3 1

Contents

Acknowledgments

The seeds of many of the arguments that appear in the following pages were planted some years ago when I was a graduate student in what is now the Rubenstein School of Environment and Natural Resources (RSENR) at the University of Vermont (UVM). While they should not be held responsible for any of the book's weaknesses, and I am sure they do not agree with everything I say here, my mentors and good friends at UVM, Bob Manning (RSENR) and Bob Pepperman Taylor (Political Science), should be credited with helping shape whatever good ideas have made it into these chapters. At UVM, I also want to thank Don Loeb (Philosophy), who introduced me to analytic moral philosophy. Although a lot of what I write in the following pages may be read as a deep criticism of that tradition, I hope he can at least appreciate the spirit of the project—and the pragmatic purpose of the critique.

Within the field of environmental philosophy, I have learned much from the work of Bryan Norton and have especially enjoyed our conversations and occasional collaborations over the years. Among other things, I hope that this book makes a small contribution to the development, which he has long championed, of a more policy- and management-relevant environmental ethics. I also want to thank a number of other environmental philosophers for sharing their insights and their various degrees of engagement along the way, including Paul Thompson, Andrew Light, Dale Jamieson, Bob Frodeman, Clark Wolf, Dane Scott, Kelly Parker, and Gary Comstock. Outside environmental philosophy, I have benefited greatly from many discussions with a number of excellent and generous policy and management scholars, including Barry Bozeman, Steve Cohen, Jan Dizard, and Dan Sarewitz.

One of the advantages of having pursued a more interdisciplinary path in environmental ethics has been the opportunity to work with many individuals and groups in the natural sciences who share my interest in the ethical dimensions of ecology and conservation. I especially want to thank my colleague and collaborator James P. Collins, whose work with me on the "ecological ethics" approach has been particularly rewarding (Jim is the co-author of Chapter 8). Likewise, I have learned much from my collaboration in recent years with forest ecologists Aaron Ellison and Kristina Stinson (Harvard Forest) on developing an applied environmental ethics program for training field ecology students and from my work with an Australian ecological research team organized by Kirsten Parris and Michael (Mick) McCarthy focused on exploring ethical trade-offs in ecological research design. Similarly, my involvement in the National Science Foundation–funded Managed Relocation Working Group, led by Jason McLaughlin, Dov Sax, Jessica Hellmann, and Mark Schwartz, has informed much of my thinking about conservation ethics and policy under global change, which is the subject of Chapter 9. The growing number of natural scientists interested in incorporating ethical concepts and arguments in their teaching and research is certainly a bright spot for applied environmental ethics and gives me hope that a more pragmatic and experimental approach to the field will lead to significant connections with the wider ecological research and conservation-management communities.

Within my home institution, I want to thank Jane Maienschein, faculty leader of the Human Dimensions group in the School of Life Sciences (SoLS) at Arizona State University (ASU) and director of the Center for Biology and Society, for her leadership and strong support of me and my work during my time at ASU. Steve Pyne and Andrew Smith, SoLS colleagues and friends, have been the source of countless valuable discussions about the intersection of the applied humanities and the life sciences; they and the rest of my Human Dimensions colleagues have helped make the SoLS a great place to research and to teach environmental ethics and policy, as have my excellent undergraduate and graduate students.

Finally, Vanessa Verri has provided steady encouragement and advice on the manuscript at various stages, for which I am most grateful. Mick Gusinde-Duffy at Temple University Press has been a strong proponent of this project from the start, and I sincerely appreciate his support, guidance, and patience.

In closing, I would like to remember James W. Wessman, a mentor in another (partial) academic life and an old friend, who recently left us all too soon. Although I do not think he ever fully forgave me for becoming an environmental ethicist rather than an anthropologist, this book, like all of my writing, bears his imprint. James meant a great deal to many people, including me, and he will be deeply missed.

This book draws from several essays that I have published previously, although the material has been significantly revised and updated (and, in many cases, rebuilt and expanded) from the original publications. Chapter 2 draws from my essay "Deweyan Democracy and Environmental Ethics," in *Democracy and the Claims of Nature: Critical Perspectives for a New Century*, edited by Ben A. Minteer and Bob Pepperman Taylor (Lanham, MD: Rowman and Littlefield, 2002), 33–48. Chapter 3 incorporates an updated and expanded version of "Environmental

Philosophy and the Public Interest: A Pragmatic Reconciliation," *Environmental Values* 14 (2005): 37–60. Chapter 4 revises and builds upon "Intrinsic Value for Pragmatists?" *Environmental Ethics* 23 (2001): 57–75. A shorter and different version of Chapter 5 appeared as "Pragmatism, Piety, and Environmental Ethics," *Worldviews: Global Religions, Culture, and Ecology* 12 (2008): 179–196. Chapter 6 borrows from and updates two essays: "Beyond Considerability: A Deweyan View of the Animal Rights/Environmental Ethics Debate," in *Animal Pragmatism,* edited by Andrew Light and Erin McKenna (Bloomington: Indiana University Press, 2004), 97–118, and "From Environmental to Ecological Ethics: Toward a Practical Ethics for Ecologists and Conservationists," *Science and Engineering Ethics* 14 (2008): 483–501. Chapter 7 incorporates and expands parts of "Pragmatism in Environmental Ethics: Democracy, Pluralism, and the Management of Nature," *Environmental Ethics* 21 (1999): 193–209, and "Environmental Ethics beyond Principle? The Case for a Pragmatic Contextualism," *Journal of Agricultural and Environmental Ethics* 17 (2004): 131–156. Finally, Chapter 8 combines a revised version of "Ecological Ethics: Building a New Tool Kit for Ecologists and Biodiversity Managers," *Conservation Biology* 19 (2005): 1803–1812, with sections of "From Environmental to Ecological Ethics."

I thank the publishers for permission to use this material here and the many anonymous referees for their helpful comments and criticisms of earlier versions of the original papers.

The work I describe in Chapter 8 was supported in part by National Science Foundation (NSF) grant #0527937 (Social Dimensions of Engineering, Science, and Technology) and NSF Integrated Research Challenges in Environmental Biology grant #DEB 0213851 to James P. Collins and twenty-two collaborators.

Refounding Environmental Ethics

1
Foundations Old and New

The Problems of (Environmental) Philosophers

On many, if not most, academic measures, the field of environmental ethics can be considered a great success. Today, courses in environmental ethics and philosophy are offered in the majority of college and university curricula; in many places, these are taught outside philosophy departments (e.g., in environmental studies programs; schools of public policy, forestry, and natural resources; and, in my own case, the life sciences). The field has produced a large and interesting literature, including major textbook anthologies, monographs, and a growing fleet of academic journals. Professional societies have been established, and dozens of national and international meetings focusing on environmental ethics issues and themes have been held. In sum, the field has, in only a few short decades, carved out its own intellectual identity and become a fixture in the applied philosophical landscape, taking its place alongside its bioethics, business ethics, and engineering ethics counterparts.

Judged on more pragmatic criteria, however, the field does not score nearly as high. In fact, a candid appraisal of environmental ethics based solely on its public policy and management impact would likely conclude that it was something of a failure. If this seems an unfair standard for evaluating an academic discipline, especially a branch of philosophy (which often measures itself by its ability to transcend the affairs of daily life), we should remember that a major part of the justification of the field when it formed in the 1970s was to provide a focused philosophical response to society's environmental problems. Species extinction and the loss of wildlands, air and water pollution, overpopulation and resource scarcity, global climate change, and the decline of ecosystem services: These problems have evoked and continue to generate serious ethical concerns and obligations, from our responsibilities to nonhuman species and ecosystems, to our character as local (and global) ecological citizens, to our duties and obligations to achieve a fair distribution of environmental benefits and burdens for present and future generations. Yet it would be difficult to mount a convincing argument that environmental ethics discourse has made a significant contribution to tackling these societal challenges or that it has played an important role in the environmental policy process or conservation planning and practice more generally.

On the contrary, the field seems to have become increasingly irrelevant to addressing the major environmental problems facing society as we move deeper into the twenty-first century. Instead of (for example) becoming a productive ally in the work of shaping, critiquing, and justifying sound environmental policy agendas or clarifying key debates and normative standards in public discussions over alternative management actions, environmental ethics has largely chosen to turn inward, becoming an increasingly specialized and insular academic discourse. Although it may be a discourse of great intellectual and professional value to philosophers and other environmental theorists, it has proven to be of comparatively little value—and to have little tangible impact—in the "real world."

This certainly seems to be the view of those who have worked in and studied the environmental policy and management domain. Donald A. Brown, an authoritative voice on the subject, with decades-long experience in the policy trenches at the state, federal, and international levels, has observed that the work of environmental ethicists "is almost never read by policy makers and infrequently considered in day-to-day decision making about pressing environmental issues" (Brown 2009, 215). Brown's view is not an unusual one. Public administration specialist Susan Buck (1997) has similarly concluded that environmental administrators and agency personnel typically have very little use for the philosophical proclivities of environmental ethicists. In Buck's experience, this attitude is largely due to the institutional culture and politics of agency decision making, especially the role of administrative discretion: "Discussions of environmental philosophy and ethics have little impact on the routine discretionary choices of government bureaucrats charged with administering environmental programs. . . . Public administrators take an oath to uphold the Constitution, not *Walden,* however much they may approve of the sentiments in the latter" (Buck 1997, 8–9).

In addition to these personal accounts, persuasive empirical evidence supports the judgment that philosophical environmental ethics has failed to break out of the confines of academic life and become a key player—or even an active participant—in the public realm. Legal scholar Christopher Stone conducted a revealing study of congressional and judicial databases in which he electronically scoured the record for explicit mention of environmental ethical concepts and authors. Stone's results were discouraging, at least for philosophers hoping to shape legal and policy tools for environmental protection. An extensive survey of these databases revealed only "sparse allusion to environmental ethicists and their literature" (Stone 2003, 15). Although Stone's study may be criticized for its narrow framing of what counts as an environmental ethical concept (see, e.g., Norton

2003), his analysis is nevertheless an illuminating investigation into the relative inability of the field to enter into the deliberations of Congress and the courts.

What explains this failure of influence and impact? Why has environmental ethics, unlike biomedical ethics (for example), been unable to escape the groves of academe and find its way into key policy, law, and management debates—the very discussions the founders of the field hoped (and still seek) to influence? I argue in this book that a number of reasons explain why this has happened, including the tendency for environmental philosophers to press ideological moral programs that do not comport with traditional (aka "anthropocentric") human values and motivations shaping public policy and management. These same programs, moreover, do not articulate well with many of the established intellectual and methodological commitments within mainstream normative ethics, political theory, and the experimental social sciences. This creates further tensions between the field and the scholarly discourses that have historically been important to the justification of environmental public policy and management. Indeed, the dogmatic nature and disciplinary purity of much environmental ethical theorizing frequently renders it an oppositional force in public policy and management discussions, a style of argument that too often tries to confront and commandeer environmental decision making rather than clarify and enrich it. In my view, this produces a philosophical posture that fails to reflect (and often attempts to constrain) the diversity of interests and values at stake in particular environmental dilemmas. It is a move that I would argue ultimately prevents philosophers from making significant contributions to integrative and intelligent policy and problem solutions.

I believe that a critical choice needs to be made here, one that will do much to determine the public impact of environmental ethics in the coming decades. The field can remain a closed discussion among philosophers and environmental theorists, insulated from the empirical details and demands of policy and practice and theoretically and methodologically walled off from the other disciplines key to understanding and managing the human-nature relationship. Or it can choose a different path, one more appropriate to a pragmatic, collaborative, and inclusive style of practical philosophy that attempts to make good on the field's original promise: to help us make sense of our environmental values and choices as moral agents and democratic citizens within a mixed (i.e., human and natural) community.

Refounding Environmental Ethics is my argument for taking this other path—that is, for choosing policy pragmatism over philosophical purity, democracy over dogma, and impact over ideology. The book makes a case for a major reorganization of environmental ethics as a branch of applied philosophy—in particular the reconstruction of its normative structure and methodological orientation—and a fundamental rethinking of the field's wider political and policy ambitions. Specifically, in the chapters that follow, I try to sketch an image of a more problem-focused, more experimental (and less ideological), more integrative and interdisciplinary environmental ethics. This vision reflects my conviction that a philosophically sound and policy-relevant environmental ethics will necessarily be a pluralistic, naturalistic, and collaborative environmental ethics.

The "refounding" of environmental ethics I advocate in these pages is heavily shaped by my reading of a critical set of philosophical and methodological commitments in American pragmatic philosophy and democratic thought. In some cases, it is a direct derivation, employing the tools and arguments of this tradition to critique dominant tendencies in the field that I suggest are holding environmental ethics back from achieving its full potential as a policy-relevant, practical philosophy of human-environment relationships. In other places, it is a more general attempt to reconstruct environmental ethics to make it more compatible with other disciplines and frameworks key to understanding and resolving environmental problems, most notably the social and life sciences.

Writing in 1917, John Dewey, a founding figure in American pragmatism (and whose work informs many of the arguments and proposals in this book), articulated a revisionist view of the philosophical project that provides a touchstone for this more pragmatic understanding of environmental ethics. "Philosophy recovers itself," he suggested, "when it ceases to be a device for dealing with the problems of philosophers and becomes a method, cultivated by philosophers, for dealing with the problems of men" (Dewey 1917, 46). For present purposes, I would like to revise and adapt Dewey's conclusion to the following: "*Environmental* philosophy recovers itself when it ceases to be a device for dealing with the problems of philosophers, and becomes a method, cultivated by philosophers *and others*, for dealing with the *environmental* problems of *society*" [emphasis added]. I describe, defend, and illustrate exactly what I mean by this modified Deweyan ideal in the chapters that follow.

Before we go any further, however, a quick sketch of the development of academic environmental ethics is necessary, because it will provide a fuller account of how we arrived at the crossroads I mention above. I also hope it will make clearer the challenges confronting any attempt to refound environmental ethics as a pragmatic field of inquiry.

The Origins of Environmental Ethics in the 1970s

Although it is fairly common today to hear talk of our having ethical obligations to conserve wild species, restore degraded ecosystems, combat global climate change, and so forth, explicitly moral rhetoric regarding the land and its nonhuman inhabitants was quite unusual until the later decades of the twentieth century. Writing in 1949, conservationist-philosopher Aldo Leopold, who would eventually become the most significant historical figure in the development of academic environmental ethics, observed that "there is as yet no ethic dealing with man's relation to land and to the animals and plants which grow upon it. . . . The land-relation is still strictly economic, entailing privileges but not obligations" (Leopold 1949, 203). Accordingly, Leopold proposed a new "land ethic" that he suggested should serve as a normative standard for evaluating good from bad land use (and ethical behavior toward nonhuman nature more generally). His words are by now quite familiar to environmental philosophers and conservationists: "A thing is right," he concluded, "when it tends to preserve the integrity, stability, and beauty of the biotic community. It is wrong when it tends otherwise" (224). Decades later, Leopold's ethical dictum continues to challenge and inspire environmental ethicists as well as land-use planners, foresters, conservation scientists, and others seeking to apply and defend his fundamental ethical breakthrough to the landscape (e.g., Callicott 1989; Beatley 1994; List 2000; Knight and Riedel 2002; Freyfogle 2003; Norton 2005).

Leopold's land ethic (and his other writing collected in his well-known book, *A Sand County Almanac*) would cast a long shadow over the development of academic environmental ethics when it emerged in the early 1970s. Yet the field was ultimately the product of a fairly complex public and scholarly environment, which may be described as the convergence of "external" social, political, and cultural forces and more academic trends within the discipline of philosophy during this time. The rise of the U.S. environmental movement in the 1960s was the popular stimulus for the development of an applied ethics focused on environmental problems, the attempt to bring the analytical resources of moral philosophy to the "ecological crisis" (e.g., White 1967). As mentioned above, the indicators of environmental decline (then as now) were many and evident across a range of media: air and water pollution, endangered species and the loss of wilderness, resource shortages and human overpopulation.

The popularization of the science of ecology during this same time was another contributing factor, providing the descriptive foundations upon which many philosophers would attempt to build a comprehensive worldview and value system that accounted for the integrity and richness of natural processes and biological entities. From the publication of Rachel Carson's *Silent Spring* in 1962—often considered to be the literary fountainhead of American environmentalism—to the work of Paul Ehrlich (1968) and Barry Commoner (1971), which warned the nation (if not the world) of the ecological and social dangers of human overconsumption, overpopulation, and rapid technological development, the ecological conception of human-environment relations would directly feed into environmental ethics (albeit in often wildly disparate ways), shaping ethicists' understanding of human impacts on biological populations, species, and ecosystems.

Internal developments in academic philosophy also provided the context for the birth of environmental ethics in the 1970s, particularly the revival of interest in social and political philosophy signified by the appearance of such works as John Rawls's *A Theory of Justice* (1971) and Robert Nozick's *Anarchy, State, and Utopia* (1974). The founding of the journal *Philosophy and Public Affairs* in the early 1970s as an outlet for a more socially and politically engaged mode of philosophical writing was another indication that philosophers were becoming increasingly concerned with examining challenging and controversial societal issues, such as poverty, warfare, and abortion. Environmental ethics was therefore part of the larger applied ethics movement that arose in this period, which also included (among other domains) biomedical ethics, engineering ethics, and business ethics. Perhaps the most influential philosopher working in this new applied and publicly engaged mode was Peter Singer, whose work (again, then as now) provided a critical ethical assessment of a wide range of social practices, including the treatment of animals, famine relief, and euthanasia (e.g., Singer 1975, 1979).

The origins of environmental ethics thus reflect societal and academic trends in the 1960s and 1970s that found philosophers seeking to respond to environmental decline as part of a more engaged style of moral philosophy. Since its beginnings, the field has evolved primarily as a nonanthropocentric moral discourse—that is, as a series of normative arguments for preserving wilderness, wildlife, natural communities, and so on for their own sake rather than any contribution they might make to human welfare or well-being. As part of this project, nonanthropocentric philosophers also were determined to highlight and ultimately dismantle the "arrogant humanism" of modern attitudes toward the natural world (i.e., anthropocentrism). Picking up on the antianthropocentric theme sounded by historian Lynn White, Jr., in his widely discussed essay published in 1967 in the magazine *Science*, early papers by Richard Routley (1973), Holmes Rolston (1975), and Kenneth Goodpaster (1978) set the stage for much of the field's subsequent development along nonanthropocentric lines, whereas work by legal scholar Stone made a parallel case for the rights of natural entities (Stone 1972). The nature-centered worldview and ethical system would be advanced in a steady stream of book-length arguments published in the following decades by Paul Taylor (1986), Rolston (1986, 1988, 1994), Laura Westra (1994), Eric Katz (1997), and J. Baird Callicott (1989, 1999a), among many others.

Although important differences existed among these approaches, such as whether a nonanthropocentric ethic should target individual organisms (biocentrism) or ecological communities (ecocentrism), whether intrinsic value in nature was viewed as being independent of (or dependent upon) human consciousness and valuation, and so on, they were generally united in the view, alluded to above, that environmental problems were the consequence of a flawed anthropocentric ontology and ethics. These philosophical failures, nonanthropocentric theorists argued, needed to be corrected by the adoption of a value framework able to account for the intrinsic value or inherent worth of nature within a biologically or ecologically defined metaphysical system. One of the more significant conclusions that the nonanthropocentrists drew was that many of the resources of the Western philosophical tradition, hobbled by an exclusivist concern with the "interests" or "moral considerability" of human beings, was incapable of motivating and justifying pro-environmental attitudes and practices, at least in their conventional humanist forms.

Not everyone shared this view during the field's formative period, however. For example, philosophers John Passmore (1974) and Bryan Norton (1984) argued that a nature-centered moral philosophy was not necessary to support conservation policies and environmental protection. Passmore argued that sufficient moral resources were already present in established humanistic philosophical traditions, while Norton's version of "weak anthropocentrism" made a critical distinction between exploitative readings of anthropocentrism and more enlightened, idealistic formulations of "human-centeredness" that could effectively guide pro-environmental policies and practices (I discuss this in more detail in Chapters

4 and 5). These dissenting humanist arguments in the field were largely made in isolation until the mid-1990s, which saw the development of what would become known as "environmental pragmatism," following the title of an influential anthology of papers edited by Andrew Light and Katz (1996). Although this general designation masked a fair amount of philosophical diversity, it captured an important familial relationship linking the work of more practice-oriented and pluralistic approaches in environmental ethics that represented a significant departure from the field's prevailing nonanthropocentrism.

The Pragmatic Turn

Indeed, the new environmental pragmatists (among whom Norton was the most prominent) would soon become identified by a number of methodological and theoretical attributes that distinguished their work from that of the biocentric and ecocentric writers in the field. Perhaps the most notable was the adoption of a general empirical temperament toward environmental values and principles. Many of the pragmatists in environmental ethics would devote their energy in the early years of the movement to making a variety of arguments for paying more attention to using philosophical tools to make more significant and useful contributions to the realms of public policy and problem solving (e.g., Norton 1991; Light and Katz 1996). In doing so, they were following in the tradition of American pragmatist philosophy, a school originally associated with the writing and thought of such late-nineteenth- and early-twentieth-century philosophers as Charles Sanders Peirce (1839–1914), William James (1842–1910), and Dewey (1859–1952). Although I elaborate many of the significant themes of pragmatism and its implications for environmental ethics throughout this book, I would like to briefly highlight some of the tradition's key features and commitments here, with some additional explication in the next section, where I outline the book in more detail.

For starters, it is helpful to make a basic semantic distinction relevant to understanding what it means to refer to a philosophical approach as "pragmatic," especially given that "pragmatism" is one of those crossover terms that has currency in popular speech and in philosophical discourse. In its everyday, nontechnical usage, being pragmatic typically implies that one is focused more on achieving results rather than conforming to higher principles or doctrinal purity. In its least flattering articulation, pragmatism becomes synonymous with political expediency, a semantic shading that suggests a sharp division between pragmatism and ethical integrity. Although aspects of the popular meaning of pragmatism do parallel its philosophical expression, the latter is much more sophisticated (epistemologically and ethically) than the commonsense usage might lead one to believe.

Historically, the pragmatist tradition in philosophy may be traced back to the "Metaphysical Club," a short-lived philosophical discussion group that met in Cambridge, Massachusetts, in the early 1870s (Menand 2001). Its members included first-generation pragmatist philosophers, such as Peirce and James, who sought to reconstruct philosophical concepts and methods to comport with a

Darwinian and post-Cartesian worldview (which entailed the rejection of fixed essences and a priori truths). The classical pragmatist tradition would reach its peak with the work of Dewey in the early decades of the twentieth century. Dewey's "instrumentalist" version of pragmatism is especially known for its attempt to make philosophical analysis relevant to pressing ethical, social, and political questions. His project was the most politically and socially engaged of the classical pragmatists; as a result, and as I argue in various ways in the ensuing chapters, Dewey's reconstruction of the traditional philosophical methods and categories is especially valuable for a pragmatic refounding of environmental ethics.

Pragmatism's influence in academic philosophy waned greatly by the 1940s, when it became overshadowed by the rise of logical positivism and logical empiricism, which were much more concerned than pragmatism with the formal study of logic, language, and semantics. The eclipse of pragmatism in academic philosophy was not total during this period, however, as quasi-pragmatist ideas were kept alive in the work of such philosophers as W.V.O. Quine and Rudolf Carnap, who are sometimes considered "analytic pragmatists." Pragmatism would eventually experience a significant resurgence in philosophy beginning in the 1970s, a rebirth largely attributable to the work of what came to be called "neopragmatist" philosophers, such as Richard Bernstein, Cornel West, Hilary Putnam, Jurgen Habermas, and especially Richard Rorty.

The philosophical heterogeneity of American pragmatism (past and present) makes it challenging to offer accurate generalizations about the tradition as a whole, especially those regarding the familial linkages between the prominent neo- and classical pragmatists. Some contemporary neopragmatists, for example, reject much of the epistemological and metaphysical trappings of historical pragmatism; Rorty's postmodernist makeover of Deweyan pragmatism is notorious for attempting to jettison any trace of Dewey's strong commitment to science and the logic of experimental inquiry (I have more to say about this in the next chapter). To make matters even more taxonomically complicated, pragmatism has captured the imagination of a diverse assortment of scholars outside philosophy, including those within cultural theory, law, history, politics, religion, and economics (see, e.g., Brint and Weaver 1991; Gunn 1992; Feffer 1993; Festenstein 1997; Hamner 2002; Posner 2003; Bromley 2006).

In its philosophical mode, pragmatism evokes a loosely connected set of theories about truth, meaning, inquiry, and value. The "pragmatic maxim" first stated by Peirce—the idea that a belief regarding an idea or object is properly fixed by inquiry into its practical consequences—provides a basic logical entrée to pragmatist philosophy, although we can identify a few related commitments and concepts that begin to flesh out the tradition in more detail.

One of the defining philosophical moves within pragmatism is the rejection of foundationalism—that is, the denial by pragmatists of the idea (shared by traditional rationalists and empiricists) that knowledge and belief must be grounded in a class of certain, fixed, and basic beliefs that themselves require no justification (i.e., they are self-evident or self-justifying in some manner). In questioning the existence of such foundational truths, such pragmatists as Dewey thus rejected traditional philosophy's "quest for certainty" and embraced a more experimental and fallibilistic view of knowledge in which all beliefs—even those we have good reason to hold based upon previous experience—are open to criticism, revision, and replacement (Kloppenberg 1998, 85). As I describe in more detail in the next chapter, the foundationalist impulse has significant implications not only for epistemology but also for wider arguments in moral and political philosophy. The search for fixed and immutable beliefs or standards for ethical and political life, for example, conflicts with an explicitly pragmatic and contextual approach to ethical judgment and democratic politics; unlike foundationalist approaches, the latter rest upon the contingent beliefs and practices of particular communities rather than universalist and absolutist claims to certainty and moral purity (Festenstein 1997, 4).

The rejection of foundational anchoring for knowledge, however, did not entail the wholesale surrender to skepticism for the pragmatists; as philosopher Putnam has suggested, the notion that one could be a fallibilist and an antiskeptic is perhaps the most novel epistemological insight of pragmatism (Putnam 1994, 152). Instead, the pragmatist embrace of fallibilism leads necessarily to a pluralistic rather than a singular or reductionistic view of belief, value, and the good. Given that individuals and communities are differently situated and are shaped to a significant degree by dissimilar traditions and experiences, as well as the fact that novel ethical situations and empirical problem contexts are always emerging (and with them, new tests for previously held beliefs and values), pragmatists view adherence to any single belief, moral principle, or rule in the face of such complexity and change as unacceptably dogmatic and ill-advised. The pragmatist commitment to pluralism, in turn, reinforces the embrace of fallibilism: As Bernstein (1989) points out, the adoption of a pluralistic ethos requires taking seriously the condition of contingency and human fallibility, for no matter how committed we are to our own beliefs and values, we must be willing to listen to others with different ideas, demonstrating the virtues of open-mindedness and tolerance for opposing views that are among the most significant features of pragmatism as an anti-ideological and experimental philosophical system.

Classical pragmatists did not ignore the incommensurability and even open conflict among disparate values, however; indeed, it was well understood by Dewey, whose hopes for a more naturalistic and scientific approach to value formation and ethical judgment may be read as an attempt to cope with the inescapable challenge of having to choose among competing goods, beliefs, and courses of social action. In Dewey's work, this led to a method of humanistic inquiry modeled after the workings of the scientific community—that is, the view that we should turn to the "laboratory" of lived human experience to determine what is in fact good and right for any given community attempting to solve its own particularized dilemmas and problematic situations. Indeed, Dewey and Peirce believed that working in concert, a diverse association of experimental "inquirers" (which could include experts, citizens, or, ideally, both) was better positioned to identify relevant facts and to construct problem solutions—and to root out factual error and distorting forces—than were individuals operating by themselves, constrained by their idiosyncratic perspectives and biases. For Peirce, who sought to develop pragmatism as a scientific metaphysics, truth would eventually emerge from the ideal workings of organized experimental inquiry over the long run (Haack 2004). For Dewey, truth and good would emerge from a similar yet less formalized process of discussion, debate, and persuasion within a community of inquirers, a method of "social intelligence" that was supported by and in turn secured a democratic social order (Westbrook 2005).

Antifoundationalism, fallibilism, pluralism, experimentalism, empiricism: These are a few core features of philosophical pragmatism (to this list, we could also add further commitments, including the moral and linguistic emphasis on community; e.g., Bernstein 1989, Campbell 1992). But returning to environmental ethics, we can now see just how pragmatist environmental philosophers at the end of the twentieth century would begin to develop a number of themes found in the work of the classical pragmatists, including the embrace of value pluralism, humanism, and a strong methodological naturalism that found pragmatically minded ethicists seeking empirical resolution for many of the philosophical and ethical questions facing environmental philosophers, professionals, and activists (e.g., Norton 1991; Light and Katz 1996; Minteer 1998; Minteer and Manning 2000). In doing so, environmental pragmatists were thus launching a fundamental challenge to the dominant philosophical project in environmental ethics—that is, monistic nonanthropocentrism. In particular, pragmatists criticized nonanthropocentrists' rejection of humanistic value systems and justifications for environmental policies and practices as being metaphysically and epistemologically flawed—and a move that would likely undercut the desire of citizens and decision makers to support a sufficiently strong environmental policy agenda (e.g., Norton 1992, 1996; Light 2000). Instead, environmental pragmatists saw the broad instrumentalism, experimentalism, pluralism, and, above all, practical temperament of the tradition of Peirce, James, and Dewey as offering a more compelling philosophical backdrop to nature conservation and environmental protection, even for those who drew upon the tradition more for methodological inspiration than for substantive philosophical content (e.g., Light 2002, 2004).

Not surprisingly, the reception of environmental pragmatism among most nonanthropocentric philosophers in the field has been chilly at best (e.g., Katz 1997, 2009; Rolston 1998, 2009; Callicott 1999b, 2002a; Westra 2009). Even though environmental pragmatists subscribe to a more pluralistic and far less environmentally aggressive form of humanism than the "strong anthropocentric" attitude characteristic of mainstream economics and certain strands of traditional ethical theory, many still see the pragmatists' rejection of strong nonanthropocentric theories of intrinsic value as a kind of philosophical revolt, a direct challenge to what it means to be doing environmental ethics in the first place. Nevertheless, most environmental pragmatists argue that the "nature-centered" ethic of the nonanthropocentrists—which many take to be the field's unique contribution to applied ethics—is philosophically unpersuasive and that, regardless, it is a politically ineffective and ultimately unnecessary position. A liberal, pluralistic environmentalism in which the normative focus is shifted to the full array of human values provided by nature can, pragmatists suggest, effectively explain and justify sound environmental practices and policy choices, including the transition to a more sustainable society (e.g., Norton 1991; Norton and Minteer 2002; Norton 2005).

Despite the gloomy appraisals of the legal and policy influence of the field discussed above, some philosophers, such as Callicott (2002a), have long maintained that theoretical environmental ethics—which typically means investigations into and defenses of the intrinsic value of nature—is nevertheless having a significant impact in the public realm, transforming the discourse of environmental value among activists and environmental professionals in much the way the language of human rights changed the legal and political culture of the West. For example, Callicott (2009) has recently argued that an analysis of judicial decisions in the wake of the passage of the Endangered Species Act of 1973 provides powerful evidence in support of the view that nonanthropocentric ideas are increasingly significant in the protection of listed species, a view that the pragmatist Norton (2009) has disputed. Although the debate between nonanthropocentrists and pragmatists over the empirical evidence for philosophical impact will likely continue, it is worth mentioning that even those observers with very little at stake in the debate over value theory in the field—and no particular loyalty to the pragmatist position—have noted that the field has not had much of an impact in the public realm, certainly not as much as many environmental philosophers had hoped (e.g., Frodeman 2006).

Accordingly, in *Refounding Environmental Ethics,* I argue that the field needs to focus on improving its methods of inquiry and becoming more open to a public mode of ethical and policy deliberation, one strongly supportive of environmental value pluralism and an experimental and contextual approach to ethical reasoning (of the latter, more is said in Chapters 4 and 7). Unlike most nonanthropocentric philosophers, I do not think that additional forays into moral ontology (i.e., what things in the world "count" or have moral status in ethical deliberations) will do much to settle what have become intractable disputes over value theory in environmental ethics, nor would a theoretical consensus on this score (highly unlikely as it is) make the field more useful and relevant to policy makers and administrators. This does not mean, however, that the pragmatic alternative rejects theory building in environmental ethics; the approach I advocate in the chapters that follow requires working through some of the more critical philosophical and political questions bearing on the relationship between moral principles, democratic values, and the methods of moral inquiry, deliberation, and public judgment. The argument for paying more attention to the pragmatics of policy and practice in environmental ethics is therefore *not* "anti-philosophy" as Callicott has claimed (e.g., 1999a, 30–32). But it is true that the model I encourage is critical of the arid theorizing and parochial character of traditional environmental ethics and that it supports calls for a considerably more applied empirical and integrative approach to normative debates and projects in the field.

Another way to put this is that, rather than seeing environmental policy and management problems as a failure of moral *principle*—that is, the result of the failure to adopt the single, correct moral attitude toward threatened species, wilderness, or the biosphere—the model of environmental ethics I outline and illustrate in this book views environmental problems as primarily a failure of moral *intelligence*. That is, I suggest that environmental problems, from the vantage point of environmental ethics, should be understood as the result of the collective failure to adopt experimental methods and a tolerant and inclusive view of the range of human and environmental values over the long run. When such values are properly examined, critiqued, and integrated via debate, discussion, and deliberation, ethical judgment in conservation decision making and environmental management and policy contexts becomes more normatively robust—and therefore more durable.

Toward Refounding

In the chapters that follow, I argue for the reformation of environmental ethics on several fronts, from the philosophical to the methodological and political. This agenda includes (1) a call for the field to move away from stalled foundational value debates and increasingly vexed questions of moral considerability; (2) a set of arguments about the need to adopt a less ideological, more democratic stance toward alternative environmental values and ethical decision making; (3) a plea to take more seriously public environmental opinion and attitudes toward nature in environmental policy and management proposals; (4) a philosophical, political, and empirical defense of pluralism, particularism, and contextualism in environmental value theory; and (5) a focused ethical reconsideration of environmental practice and policy, including ecological research, natural resource management, and nature conservation under global change. Although each chapter examines a specific question in either the theory or application of environmental ethics to conservation action or to environmental policy and management dilemmas, together they can be read as an exploration and defense of those pragmatist themes I believe are key elements in the attempts to refound environmental ethics as a more inclusive, experimental, and effective form of normative discourse in public environmental affairs.

Chapters 2 and 3 develop an aspect of the political tradition within American pragmatism, arguing that much nonanthropocentric environmentalism has been too skeptical of democratic values and processes, especially as these bear upon the traditional appeal to foundational moral principles in environmental decision making. Chapter 2 provides a justification for democratic life that rests on an epistemological move in pragmatism, most clearly articulated in Dewey's work, that views democratic social conditions as a precondition for experimental inquiry and intelligent problem solving. It is an argument that I believe should be seriously considered by environmental philosophers seeking to influence public policy and to contribute to the resolution of environmental policy and management debates. In Chapter 3, I elaborate this position by homing in on the "public interest" as a normative standard for political judgment and policy action, appeals to which are common to the philosophy of public administration and American pragmatist thought. In particular, I uncover a deliberative strain of public interest theory in Dewey's democratic writing that I suggest can help environmental ethics reconnect to a core concept in conventional political, policy, and administrative discourse and in the process become an important force in shaping this expression around environmental values as critical dimensions of the public interest in specific policy discussions.

Chapters 4 and 5 turn more toward value theory, including procedural and substantive arguments for rethinking and revising the historical emphasis on nonanthropocentric theories of value in environmental ethics. In Chapter 4, I argue that, contrary to the conventional wisdom, pragmatists in environmental ethics are not precluded from embracing certain kinds of intrinsic value arguments in particular situations, a claim that I illustrate by examining the guarded receptivity to intrinsic value by Norton (often thought to be one of the most strident critics of this concept in the field). Moreover, I suggest that pragmatic appropriations of intrinsic value can prove quite useful and effective in certain environmental policy and management contexts. I close the chapter with a discussion of the use of intrinsic value theory in international conservation arguments, including a detailed rejoinder to Rolston's example of the plight of biodiversity conservation and development in Nepal's Chitwan National Park. In Chapter 5, I attempt to recover an underappreciated aspect of the pragmatist tradition—Dewey's religious thought—in an effort to enrich the normative discourse of environmental pragmatism. Specifically, I argue for the value of Dewey's understanding of "natural piety" for shaping a more idealist understanding of pragmatic instrumentalism that captures many of the ethical intuitions of the nonanthropocentrists without requiring a metaphysical commitment to the intrinsic value of nature.

One of the recurring themes in *Refounding Environmental Ethics* is the need to reconceive environmental ethics as a dynamic and adaptive process of problem solving, a procedural model of ethical inquiry that sees the field operating more in the mode of a deliberative political argument, or, as I argue in several places, as a form of dispute resolution. In this vein, Chapter 6 examines a central normative debate in environmental ethics: the conflict between holistic environmental ethics and individualistic animal welfare and rights approaches. I argue in this chapter that, although discussions of moral considerability in environmental ethics have served an important purpose (i.e., they have turned our attention to the question of "what counts" in nature), they have unfortunately produced intellectual stalemates, as environmental holists and animal individualists dig further into long-entrenched positions. I advocate a move away from repeated claims of moral considerability toward a process of coordinated dispute resolution and consensus building in particular problem contexts.

The next two chapters attempt to advance several pragmatist tenets in environmental ethics, including the commitment to value pluralism and contextualism as well as the need to pursue a more practical agenda in the field. Together, these two chapters also make a case for greater interdisciplinarity in environmental ethics in terms of methodology and application. In Chapter 7, I employ theoretical argument and empirical data to make the case for a pluralistic, naturalistic, and contextual reading of environmental ethical inquiry and judgment. I turn to the ethical thought of Dewey to defend the rejection of moral monism in environmental ethics (the reduction of a complex field of environmental values to a single worldview and small set of moral principles) and to justify the incorporation of social scientific/empirical methods of inquiry into ethical analysis. The chapter includes the results of public opinion surveys I have conducted on New Englanders' environmental ethical commitments and their attitudes toward natural resource management (specifically, public lands and wildlife), and demonstrates the value of taking a methodologically naturalistic approach to core environmental philosophical topics.

Chapter 8 continues the theme of interdisciplinarity and pragmatic engagement by bringing the tools of environmental ethics to the dilemmas and problems that emerge within the life sciences and biodiversity management. This chapter, written with ecologist James P. Collins, argues for a new practical extension of environmental ethics to the ecological research and conservation management community. Ecological research and biodiversity management often raise unique ethical questions in areas that include responsibilities and duties to the scientific community, public welfare, research animals, species, and ecosystems. Answering these ethical questions is challenging, because ecologists and biodiversity managers do not have the equivalent of bioethics, an established field with a support network for biomedical researchers and clinicians, to guide them in making decisions. Traditional environmental ethics provides some insight into environmental values and the duties these may impose on humans. But for the most part, those in the field do not take into consideration many of the common responsibilities and obligations ecologists and managers have to the scientific profession or to public welfare. This chapter presents a series of cases to illustrate the kinds of ethical questions faced by ecological researchers and biodiversity managers in practice. Collins and I argue for the creation of an extensive case database and a pluralistic and integrated ethical framework, one that draws pragmatically from the theoretical (normative), research, animal, and environmental ethics traditions.

The book's final chapter takes stock of several changes currently taking place—and anticipated in the coming decades—in conservation policy as a result of global environmental change. There, I suggest that we are moving toward a new paradigm of nature conservation, one in which older ideals and norms of preservation, wildness, native species, and so on are becoming eclipsed by more relativistic and dynamic standards and concepts. The emerging legal and policy regime under global change in turn demands a more interventionist and anticipatory conservation philosophy. I argue that traditional preservationist arguments for saving species and wildlands, and the anti-interventionist nonanthropocentric principles that frequently support them, will become increasingly untenable in novel environments that bear little resemblance to the historical systems of the past. The challenge for a pragmatic environmental ethics within this new model of conservation action and policy is to guide acceptable environmental change in an increasingly dynamic ecological order while also providing sufficient moral restraint on the destructive human modification of nature. It is a formidable challenge, to be sure, but I believe it is one that the field must meet head on if it is to play a meaningful role in nature conservation under global change in the twenty-first century.

To wrap up this Introduction, I want to be clear about what this book is and what it is not. Although I cover many of the major traditions and debates in contemporary environmental ethics and engage the work of many important philosophers in the field, such as Rolston, Callicott, Norton, and others, *Refounding Environmental Ethics* is not intended as a general introduction to the subject, nor does it attempt a systematic overview of the field's theoretical development and applications. Many fine books undertake this important project, including a growing list of anthologies designed for classroom use (some of the better collections are Light and Rolston 2002, VanDeVeer and Pierce 2002, and Pojman and Pojman 2007). Recent synthetic accounts of environmental philosophy by John O'Neill, Alan Holland, and Light (2008) and Dale Jamieson (2008) are also good places to turn for a more comprehensive treatment of the field.

What this book offers instead is a critique of mainstream environmental ethics and a defense of my own pragmatist alternative, one that seeks to integrate environmental ethical theory, democratic thought, and the empirical demands of environmental practice in an effort to widen the field's appeal and influence. Although I include ample discussion of theory in environmental ethics, especially in the early chapters, I have tried to expand the theoretical conversation beyond narrow environmental value theory to include arguments in classical and neopragmatism, democratic theory, and the philosophy of public administration, among other traditions. The book should therefore pair well with the standard anthologies or monographs, serving as a pragmatic counterpoint to the field's traditional nonanthropocentric—and more "principle-driven"—approaches to environmental ethics.

I have also sought to illustrate my brief for a pragmatic environmental ethics with numerous case discussions, from the management of invasive species and the impacts of ecological research, to park-people conflicts and public-lands management, to species conservation under climate change. I hope that these and other cases and issues presented in the book work to clarify and also to defend the theoretical arguments made throughout *Refounding Environmental Ethics.* I also hope that they will encourage students and educators from a variety of fields—for example, environmental policy and politics, the human dimensions of natural resources and ecology, and conservation biology—to engage in more concrete discussions and debates surrounding the ethical dimensions of environmental practice. Finally, although it is impossible to engage on the literature of environmental ethics without recourse to the field's often-esoteric jargon, in the pages that follow, I have tried my best to present these ideas and arguments in the clearest possible terms and in a style that I hope will be accessible to readers across a wide range of environmental disciplines, especially those beyond academic philosophy.

2

Democracy and Environmental Ethics

A Justification

Introduction: The Price of Purity

In Chapter 1, I describe the rise and development of academic environmental ethics in the 1970s and 1980s as a quest for a radically new environmental worldview and value framework that would be unequivocally nonanthropocentric, recognizing the intrinsic value of natural entities and processes and establishing direct duties to promote the good or interests of nature. The emergence of a pragmatist counterpoint to this nonanthropocentric project in the 1990s was driven by a deep dissatisfaction among some philosophers with the ethical and methodological bent of this form of theory in environmental ethics. These dissenting writers argued that the nonanthropocentric position, at least as some of the field's leading thinkers advocated it, was too dismissive of human values and motivations for conservation efforts and policy argument and too removed from the real-world pragmatics of environmental decision making to be of much use to environmental managers and policy makers. This critique, and the constructive call for a more humanistic, pluralistic, and practical philosophical project (under the banner of "environmental pragmatism"), characterizes the first wave of pragmatist writing in environmental ethics (Light and Katz 1996).

The pragmatist assessment of mainstream (i.e., nonanthropocentric) environmental ethics resonated strongly with me when I began studying in environmental philosophy in the mid-1990s. As I continued my work in the field over the next decade, I, too, would become increasingly concerned about the flight from the humanistic values of culture and experience by many nonanthropocentric philosophers, a move that I viewed then—and still see—as undercutting rather than supporting sound environmental policy goals. It is a style of philosophical argument that I believe also creates serious and often unnecessary tensions with traditional societal ethical obligations. In a "thin" pragmatic or strategic sense, I worry that when such philosophers belittle "anthropocentric" appeals to human culture, tradition, duties to future generations, and so forth, they ultimately erode public support for nature protection and sustainability given the currency and influence of such "enlightened" humanist claims in environmental legislation and policy making (see, e.g., Flourney 2003; Cohen 2006), as well as in the structure of environmental public opinion (Minteer and Manning 1999, 2000; Chapter 7 of this book). Even if these writers are personally opposed to human-oriented approaches to environmental obligation and policy agenda setting, this does not seem like an intelligent or politically savvy move for the field as a whole to make, given the need to build broad coalitions and constituencies for conservation and environmental protection.

On normative ethical grounds, too, it seemed to me that the narrow nature-centered orientation of such positions ran the risk of downplaying other pressing ethical obligations and concerns, especially critical issues of human welfare and social justice, thus inelegantly exposing environmental philosophers to damaging charges of misanthropy and "green imperialism." Indeed, criticisms of nature protectionists as wholly insensitive to the (anthropocentric) concerns of social justice and the plight of local peoples—often poor and powerless—in international conservation projects centered on the protection of threatened species and landscapes have become all too common in recent decades, suggesting a profound rift between the discourse of nonanthropocentric environmentalism and that of poverty alleviation and rural development (see, e.g., Dowie 2009; Miller, Minteer, and Malan 2011). This is unfortunate, especially given the widely recognized imperative to develop integrative policy linkages among international health and development projects, the maintenance of ecosystem services, and long-term biodiversity protection (see, e.g., Roe and Elliot 2004; Millennium Ecosystem Assessment 2005; Sachs et al. 2009). These converging social and conservation agendas are ill served, however, by nonanthropocentric philosophers' (and like-minded conservation advocates') desire to create an ethical and policy schism between the goals of nature protection and human well-being (e.g., Katz and Oechsli 1993; Rolston 1998; Terborgh 1999).

But one of the most distressing aspects of this mode of environmental ethics—and a problem that I believe has not disappeared from the literature—is the highly ideological and potentially undemocratic character of the strong version of the nonanthropocentric program. In particular, I am wary of the common epistemic and rhetorical move in which some prominent writers in the field argue that "true" environmental ethic, and an ethically defensible environmental policy agenda, *must* be justified by nonanthropocentric arguments (and purged of objectionable anthropocentric elements) for these views to be philosophically valid and politically effective. Philosophers who argue this position typically advocate universal conversion to the normative view that biodiversity (i.e., wildlife and plant populations/species), ecological systems, and so on possess intrinsic value. It usually follows from this that citizens and policy makers, to be truly "ethical" *vis-à-vis* nature, are encouraged to forswear more traditional and widely held anthropocentric outlooks in which such entities have "only" instrumental value, regardless of how liberal (i.e., nonconsumptive) such notions of "use" are construed. These anthropocentric commitments—even idealist values that depart from economistic principles—are viewed by ideological nonanthropocentrists as ethically vacuous and "incorrect" views for citizens to hold.

This sentiment, which, again, I believe is widespread among many nonanthropocentric writers, is perhaps most powerfully expressed in the work of Holmes Rolston, one of the founders of the field and perhaps the most zealous defender of the need to recognize and promote nature's intrinsic value as a universal ethical duty. Consider how Rolston describes the ethos of historically timber-dependent communities of the Pacific Northwest, communities that have struggled in recent decades to transition from an older forest products–based economy toward a more diversified economic model:

> They once lived in a community with a worldview that saw the great forests of the Northwest as a resource to be taken possession of, exploited. But that is not an appropriate worldview; it sees nature as a commodity for human gratification, and nothing else. The idea of winning is to consume, the more the better. When the goalposts are moved these "losers" at the exploitation game will come to live in a community with a new worldview, that of a sustainable relationship with the forested landscape, and that is a new idea of "winning." What they really lose is what it is a good thing to lose: an exploitative attitude toward forests. What they gain is a good thing to gain: a land ethic. (2009, 116)

Rolston characterizes the citizens in this large and diverse region as thoroughly homogenous with respect to their environmental values and worldview; in his telling, the conversion of these communities from their universally held and "inappropriate" exploitationist attitudes to an ethic of sustainability will turn these "losers" into environmentalist "winners." This kind of sweeping statement—not to mention Rolston's Manichean view of the ethical sensibilities and policy attitudes of forest-dependent communities—would surely raise the eyebrows of environmental social scientists who actually study the complex and disparate environmental attitudes and values of these citizens. In reality, theirs is a normative landscape that resists such simplistic, one-note characterizations, as, of course, does any modern community comprising people with different cultural backgrounds, social roles, and demographic characteristics.

Of course, this does not mean that the search for a more sustainable economy and culture in the Pacific Northwest is not a good thing for the ecosystems of the region and the long-term economic health of communities mired in an eroding natural resource–based market. Rather, it is only to highlight the stark ethical vision of nonanthropocentrists, such as Rolston, who see environmental ethical options as a kind of binary, all-or-nothing contest, one between a correct or "appropriate" nature-centered worldview and an incorrect, consumptive anthropocentrism. Although most nonanthropocentric philosophers are highly critical of anthropocentrism in environmental ethics, Rolston's animus toward humanist values is distinctive for its unwavering consistency and for its focus on the deeper implications for character development. "Both anthropocentric and anthropogenic values," he has declared, "have to come to an end before we can become the best persons. We have to discover intrinsic natural values" (1994, 166).

Rolston's nonanthropocentric vision of moral perfectionism is notable for its boldness and candor, but the judgment that an anthropocentric value framework is ethically and ontologically defective and thus must be replaced by a nonanthropocentric one is a widely held view in the field. For example, Eric Katz, another influential nonanthropocentric philosopher, has similarly argued that the wholesale conversion to a nature-centered ethic must take place to secure good environmental policy outcomes. "A shift in values will be required for the successful implementation of any environmental policy," he writes, asserting that "even a policy of sustainable development will have to be based on the intrinsic respect for that which is being sustained, the natural environment" (1997, 171). Katz is obviously worried about the temptation environmentalists may feel to appeal to human-centered justifications in articulating their policy arguments. He therefore cautions against making concessions to anthropocentric interests, regardless of their historical influence and political efficacy in the public realm: "Nonanthropocentrism must resist anthropocentric compromises in policy and must focus all of its energies on the protection and preservation of natural entities and systems" (2009, 194).

The eliminativist and uncompromising attitude toward commonly held anthropocentric values—and the accompanying judgment that those who hold them are mistaken or, in Rolston's view, ethically stunted—has long been a fixture of environmental ethical writing. Indeed, such skepticism may be found among even more nuanced nonanthropocentric theorists, such as J. Baird Callicott, who has frankly acknowledged the pragmatic value of appealing to traditional human goods and interests in environmental policy arguments. At the same time, however, Callicott makes it clear that such appeals should not be taken to imply *philosophical* validation of such anthropocentric views. Although humanist religious and intellectual commitments may be evoked to support pro-environmental policies and practices, Callicott writes, these beliefs do not, in his words, comprise the "real reasons" for protecting nature. For Callicott, this special epistemic and ethical status is apparently reserved only for intrinsic value of nature claims (1999a, 33).

My main objection to this way of thinking is that the ethical and policy projects of such writers as Rolston, Callicott, and Katz seem to include very little space for meaningful public discussion, debate, and critical analysis that could inform, and possibly challenge, their claims about the necessity of adopting a nonanthropocentric worldview. That is, these interlinked ethical and (very generalized) normative policy arguments offer little room for inquiry into the merit of those dogmatic intrinsic value of nature claims and scrutiny of the parallel directive that we *must* adopt a nonanthropocentric worldview (and jettison our anthropocentric beliefs) before we can make proper environmental decisions, engage in pro-environmental behaviors, support effective environmental policies, and become the "best persons." In seeking to narrow the frame of value to a singular program of nonanthropocentric ethics, philosophers ethically and politically disenfranchise individuals who hold different (yet appreciative) normative views about the value of nonhuman nature and the obligations we may have to conserve and protect it, now and in the future. They assume the moral truth of this position and believe that this should compel the political community to convert to them and consequently to pursue those policies they believe are entailed by the commitment to nature's intrinsic value (and the rejection of anthropocentric values).

I predict, though, that it would be politically disastrous if philosophers and advocates insisted on public adherence to nonanthropocentric views as preconditions to any serious policy argument. This is certainly not the posture assumed by the major conservation and environmental nongovernmental organizations (NGOs), such as the Nature Conservancy, WWF, and Conservation International, which overwhelmingly appeal to human interests (often in economic or utilitarian terms) in their vision and mission statements and allude to the intrinsic value of nature very rarely—if at all (Campagna and Fernández 2007). Although such philosophers as Katz and Rolston assert the necessity of nonanthropocentric claims for nature conservation and environmental policy making, there is in fact scant empirical evidence that such arguments are *essential* to these efforts.

Instead, and as these organizations are well aware, many examples demonstrate the effectiveness of broadly anthropocentric arguments (especially in the form of appeals to welfare-serving ecosystem services and the well-being of future generations) for protecting plant and animal species, sustaining ecological systems and processes, and motivating other significant conservation and environmental policy goals around the globe.

Certainly, broadly humanistic ethical arguments are and will continue to be central to political and policy actions responding to anthropogenic climate change, perhaps the most daunting environmental issue facing citizens and decision makers today. Although nature-centered ethical arguments may play a secondary role in these discussions, from an ethical perspective it seems clear that the political debate over climate change, and the working out of any lasting and just set of policy responses, will hinge far more on clarifying and resolving *anthropocentric* concerns regarding the economic, physical, and social well-being of present and future generations. It will also depend upon addressing critical questions of procedural and social justice in climate negotiations and outcomes as well as the ethical implications (for future people) of relying too heavily on discounted benefits and costs of climate change actions, the responsibility of the biggest greenhouse-gas (GHG) emitters (such as the United States) to take the lead in the global political response to the problem, and related concerns (see, e.g., Jamieson 2001; Singer 2002b; Broome 2008; Stern 2009).

For example, one of the more significant normative debates in climate change policy is whether we should emphasize mitigation or adaptation strategies to deal with the consequences of a variously warming and changing global environment.

Those promoting a more significant role for adaptive responses to climate change argue that, because of time lags in the climate system, a significant degree of global warming is unavoidable, even if a strong and enforceable mitigation policy were put into effect today. They also caution that emphasis on mitigation alone will come at the cost of undertaking adaptive measures in the near term to increase ecological and social resilience to climate shifts (including those not directly linked to GHG emissions), a concern that responds in part to the demands of more vulnerable societies today to potentially damaging climate events (e.g., Adger et al. 2006; Pielke et al. 2007). Critics of embracing the adaptationist position too strongly, on the other hand, argue that this approach will fail in cases of sudden, catastrophic climate change and that a policy emphasizing adaptation leaves the more vulnerable and poorer parts of the world in a worse position given their inability to pay for adaptive measures (e.g., construction of sea walls, modifications of planning and architecture, and planting of drought-resistant crops; see, e.g., Jamieson 2005). It would be difficult to argue that these are not pivotal ethical questions surrounding the policy response to anthropogenic climate change. It would be equally difficult to argue that a nonanthropocentric environmental ethics is *essential* to making progress in such discussions and that we must adopt this moral position before we can address these policy issues fairly and effectively.

In sum, the ideological and exclusivist character of much nonanthropocentric writing and rhetoric in environmental ethics should, I think, be of great concern to those who wish to respect philosophical and public ethical pluralism while making an effective case for conservation and environmental sustainability in today's pressing management, policy, and regulatory debates. In my view, this purist form of ethical argument runs counter to the kind of experimental and democratic attitude toward the values and beliefs of citizens that I think is critical for philosophers and activists to hold in an era shaped by the complex forces of global environmental change, especially given the ecological dynamism and ethical diversity that characterizes our historical moment—conditions that ultimately shape the environmental political and policy context (I have more to say about these issues in Chapters 7, 8, and 9). Instead of pushing moral conversion to a unidimensional nonanthropocentric ethic, philosophers should, it seems to me, seek to better understand and enlist the potential practical wisdom of a full range of perspectives on the human-nature relationship while at the same time respecting the right of individuals to hold a variety of environmental ethical views—even if they do not correspond to the tenets of doctrinaire nonanthropocentrism.

Again, this does not mean that intrinsic value of nature claims do not have a place—perhaps in some instances an important one—in the public discourse of environmental ethics. As I discuss in Chapter 4, I believe that a commitment to environmental value pluralism and the role of public deliberation in the justification of environmental ethical claims does not preclude the appeal to the intrinsic value of nature in certain contexts. Rather, I argue that the pragmatic approach properly views such claims as but one of a set of normative principles that citizens may hold and that may or may not prove effective in particular decision-making/problem-solving situations. But, as I explain, the pragmatic understanding of intrinsic value that I support is quite different from the ideological and metaphysical renderings of the concept by such philosophers as Rolston and Callicott.

Regardless of the eventual normative content of any particular argument for conserving wild species, restoring and maintaining stressed ecosystem services, or creating more sustainable energy and transportation systems, public debate, deliberation, and criticism—and an experimental and fallibilist view toward environmental values and policy goals—should be seen as essential to the political and ethical justification of environmental ethics and the formulation of intelligent and democratic environmental policy. In other words, I do not believe that environmental ethicists should be in the business of requiring citizens, environmental professionals, and policy makers to embrace particular nonanthropocentric principles—or, for that matter, any particular *anthropocentric* principles—before collective inquiry, discussion, and debate about such commitments and the policy ends they justify. Environmental ethics can certainly provide a language to describe such values and construct more or less compelling philosophical justifications and historical lineages for them, but we must recognize that the social legitimacy and political authority of these claims—not to mention their modalities in particular policy and problem contexts—ultimately will flow from the processes of public deliberation and inquiry rather than the method of philosophical decree.

This procedural and democratic model of ethical inquiry is, of course, a hallmark of certain strands of philosophical pragmatism, especially the political and ethical writing of John Dewey. A "culture of democracy" in the Deweyan sense—that is, a democratic temperament exhibited in the method and substance of ethical inquiry into the human-nature relationship—will, I argue throughout this book, enable the field of environmental ethics is to avoid its longstanding ideological and absolutist tendencies and respect the values of democratic life in spirit and in practice.

A Challenge

When I first began articulating a version of these criticisms some years ago, I framed the problem then as the tension between "foundationalist" approaches in environmental ethics—well represented by the work of the nonanthropocentric writers described above—and a more pragmatic/democratic mode of ethical theorizing and argumentation as advocated most powerfully by Dewey in the classical pragmatist tradition (see, e.g., Minteer 1998). My usage of the term "foundationalism" in this context was partly epistemological but mostly political; I was inspired by the work of political theorist Michael Walzer, who has written compellingly (in my view) of the undemocratic implications of philosophical "founding." This method, as Walzer describes it, involved the tradition of philosophers' seeking intellectual purification and abstraction from the political community to discover and inject preexperiential and prepolitical notions of "truth," "right," and "good" into the stream of lived experience. Walzer's point (summarized very simply) is that in the realm of democratic politics, beliefs and ethical principles instead are properly seen as receiving validation and earning their social authority through the messy and context-bound processes of public argument, interpretation, and criticism within the political community. This process, and the political authenticity it subsequently bestows upon normative and empirical claims bearing on the interests of the public, is, Walzer argues, something quite different from the hypothetical ruminations of philosophers constructing moral projects through analytical invention and testing them via stylized "thought experiments" (Walzer 2007; orig. 1981). Walzer's identification of the deep gulf separating foundationalist philosophy (in his sense) and democratic politics clearly has an antecedent in the antifoundationalism and fallibilism of the pragmatists (described in Chapter 1), especially Dewey, who rails against the "quest for certainty" in Western philosophy and the intellectual and political vices of anti-experimental and absolutist philosophical methods and projects.

My original critique of the foundationalist tendencies of nonanthropocentric theorists—and the implications of such work for a more democratic environmental ethics—elicited a forceful response from Callicott, one of the theorists whom I single out in my earlier discussion (Minteer 1998). In his original rebuttal to my arguments, Callicott (1999b) objected to the fact that, despite my call for a more democratic temperament in environmental ethical argument, I offered no reasons "for a commitment to democracy" (511). He therefore thought that my motivations for seeking to place such considerations front and center in environmental ethics were "cryptic," "insidious," and ironically *un*democratic, given the substance of my claims. "Minteer assumes," Callicott wrote, "that democracy and democratic values are unquestionably good things, but in pretending to eschew foundations, he slyly puts the foundations of democracy and democratic values beyond discussion and debate" (512).

I take Callicott's remarks as a provocative challenge for me to offer some sort of *justification* for a commitment to democratic values and practices that I trumpet in that earlier paper (and endorse above)—that is, a basic philosophical argument from which democratic principles and institutions, such as freedom of speech, thought, self-determination, and so on, may be deduced with great certainty. Indeed, as his words here and elsewhere suggest, Callicott appears to be looking some sort of foundationalist argument to back up a normative political commitment—that is, a prepolitical claim regarding the essence of human nature, or perhaps the existence of certain natural rights, that may be evoked to support our intuitive, shared understanding of democratic principles and institutions. Unfortunately, I do not think a convincing and coherent philosophical defense of democracy can be made along these lines. But this is a modest concession and should not frighten democrats—in environmental ethics or elsewhere—into abandoning their principles because they lack a foundational, "valid-in-all-possible-worlds" justification. It does nothing to warrant skepticism toward democracy, nor does it call into question the particular status and legitimacy of democratic values and practices in environmental ethics. Rather, I would suggest that it only challenges the presupposition that such foundationalist claims are, in fact, *necessary* to the justification of democratic values and decision making (and, by extension, democratic environmentalism) in the first place.

Thankfully, philosophical founding is not the only way to go about justifying democracy as a shared experience, or a "way of life," as Dewey so memorably puts it. One alternative strategy, appealing to many of the postmodern persuasion, would be to suggest that our commitment to democratic practices and norms is nothing more than a historically contingent set of attitudes that has, better than any alternative, allowed us to "cope" with social existence in the modern era. On this reading, democratic values and principles rest upon nothing more than constructed cultural conventions (especially, linguistic practices) and the "social hopes" of individuals *qua* democratic citizens. This is, of course, the sort of strong antifoundationalist move preferred by "neopragmatists," such as Stanley Fish and the late Richard Rorty, theorists who wish to completely dispense with the idea that our democratic politics require *any* sort of philosophical justification, especially (but not only) metaphysical "back-up." As I go on to discuss, I am not persuaded by their position, mostly because I do not think they are consistent with the very pragmatic tradition they rely on in advancing their deconstructive arguments. So if I am to respond to Callicott's important challenge to justify a commitment to democracy in environmental ethics, I must turn to something other than this.

What, though, remains if we want to avoid the fruitless search for democracy's immutable foundations, yet we find the reduction of democratic commitments to an airy therapeutic vocabulary too close to moral skepticism for comfort? I think another path—one perhaps between these two poles—is open to us. It would find us looking for the justification of our democratic values and beliefs in something more substantial than Rorty's and Fish's ungrounded linguistic practices but in something less objectionable than a philosophical foundation posited to exist outside (and prior to) human experience. I believe this type of support is indeed found in Dewey's pragmatism, though my understanding here is clearly at odds with Rorty's and others' claiming of Dewey as special kind of radical antifoundationalist *and* radical antiformalist—that is, a pragmatist "without method." In particular, and following the reading of pragmatist scholars Hilary Putnam (1992) and Robert Westbrook (2005), I believe we can find in Dewey's work a powerful and persuasive instrumentalist (or, more precisely, "logical") defense of democratic commitments and institutions, even though, as Westbrook points out, Dewey does not always make this argument in a direct and explicit way (2005, 179–180). I suggest that it is an even more convincing argument in the environmental context, at least to the degree that we are searching (as I believe we should be in environmental ethics) for effective ways to resolve thorny environmental disputes and policy dilemmas.

Before I discuss this justification of democracy that may be found in Dewey's work, however, I discuss how the question regarding the political consequences of philosophical pragmatism (focusing on Dewey's project) has created an interesting rift in contemporary pragmatic philosophy between, on the one hand, "neopragmatists," such as Rorty and Fish, and, on the other, "paleopragmatists" (to borrow a term from Westbrook), such as James Gouinlock and Putnam. I do not hesitate to take sides in this debate. As mentioned above, I believe that the latter camp has pretty much got Dewey right, and I attempt to defend this interpretation by providing a short overview of Dewey's instrumentalist theory of inquiry and its connection to democratic values and institutions. With this piece in place, in the final section of the chapter, I return to highlighting the critical differences between Deweyan democracy as I understand it (and the method of inquiry that supports and is reinforced by it) and the approach to environmental valuation and policy argument that environmental ethicists commonly take.

Pragmatists and Democracy: A House Divided

The resurgence of pragmatism in social, philosophical, and legal circles that began in the late twentieth century owes much to Rorty's high-profile efforts to elevate Dewey and the pragmatists' intellectual stature in Western philosophy. His somewhat idiosyncratic interpretation of Dewey as a thoroughgoing historicist and radical relativist (though Rorty eschewed the latter term), however, has raised more than a few hackles among Dewey scholars. This tension has only been exacerbated by Rorty's unlikely claiming of Dewey as a fellow traveler of "post-Nietzschean" European philosophers, such as Martin Heidegger and Ludwig Wittgenstein, and French postmodernists Jacques Derrida and Michel Foucault. To my mind, though, and as I indicate above, one of the most significant objections raised against Rorty and his postmodernist makeover of Dewey is his desire to decouple Dewey's politics—his "renascent liberalism" and democratic faith—from his philosophical views, particularly those relating to Dewey's writings on logic and his theory of inquiry. According to Rorty, Dewey never attempts to justify his unflagging commitment to democratic principles and practices—certainly not, at least, in any meaningful philosophical sense. Instead, Rorty suggests that Dewey offers only "inspiring narratives and fuzzy utopias" (1999, 120), a political vocabulary articulating nothing more than a purely conventional "anti-ideological liberalism" (1991, 64).

Rorty thus claims that Dewey "saw democracy not as founded upon the nature of man or reason or reality but as a promising *experiment*" (1999, 120; emphasis added), an endeavor whereby Dewey "asks us to put our faith in ourselves—in the utopian hope characteristic of a democratic community—rather than ask for reassurance or backup from outside (119–120). Rorty's characterization of democracy as an ungrounded "experiment" is interesting, and I have more to say about this shortly. For now, though, the significant point to make is that Rorty thinks Dewey's adherence to democratic values and politics has very little to do with his possessing any particular *philosophical* beliefs, including not only metaphysical and epistemological claims but also, as we shall see momentarily, notions about the logical method of experimental inquiry.

Rorty's dismissal of attempts to read Dewey, and pragmatic philosophy more generally, as justifying or entailing a particular political project (democratic or otherwise) is wholeheartedly embraced by literary theorist Fish, whose forays into legal and social theory show him to be an even more rabid deconstructive neopragmatist than Rorty. In his provocative book *The Trouble with Principle* (1999), Fish cautions us to remember that pragmatists' deep commitment to fallibilism cuts both ways. "If pragmatism points out that its rivals cannot deliver what they promise—once-and-for-all answers to always relevant questions," he writes, "pragmatism should itself know enough not to promise anything. If pragmatism is true, it has nothing to say to us; no politics follows from it or is blocked by it; no morality attaches to it or is enjoined by it" (295). As his remarks here suggest, Fish favors a view of pragmatism that emphasizes its radical contingency and antiformalism, and his work vigorously rejects all attempts to found and apply lawlike, algorithmic principles to existential situations. Pragmatists, Fish believes, inevitably must slide down a slippery slope to complete epistemic and moral relativism. To his mind, this is an unarguably good thing: "Once you start going down the antiformalist road (with pragmatism or any other form of antifoundationalist thought)," he surmises, "there is no place to stop. Once contextualism is given its head and apparently firm meanings are made to shift and blur whenever a speaker is reimagined or a setting varied, no mechanism, not even the reification of context itself, will suffice to put on the breaks" (294). Like Rorty, Fish wants to deny the necessity as well as the desirability of having our politics underwritten by theoretical arguments *of any kind*, especially the dreaded "neutral principles" to which Fish believes the philosophical justification of political and legal practices must ultimately resort. "If democracy has to some extent worked," he concludes, "it is because certain political structures are firmly in place and not because its citizens have internalized the sayings of Emerson, Dewey and James" (301). Our political experience comes first, and it is composed of only a set of (unjustified) public practices that we happen to have adopted within our liberal culture at a particular time and place.

What may be said of this neopragmatic skepticism toward the relationship between pragmatism and democracy? For starters, Rorty's and Fish's claims appear, at least to many "paleopragmatist" observers (and I count myself among them), to completely miss the core of Dewey's project: his tireless commitment to the logical refinement and practical application of a unified method of inquiry to moral, social, and political life. Philosopher Gouinlock makes one of the more persuasive and consistent cases for this reading of Dewey's work:

> In Dewey's ideal, experimental inquiry and democratic behavior become fused. The nature of their combination can perhaps best be suggested by thinking of them as a union of certain moral and intellectual virtues—with the distinction between moral and intellectual less fixed than it seemed to be for Aristotle. The virtues include a willingness to question, investigate, and learn; a determination to search for clarity in discourse and evidence in argument. There is also a readiness to hear and respect the views of others, to consider alternatives thoroughly and impartially, and to communicate in a like manner in return. . . . These might be viewed as the virtues of the experimental inquirer, but they are also virtues in the process of collective moral deliberation. What makes democratic behavior more than free speech and counting votes is that the participants use *scientific intelligence* in determining the nature of their situation and in formulating plans of action, and they are not stuck on foregone conclusions. (1990, 267; emphasis added)

This "fusing" of norms of experimental inquiry and democratic practice and the reliance of inquiry on what Gouinlock refers to as "scientific intelligence" are the very moves and commitments Rorty and Fish would like to read out of the pragmatic canon. As we shall see below, Rorty is not at all comfortable with Dewey's attention to and high opinion of scientific method, a hostility doubtless owing to Rorty's strong efforts to deprivilege the epistemic authority of science as producing "special" truths corresponding to an objective, external world. But, as we shall also see, Dewey's articulation of method and inquiry avoids this criticism by firmly grounding itself within the practices of concrete human experience.

I believe the textual evidence shows that Dewey is quite clear and consistent about the connection between the method of inquiry (inclusive of, but not reducible to, those forms employed in the natural sciences) and democracy. Consider, for example, the following places (and these are only a smattering of quotes from an overwhelmingly vast corpus of work) where Dewey speaks directly to this connection:

From *The Public and Its Problems*:

> There can be no public without full publicity in respect to all consequences which concern it. Whatever obstructs and restricts publicity, limits and distorts public opinion and checks and distorts thinking on social affairs. *Without freedom of expression, not even methods of social inquiry can be developed.* For tools can be evolved and perfected only in operation; in application to observing, reporting and organizing actual subject matter; and this application cannot occur save through free and systematic communication. (1927, 339–340; emphasis added)

From *Ethics*:

> The alternative method [to dogmatism] may be called experimental. It implies that reflective morality demands observation of particular situations, rather than fixed adherence to *a priori* principles; that free inquiry and freedom of publication and discussion must be encouraged and not merely grudgingly tolerated; that opportunity at different times and places must be given for trying different measures so that their effects may be capable of observation and of comparison with one another. It is, in short, *the method of democracy*, of a positive toleration which amounts to sympathetic regard for the intelligence and personality of others, even if they hold views opposed to ours, and of *scientific inquiry into facts and testing of ideas.* (1932, 329; emphasis added)

From *Liberalism and Social Action*:

> *The method of democracy—inasfar as it is that of organized intelligence—*is to bring these conflicts [conflicting private and social interests] out into the open where their special claims can be seen and appraised, where they can be discussed and judged in the light of more inclusive interests than are represented by either of them separately. . . . Democracy has been a fighting faith. When its ideals are *reenforced by those of scientific method and experimental*

> *intelligence*, it cannot be that it is incapable of evoking discipline, ardor and organization. (1935, 56, 64; emphasis added)

From "Creative Democracy—The Task before Us":

> For what is the faith of democracy in the role of consultation, of conference, of persuasion, of discussion, in formation of public opinion, which in the long run is self-corrective, except *faith in the capacity of the intelligence of the common man to respond with commonsense to the free play of facts and ideas which are secured by effective guarantees of free inquiry, free assembly and free communication*? (1939a, 227; emphasis added)

If Rorty wants to purge Dewey's thought of any discussion of the relationship between democratic commitments and scientific inquiry, he certainly has his work cut out for him. As these few excerpts show, in Dewey's view, democracy and the scientific method significantly overlap; they share a set of common virtues characteristic of properly conducted, controlled inquiry. These virtues—toleration; openness; free communication; nondogmatic, fallibilist attitude toward held beliefs; and so on—describe the normative constraints of sound scientific investigation. They also describe many of the normative requirements and constraints of democratic deliberation. Indeed, by "securing effective guarantees of free inquiry, free assembly and free communication," democratic institutions and their articulated moral principles provide the experiential matrix in which intelligent, socially organized inquiry and cooperative problem solving can occur.

This need to provide a suitable environment for social inquiry, where "conflicts are brought out into the open"—and which terminates in warranted public knowledge ("which in the long run is self-corrective")—is thus part of the justification for the existence of democratic values and practices: an "instrumentalist" justification of democracy. I have more to say about this process in the next chapter, but here we can that, in a society where public speech and free communication are curtailed or denied, where openness and publicity are replaced by secrecy and the suppression of information, and where the freedom to assemble in the streets and the meeting hall is authoritatively discouraged or withheld from citizens, no meaningful or effective intelligent inquiry into social problems can occur. As Putnam succinctly puts it, democracy for Dewey "is not just one form of social life among other workable forms of social life; it is the *precondition for the full application of intelligence to the solution of social problems*" (1992, 180; emphasis added).

Democratic institutions are justified, in other words, by the "requirements of scientific procedure in general: the unimpeded flow of information and the freedom to offer and to criticize hypotheses" (Putnam 1992, 188). Although democracy obviously rests upon additional commitments as well—for example, the moral conviction that individual citizens have a presumptive "right" to contribute to the ongoing shaping of values and goals guiding the community—this instrumentalist/methodological justification plays a major part in Dewey's thinking about the pressing need for basic democratic freedoms and protections. Furthermore, this relationship between democracy and the experimental method of inquiry is a two-way street: The practice of inquiry turns back on and enriches democratic practices and principles by assisting in the effective resolution of politically divisive public problems and dilemmas.

Rorty, not surprisingly, is unconvinced by such talk. Responding to Gouinlock's argument about the central role of the experimental inquiry in Dewey's writings, Rorty concedes the point but downplays its significance. "Granted that Dewey never stopped talking about scientific method, I submit that he never had anything very useful to say about it," he quips. Furthermore, Rorty issues a challenge to Gouinlock and his other paleopragmatist opponents on this front: "Those who think I am overstating my case here should, I think, tell us what this thing called 'method'—which is neither a set of rules nor a character trait nor a collection of techniques—is supposed to be" (1995, 94). Rorty's remarks here essentially restate the views expressed in his earlier paper, "Pragmatism without Method," where he explicitly spells out his objection to those claiming the significance of Dewey's theory of inquiry for his philosophical and political thought. As he writes there, "If one takes the core of pragmatism to be its attempt to replace the notion of true beliefs as representations of 'the nature of things' and instead to think of them as successful rule of action," as Rorty clearly does, "then it becomes easy to recommend an experimental, fallibilist attitude, but hard to isolate a 'method' that will embody this attitude" (1991, 65–66).

Rorty is quite correct that Dewey never offers a distinct method encapsulating the experimentalist attitude, if by "method" he means an *a priori,* formal process set down in schematic detail. Such an unwieldy instrument would not have been compatible with Dewey's emphasis on the creative role of deliberation within problematic situations, nor would it, I think, have fit with his elevation of the place of unique contextual considerations within moral and political experience. But if we relax the definition of "experimental method" to refer to something less than a rigid set of formal procedures guiding inquiry—or a collection of specialized techniques—then Dewey clearly has much to say about the method of intelligent inquiry.

Moreover, his instructions here are significantly more substantial and rigorous than the modest endorsement of the need for individuals to display "reasonable" and "tolerant" characters in their cooperative problem-solving activities. Dewey devotes his monumental 1938 work, *Logic: The Theory of Inquiry,* to the elaboration of this method and the pattern he believes all successful inquiries assume. In summary form, this pattern is defined by a progression of operational stages: (1) the formulation of a "problematic situation," or the judgment that a particular "indeterminate" situation—that is, one characterized by a perceived instability or disturbance—requires investigation; (2) the contextual analysis and generation of various action-guiding hypotheses; (3) the reasoning through, rehearsing, and testing of these hypotheses; and (4) the construction of a reflective and terminating judgment resolving the problem at hand (although a decision is open to revision and replacement in the light of future inquiry).

In arguing that this pattern of inquiry be implemented in social, moral, and political experience, Dewey avoids charges of vulgar "scientism" and positivism by making it clear that he is not suggesting that scientific methods (as employed in the natural sciences) simply be lifted root and branch and transplanted to other realms of human culture:

> When we say that thinking and beliefs should be experimental, not absolutistic, we have then in mind a certain logic of method, not, primarily, the carrying on of experimentation like that of laboratories. Such a logic involves the following factors: First, that those concepts, general principles, theories and dialectical developments which are indispensable to any systematic knowledge be shaped and tested as tools of inquiry. Secondly, that policies and proposals for social action be treated as working hypotheses, not as programs to be rigidly adhered to and executed. They will be experimental in the sense that they will be entertained subject to constant and well-equipped observation of the consequences they entail when acted upon, and subject to ready and flexible revision in light of observed consequences. (1927, 361–362)

The method of inquiry Dewey has in mind is inclusive of science, to be sure, but he sees it also as a general pattern of problem solving to a lesser degree operational in the arts, historical analysis, jurisprudence, and other "nonscientific" domains of experience. As Larry Hickman (2001, 53) writes, Dewey's argument is simply that the method he describes works better than any other in resolving social problems, wherever they occur, and that if the method is authoritative, it is not because of any "correspondence" to a metaphysically defined reality, but rather because experience has shown it to outperform its rivals. Dewey says as much in *Logic*:

> We know that some methods of inquiry are better than others in just the same way in which we know that some methods of surgery, farming, road-building, navigating or what-not are better than others. It does not follow in any of these cases that the "better" methods are ideally perfect, or that they are regulative or "normative" because of conformity to some absolute form. They are the methods which experience up to the present time shows to be the best methods available for achieving certain results, while abstraction of these methods does supply a (relative) norm or standard for further undertakings. (1938, 108)

For Dewey, the method of inquiry arose from reflective study of *actual* successful inquiries in the arts and sciences and the consideration of their constituent elements and processes, not from some transcendental realm "outside ourselves." It is not a rationalistic instrument to reveal the hidden order of the cosmos, nor is it a special philosophical tool to make the universal voice of nature articulate. It is instead an evolving and fallible social process for transforming problematic situations into ones that are more settled and secure. And the continual revision and refinement of this method, guided by informal logic and substantively infused with the empirical failures and achievements of particular experiments in social life, keeps Dewey's model free from the more objectionable formalistic trappings and maintains a significant, if not critical, link between reflective activity—thought—and the world of lived experience.

And although this notion of inquiry reflects an ambitious and hopeful attitude toward the ability of ordered intelligence to resolve pressing ethical, social, and scientific problems, Dewey's understanding of inquiry is also tempered by his own Darwinian naturalism, which ensures that it retains a vital sense of conditionality and epistemic fallibility. In *The Undiscovered Dewey* (2008), Melvin Rogers's interesting and provocative reexamination of Dewey's intellectual project, the political theorist argues that the great American philosopher's view of experimental inquiry is heavily conditioned by this circumspect worldview. "For Dewey," Rogers suggests, "humility is the gift of inquiry. Inquiry ascertains meanings otherwise not there and satisfies fractures in human life, but also may fail to do so—that is, our projections into the world may fall short of what they attempt to satisfy, manage, or negotiate" (101). According to Rogers, the Darwinian commitment to the natural conditions of contingency, change, and unpredictability had an enormous influence on Dewey's philosophical system, chastening his Enlightenment convictions regarding human progress (or, at least, the unquestioned faith in human progress as a kind of metaphysical belief), making him on the whole much more cautious and circumspect toward ethical, epistemic, and political claims than many supporters and critics of his work have suggested. Although I think he slightly overstates his case, I do concur with Rogers that a greater degree of humility and temperance is on display in Dewey's experimentalism and progressivism than his critics (past and present) acknowledge.

But back to Rorty: What is curious is that, as his remarks above suggest, Rorty does in fact recognize that Dewey views democratic life through the lens of inquiry: "Dewey saw democracy not as founded upon the nature of man or reason or reality but as *a promising experiment*" (1999, 120; emphasis added). But after making this observation, Rorty mistakenly concludes that the "promising experiment" Dewey finds in democracy rests only upon ungrounded "social hope" and his "fuzzy" utopian vision of democratic culture. I think this misses the heart of Dewey's project. The elaboration and defense of the method of inquiry as appropriate to the whole of human experience, including moral and political life, is an unmistakable preoccupation of Dewey's work. Although he offers much more than the instrumental justification outlined here, this justification is, I believe, powerful in Dewey's project, despite Rorty's and Fish's postmodernist attempts to expunge it from pragmatic accounts of democratic politics and values.

Deweyan Democracy and Environmental Ethics

So Dewey reminds us that if effective inquiry into our common social problems is to be realized, we must see to it that the social institutions and practices necessary for undertaking this inquiry are put into place and vigorously defended. Democracy, in this reading, is therefore a requirement of the general method of intelligent problem solving and dispute resolution, a method we see most fully expressed in the experimental sciences. Over time, and by its fruits, this method has shown itself to be the best means available for transforming our myriad problems and conflicts in the sciences and technical arts into settled, stable, and secure situations. Dewey thus concludes that the application of the experimental method to the improvement of the moral and political realms of the human estate is warranted by such past experience. The task, therefore, is for citizens to develop the proper intellectual habits and to support social conditions capable of promoting this method in all aspects of daily life.

Robyn Eckersley (2002), a nonanthropocentric political theorist, suggests that classical and contemporary pragmatists' focus on this activity of problem solving results in a toothless, piecemeal politics incapable of developing a sufficiently radical critique of our social problems, including the environmental predicament: "The greatest weakness of such an orientation [pragmatic problem solving] is that it has a tendency to be conservative, *to take too much as given*, to avoid any critical inquiry into the 'big picture' and to work with rather than against the grain of existing structures and discourses" (65; emphasis original). But this conclusion is challenged by Dewey's own radical conception of democracy, his reconstructed liberalism that favors a communal understanding of economic life and politically coordinated social action:

> Liberalism can be true to its ideals only as it takes the course that leads to their attainment. The notion that organized social control of economic forces lies outside the historic path of liberalism shows that liberalism is still impeded by remnants of its earlier *laissez faire* phase, with its opposition of society and the individual. The thing which now dampens liberal ardor and paralyzes its efforts is the conception that liberty and development of individuality as ends exclude the use of organized social effort as means. . . . We must reverse the perspective and see that socialized economy is the means of free individual development as the end. . . . Organized unity of action attended by consensus of beliefs will come about in the degree in which social control of economic forces is made the goal of liberal action. (1935, 63)

Dewey is not John Locke, nor is he Adam Smith. Far from an endorsement of the status quo, Dewey's project of socialized liberalism requires the planned transformation of productive life to a more "democratic" order, one where each citizen can experience "effective liberty": the positive freedom defined by the institutional encouragement of the growth of our cultural selves in a socially organized manner. Political theorists often overlook Dewey's sharp critique of the metaphysical atomism and methodological individualism of classical liberalism, even though the reclamation of his strong democratic credentials has been underway for decades (e.g., Westbrook 1991; Rogers 2008). Contrary to Eckersley's judgment, Dewey is seriously concerned with the "big picture" of American political economic structures; moreover, his call to fully democratize such structures is a necessary move if the method of social intelligence he advocates could be effectively brought to bear on vexing public problems.

This now brings me back to Callicott's challenge to justify democracy in environmental ethics. I have attempted to offer just such a defense of democracy;

or, more accurately, I have highlighted and endorsed what to my mind (and to such interpreters as Putnam and Westbrook) is one of the most compelling arguments in support of democratic values and practices to be found in Dewey's writing. As I mention earlier, I believe that this particular, instrumental justification of democracy also holds a special connection to environmental ethical inquiry, or at least my view of how such inquiry should be conducted. Given the empirical evidence supporting the existence of robust public value pluralism toward the environment (e.g., Minteer and Manning 1999, 2000; see also Chapter 7), as well as the undeniable complexity and scientific uncertainty surrounding environmental problems (more on this in Chapter 9), it seems wise to adopt a pragmatic and provisional approach to environmental ethical and policy inquiry, an approach that embraces the democratic ethos in Dewey's work, and its social and institutional facilitation of the experimental method in technical and public affairs, as the best means to address and resolve complex environmental policy questions.

Indeed, the thorny intergenerational normative and empirical aspects of many contemporary environmental problems, not to mention the *intra*generational value conflicts and scientific disagreements playing into discussions surrounding such issues as environmental risk assessment, biodiversity loss, global climate change policy, and the like, suggest that we would do well to assume a more explicitly pragmatic attitude toward our environmental goals and polices as well as the ethical claims offered in support of them. I think the adoption of this attitude will render our institutions and communities more dynamic and innovative—and therefore more effective and responsive to emerging environmental challenges. I also believe that it promises to stimulate the kind of social learning necessary for intelligent and dynamic forms of environmental management and problem solving, learning achieved through the practice of collective inquiry and public deliberation over alternative environmental values and policy goals.

Here we see the convergence of democratic experimentalism, environmental ethical pluralism, and the philosophy of adaptive ecosystem management, an approach that emphasizes policy experimentation and social learning within ecological systems—and that adopts a multivocal and contextual view of environmental values in this larger process. Adaptive managers acknowledge the complex structure and inherently unpredictable nature of coupled ecological and social systems and yet seek to create management interventions and manipulations of ecosystems that progressively reduce this uncertainty over time—an important step toward the ultimate end of enhancing ecological and institutional resilience (Walters 1986; Lee 1993; Gunderson, Holling, and Light 1995; Gunderson and Holling 2002; Gunderson, Anderson, and Holling 2009). With respect to environmental values, the goal in such processes is not to seek to reduce environmental values to a simplified notion of economic or intrinsic good (à la neoclassical economics and nonanthropocentric environmental ethics, respectively), but rather to design a procedure that allows stakeholders to introduce, discuss, and ultimately learn about the complex plurality of environmental and social values in a deliberative process. This process is supported by norms of democratic inquiry and aimed at producing intelligent and sustainable policy outcomes driven by community values and aspirations (Norton and Minteer 2002; Norton 2005).

As I mention in the introduction to this chapter, however, many (perhaps most) environmental philosophers do not see ethical and policy inquiry in such experimental and democratic terms. Rather than adopting the sort of epistemic and political attitude toward normative claims in policy debates I advocate here, nonanthropocentric writers, such as Callicott, prefer to dogmatically cling to a single moral "end" (intrinsic natural value)—an end advanced prior to public deliberation and inquiry—and attempt to anoint it as the *sole* principled ground for defending our environmental decisions. "One wants to offer the *right reasons* for doing the right thing—as well as to get the right thing done—irrespective of pragmatic considerations," Callicott writes (1999a, 244; emphasis added). In adhering to absolute "right reasons" in the philosophical justification of environmental decisions, such philosophers as Callicott display their commitment to a class of special and universal ethical claims (roughly, those composing nonanthropocentric holism), claims advanced as the "correct" moral justifications for all environmental public policies and practices.

This almost Kantian preoccupation with purity of moral motivation (which is somewhat surprising for an avowed Humean, such as Callicott) is, I believe, unhelpful for actual environmental problem solving and dispute resolution. In fact, and as I suggest earlier, I believe these results-driven enterprises will politically founder if environmental philosophers are successful in constraining the public debate over environmental policy alternatives to the uniquely authoritative ethical commitments they deduce from their metaphysical arguments about the true human place in nature. Again, by rejecting "pragmatic considerations," these environmental philosophers turn their backs on the arguments that have proven historically successful in safeguarding environmental health and integrity—from hunters' support for wetland policy, to recreationists' efforts to defend roadless areas in national forests, to citizens' support for sustainability initiatives as a question of long-term economic efficiency. An environmental ethics that seeks to deprivilege these and other "pragmatic reasons" for supporting the environmental agenda is one committed to staying on the policy sidelines.

Furthermore, it is a move that elides what many policy scientists believe is the real normative challenge for an applied ethics of the environment—that is, developing the means to reconcile conflicting *anthropocentric* value frameworks in real-world debates over such goals as environmental health, biodiversity conservation, and climate change policy. As Dan Sarewitz (2009) notes, environmental policy conflicts are, more often than not, driven by disagreements over which human interests—for example, short-term utility maximization or long-term aesthetic, cultural, and scientific/educational values—should prevail in policy disputes over protecting wild species and ecosystems. Donald A. Brown (2009) seconds this point, arguing that a truly useful and applied environmental ethics would focus far less on the question of the intrinsic value of nature and more on the ethical issues raised by the use of economic, legal, and scientific arguments in justifying environmental decisions. These considerations are front and center in the case of climate change policy, where, once again, it seems clear that the real ethical challenge is to reconcile conflicting (human) rights, justice, and welfare outcomes in international climate policy discussions rather than defend general nonanthropocentric theories of value.

Conclusion

A more pragmatic and experimental environmental ethics can make significant contributions to the task of democratic and intelligent environmental problem solving and policy argument. It can assist in the identification and clarification of public environmental value claims and help stakeholders and policy makers target key ecological structures and functions that account for and track such values over time and space. It can also help develop and refine better and more inclusive methods of social inquiry and valuation and work within various lay and professional communities to identify and articulate coherent and well-integrated social and environmental goals and objectives. When ethical critique is necessary, environmental philosophers can certainly provide it, although they will be doing so as politically engaged *citizens* rather than as dogmatic metaphysicians—or, worse, as environmental philosopher kings.

Although environmental ethicists may have special skills that will prove useful in specific public-policy deliberations (e.g., semantic sensitivity, the ability to make well-reasoned arguments), I do not believe we have special *knowledge* of the moral and metaphysical "truths" that must govern communities' relationship with their natural and social environments. In fact, I do not believe such absolute truths exist; some strategies are simply better or worse for achieving democratically determined environmental goals, and there are more or less adaptive behaviors and interventions in ecological systems. Because we seldom have the epistemic luxury of knowing what all these strategies and manipulations are *a priori*, we need to assume an experimental posture toward environmental ethical argument and the search for durable environmental policies that promote the values we collectively choose to pursue as a democratic community. These policies—and their ethical justifications—are, in turn, subject to further debate and modification as we continue to learn within coupled natural and social systems and as we absorb the lessons of our policy failures and successes.

Callicott responds to this line of argument by doubling down on his view of the heroic, foundationalist task of environmental philosophers, one that sees this kind of work, rather than the experimental and pragmatic method, as essential to the very existence of democracy:

> Environmental philosophers such as Rolston and I have . . . taken on . . . [a] lofty and protracted task. We would like to contribute to the kind of transformation of Western culture and civilization that philosophers in the past—such as Locke, Kant, Bentham, and Mill—have effected. . . . Democracy, the

> political practice we know and cherish, owes its existence to substantive, foundational philosophical work of the kind that Rolston and I, as well as many other contemporary environmental philosophers, wish to continue. (2002b, 107–108)

In the end, I simply have to conclude that environmental philosophers, such as Callicott, Rolston, and Katz, see the mission of environmental ethics very differently than I do. They think it is to invent the substantive metaphysical and moral foundations that will save us from our political mistakes by philosophically guaranteeing the correct environmental policy agenda while at the same time transforming "Western culture and civilization" into a nonanthropocentric order. I am wary of such guarantees—and the mission of cultural transformation—and think that environmental philosophers should stick to the philosophically more humble (though far from easy) task I describe here: the facilitation of improved methods of inquiry into specific environmental problems and the continual shoring up of the democratic social institutions that allow these methods to run free in public life. Callicott (1999b) writes that this effectively means I wish to "silence philosophers." I do not. I do, however, wish to see philosophical environmental inquiry become more democratically accountable and more experimental—and thus more publicly useful. Otherwise, I fear that, rather than building extensive coalitions for collectively agreed upon environmental policy goals and working toward the reconciliation of empirical value conflicts in critical environmental debates, ethicists will end up only preaching to our own philosophical choirs. That this would be a most regrettable development is a conclusion on which I think all of us in environmental ethics, despite our differences, can agree.

3
The Public and Its Environmental Problems

Why Are They Not Taking Environmental Philosophy More Seriously?

Although environmental ethics has (as I mention in Chapter 1) achieved significant academic success—at least, if we judge this by the number of courses offered, monographs published, and journals established—its standing within the discipline of philosophy has always been somewhat tenuous. Indeed, J. Baird Callicott once wrote that environmental philosophy was "something of a pariah" in the mainstream philosophical community (1999a, 1). Although the reputation of the field in conventional philosophy circles may be slowly changing, I believe Callicott's observation remains largely accurate. For example, even though interest in environmental ethics is growing within interdisciplinary programs and departments—for example, in environmental studies, public policy, natural resources, and the life sciences—the field's fortunes have not risen nearly as rapidly within traditional philosophy departments, where environmental ethics still seems to be viewed as a fringe discussion rather than as a serious field occupied with exploring what are considered to be the "big" philosophical questions.

In his ruminations on the relatively low status of environmental ethics in the philosophy community, Callicott offers a number of reasons—from the moral to the political—to explain the expulsion of the field to what he describes as the "applied ethics barrio" (1999a). Yet despite this, Callicott (and presumably many other philosophers in the field) remains hopeful that environmental ethics will ultimately triumph over conventional, mainstream moral philosophy and reconstruct the latter along more nonanthropocentric lines. Although I disagree with many of Callicott's philosophical and political aspirations for environmental ethics (as I hope the previous chapters make clear), I do sympathize with his frustration over the status of the field within applied philosophy. I believe, however, that environmental philosophers share some of the blame for this state of affairs. The field's historically sharp rebuke of the claims and commitments of conventional (i.e., anthropocentric) moral and political thought is, I suggest, the main reason why it has been seen as a discourse that often takes place outside the mainstream philosophical community. Moreover, and as I argue in Chapter 2, given that such received ethical and political concerns motivate citizens, legislators, and decision makers, this rejection of the humanist tradition may also be viewed as one of the primary reasons why environmental philosophy has not made significant and lasting inroads into environmental policy discussions.

For such philosophers as Callicott, Holmes Rolston, Eric Katz, and others, this scholarly exclusion is simply the price that has to be paid for advancing what is seen as radical philosophical and cultural reform. I believe, however, that it is too dear. In fact, over the long run, I suggest that the rejection of traditional philosophical and political theories and concepts only impoverishes environmental ethics as a scholarly field and as an effective participant in the formation of environmental policy arguments. I think that many environmental philosophers have been far too hasty in their abandonment of the traditions of mainstream Western thought and that the time is ripe for a reconsideration of the value and utility of this inheritance for current normative and policy discussions in the environmental realm.

In the previous chapter, I draw directly from one of the primary traditions in Western philosophical and political thought (American pragmatism) in arguing for a more experimental and democratic style of environmental ethical argument. Here, I want to build on this important linkage between pragmatism, democracy, and environmental ethics by considering what a return to the notion of the "public interest"—a core normative ideal in the history of American public policy and administration—might offer in the search for a more democratically suitable and pragmatic style of environmental ethics. A reclamation of a deliberative, nonaggregationist understanding of the public interest in environmental ethical argument, I suggest later in this chapter, not only will strengthen the connection between public environmental values and the policy process but also will help bring the field of environmental ethics—which is often seen as an "outsider" in debates over the moral and political dimensions of public life—into the mainstream of American political culture and the heart of democratic politics.

One of my primary objectives in this chapter, then, is to build a modest, but hopefully useful, bridge between the public affairs and environmental ethics communities. I also attempt to show that nonanthropocentrists and theorists of a more humanist bent can support appeals to the public interest in environmental philosophy and environmental policy discussions, provided they surrender the notion that environmental ethics competes with, rather than informs, the public interest in a democratic society.

The Public Interest and Its Eclipse in Environmental Ethics

Whether defined boldly as "the ultimate ethical goal of political relationships" (Cassinelli 1958, 48) or somewhat more prosaically as a term "used to express approval or commendation of policies adopted or proposed by government" (Flathman 1966, 4), the public interest carries an unmistakable air of political legitimacy and moral authority when evoked as a justification for public policy. Indeed, it seems woven into the very fabric of political and administrative ethics. It is difficult to imagine a successful public policy proposal that openly flouts the public interest; likewise, it is hard to think of one that does not at least implicitly incorporate a notion of the interest or good of the public in its supporting arguments. Even cynical uses of the term as an ethical "fig leaf" covering more narrow or "special" interests affirm the power of the concept in public life.

Yet despite its estimable bearing in political culture, over the course of its short history, the field of environmental ethics has strangely pitted itself *against* the concept of the public interest, at least as the term "public interest" has come to be understood. In a sense, this is somewhat surprising. One would have assumed that environmental philosophers would have by now developed a fairly robust concept of the public interest as an important normative standard in their projects, an understanding directly tied to the promotion of core environmental values. After all, if the field has a consensus goal, it is surely the improvement of human-nature relationships by advancing compelling and well-reasoned arguments for valuing the environment and, by extension, for choosing good environmental policies. Given the potential influence of the public interest as a widely recognized standard for policy choice and decision making, one would have expected the language of public interest to be widely spoken in environmental ethics—if not in the native tongue, then at least in one of its more popular dialects.

The nature of the field's professional founding, I believe, explains the eclipse of the public interest in environmental ethics. As I discuss in the previous chapters, first-generation ethicists, such as Richard Routley and Rolston, set forth what would become highly influential arguments suggesting that a radically new environmental ethic—one that found value in nature directly rather than in its contribution to the good or interests of humans—was required if humanity was to find a defensible moral footing in the environmental crisis (Routley 1973; Rolston 1975). Recall that an earlier version of this argument for a new philosophical relationship to the environment had been unfurled in the pages of *Science* by historian Lynn White, Jr., who in many respects set the agenda for many of the subsequent decades in environmental philosophy with his now-infamous analysis of the negative environmental attitudes found within Western culture, particularly the Judeo-Christian tradition and the creation story depicted in Genesis (White 1967; see also Callicott 1999a, 187–219).

It is important to remember, however, that White's much-pored-over essay is by no means simply a one-note condemnation of the anthropocentrism of the

Western philosophical and religious tradition. Indeed, his paper also raises questions about the ability of modern democratic societies to curb what White suggests are possibly inherent tendencies toward environmental exploitation. As he puts it, "Our ecologic crisis is the product of an emerging, entirely novel, democratic culture. The issue is whether a democratized world can survive its own implications." White follows this provocative question with an equally radical conclusion: "Presumably we cannot," he writes, "unless we rethink our axioms" (1967, 1204).

This call for revisiting and rethinking the philosophical roots of Western culture, which for White were the technoscientific worldview and its underlying religious and secular foundations in the medieval period, implied nothing less than an overhaul of the tradition, a foundation-razing process in which a new philosophy of science, technology, and nature—and perhaps a new, less arrogant relationship to the natural world—would be unearthed and absorbed into the modern worldview. Early environmental philosophers, such as Routley and Rolston, then, apparently following White in their call for a new ethic able to account for the independent value of the natural world, assumed that the anthropocentric worldview (and its destructive instrumentalization of nature) had to be replaced with a new, nonanthropocentric outlook. Here, White's thesis about the anti-environmental implications of the Judeo-Christian religion, particularly his sweeping claim that the latter was "the most anthropocentric religion the world has seen," offered a point of departure for environmental philosophers, who would respond in subsequent years with a series of influential criticisms of the moral humanism of the Western philosophical inheritance (e.g., Taylor 1986; Rolston 1988; Callicott 1989; Westra 1994; Katz 1997). As the field matured in the 1980s and 1990s, and as I describe in the previous chapters, an exclusivist non-anthropocentric agenda established itself as the dominant approach in the field, with a few notable exceptions (of the latter, see Passmore 1974; Norton 1984, 1991; Weston 1985; Stone 1987).

The result of these developments is that the public interest never became part of the agenda of environmental philosophy in the same way, for example, that it appears to have made lasting impressions in other branches of applied philosophy, such as business, engineering, and biomedical ethics. Concerned with what it perceived to be more pressing and fundamental questions of moral ontology—that is, with the nature of environmental values and the moral standing of nonhuman nature—environmental philosophers pursued questions self-consciously cordoned off from parallel discussions in mainstream moral and political theory, which were apparently deemed too anthropocentric to inform a philosophical field preoccupied with the separate issue of the moral standing and significance of nonhuman nature. As a consequence, instead of (for example) providing a conceptual or analytic framework for evaluating cases, practices, and policies from the perspective of ostensibly "human-centered" concepts, such as the public interest, many environmental philosophers preferred to focus exclusively on the independent status of natural values. I argue that this original failure to link environmental values and claims to recognized moral and political concerns also helps explain the relative inability of environmental philosophy to have a significant impact within public and private institutions over the years, especially when compared with other applied ethics counterparts. Environmental philosophy is and always has been concerned with "nature's interest," not that of the public.

This situation has also produced a number of unfortunate consequences for the contribution of environmental ethics to policy discussion and debate, not to mention more concrete and on-the-ground forms of social action. One example here is the largely missed opportunity for philosophers to study and contribute to some of the more important environmental reform movements and institutional initiatives of the past four decades. Chief among these developments, perhaps, is the public interest movement that developed alongside environmental ethics in the late 1960s and early 1970s, which united consumer protection with environmental advocacy through such organizations as Ralph Nader's Public Interest Research Groups (PIRGs). This list of emerging direct-action environmental movements would also have to include the growing number of grassroots organizations and groups, commonly lumped under the "environmental justice" banner, that have sought to link the concerns of public health, safety, and community well-being to environmental protection through the language and tactics of social justice and civil rights (Gottlieb 1993; Shutkin 2000; Shrader-Frechette 2002; Sandler and Pezzullo 2007). Had environmental ethics worked a serious notion of the public interest into its agenda, it doubtless would have been (and would now be) much more engaged with these influential movements in citizen environmental action, not to mention a range of discussions in such areas as risk communication, pollution prevention and regulatory reform, public understanding of science, and so on.

Part of the larger problem here stems from what I suspect is an incomplete apprehension of the concept of the public interest by environmental philosophers, a view that has in many cases resulted in theorists' advancing intrinsic value of nature claims as a normative standard for environmental policy that *competes* with the public interest in the battle for environmental protection. Environmental philosophers, when they do acknowledge the public interest, seem to assume that it is little more than aggregated individual preferences. In this strong "Benthamite" reading, environmental protection is therefore viewed as effectively being held hostage to the preponderance of exogenous and unquestionable consumer-demand values. But this rather one-dimensional utilitarian understanding is not the only, or the best, account of the public interest as an authoritative standard for public policy. Environmental philosophers are not entirely to blame for this limited view, however, because the liberal utilitarian version of the public interest (and its corollaries) has shaped public thinking about the concept in the modern period. We therefore need to examine the concept of the public interest a bit more closely if we are to accurately gauge its utility in environmental philosophy and policy discussions.

The Public Interest: A Pragmatic Retrieval

It is common for observers of the public interest to note its association with two broad traditions in political thought (Benditt 1973). The first, and clearly the dominant notion of the public interest in contemporary public life (and the one held, I think, by most environmental philosophers), is the "Benthamite," or liberal utilitarian, tradition mentioned above. Here, the public interest is thought to be derived directly from the mechanical or mathematical aggregation of individual interests. In this understanding, the community or "public" is not real in any meaningful sense and thus cannot properly be said to have any interest or good apart from the sum of the interests or preferences of its distinct individuals (but see James 1981). Contemporary versions of this view may be found in various public interest "proxies," such as economists' renderings of individuals' "willingness to pay," the presuppositions and decision logic of social choice theory, and pluralist models of interest politics focused on the bargaining and competition between multiple interest groups.

The second, and historically less pervasive, view is a more socialized and communal accounting of the public interest as the shared, common good of citizens composing a recognizable political community. This notion, typically associated with such thinkers as Jean-Jacques Rousseau and Edmund Burke—and, earlier, with Aristotle and Thomas Aquinas—focuses more on the moral and even metaphysical notion of common good (often in an objective sense) and thus stands in stark relief from the individualist and subjective account of interests and preferences in the liberal model (Flathman 1966; Benditt 1973; Diggs 1973). This communal reading of the public interest as common good has, however, largely been clouded over by the Benthamite understanding in modern life, although recent revivals of this tradition among political theorists and policy scientists (such as the civic republicanism that Michael Sandel [1996, 2005] advances) suggest that change is perhaps in the air. Bruce Douglass (1980) traces the historical ascendance of the liberal utilitarian public interest over communal notions to the crumbling of medieval feudalism and the capture and transformation of the idea of the common good by "Royalist" monarchs as an instrument for political power. According to Douglass, the claim to a "public interest" arose in this environment as a liberal democratic argument of the people agitating for freedom from the exploitation and abuses of the Crown (106). The public interest thus became thoroughly entangled in the moral language of individualism; in the process, it was effectively purged of its earlier communal aspects and the notion of a shared good among citizens.

Contemporary treatments of the public interest that have attempted to shine analytic light on the concept have generally met with mixed results. The problem is that the idea of the public interest has been plagued by an inordinate amount of ambiguity in its popular and academic usage. Are we, for example, to take the notion of "interest" referred to in the "public interest" to be an objective good independent of the will of individuals? Or does it refer to the subjective desires and preferences of individuals *qua* citizens (or perhaps *qua* consumers)? Or is it something else altogether? Can a policy (action, decision, proposal) be said to be in "the public interest" and yet nevertheless be *rejected* by the majority of the citizenry? Related to these questions are a host of epistemic issues, among them: How is the public interest (however it is defined) to be known? Is it indeed something that may be discovered by identifying and then aggregating hundreds, thousands—perhaps millions—of individual expressed preferences? If so, how meaningful (and feasible) can it really be as a substantive normative standard? Can the public ever be mistaken about its interests? These are just a few of the thorny questions that work to make the public interest a vexed concept in political and moral discourse. This conceptual fuzziness and, in particular, the "nonscientific" character of the public interest led Arthur F. Bentley, writing in the early part of the twentieth century, to memorably declare it an "idea ghost," one that clear-thinking political scientists would do well to avoid (1908, 167).

In spite of these difficulties, a distinct scholarly literature on the public interest began to form in the 1950s and 1960s as political scientists grappled with many of the questions listed above and attempted to cash out the significance of the public interest as an analytical tool and as a normative standard for public policy and administration (e.g., Cassinelli 1958; Barry 1965; Flathman 1966; Held 1970). Some observers, following in the skeptical footsteps of Bentley, criticized the public interest for its perceived conceptual incoherence and meaninglessness as a rational standard for public policy. Writing in this vein, Frank Souraf (1957) concludes that the various and conflicting definitions of the public interest rendered it mostly useless as a tool of political analysis, although he does acknowledge its "hair shirt" value as a symbol of the interests of the underrepresented and voiceless in power politics (639). Souraf even proposes an acceptable "minimalist" association of the public interest as the democratic method of orderly settlement of citizen conflict. Still, concerns about the imprecision of the concept of the public interest and its inability to be operationalized are fairly commonplace in this early literature. Glendon Schubert (1960), after considering the meaning and function of the public interest within several bodies of administrative theory, determines that the concept is, in the end, too general, too vague, and too inconsistent be of much use in shaping the course of public affairs.

Other scholars, however, are more receptive. Political philosopher Brian Barry devotes several chapters to a discussion of the public interest in his 1965 book, *Political Argument.* There, Barry concludes that the public interest is directly attached to the social role of the citizen, describing it as "those interests which people have in common *qua* members of the public" (190). Following Barry's lead, political theorist Robert Goodin suggests that a policy or action is in the public interest "if and only if: (1) It is an interest that people necessarily share (2) by virtue of their role as a member of the public (3) which can best or only be promoted by concerted public action" (1996, 339). The public interest in Goodin's view is therefore not contingently public, but rather necessarily so; it arises out of shared public roles and requires deliberate and coordinated collective action to secure and promote.

One of the most nuanced and extensive studies of the public interest in the literature may be found in political scientist Richard Flathman's important 1966 book on the subject. Although Flathman agrees with many of the concept's critics that "the public interest" probably has no all-inclusive and universally valid descriptive meaning, he argues that descriptive meaning could nevertheless be determined in specific contextual situations as reasoned discourse worked to "relate the anticipated effects of a policy to community values and to test that relation by formal principles" (82). These formal principles include a utilitarian principle that directs inquirers to look for the full consequences of proposed policies and a "universalizability" principle by which individual interests are to be generalized and subsumed under rules or maxims that flow from shared community values. As Clark Cochran (1974) observes, Flathman's approach, although largely procedural in nature due to its reliance on the method of vetting community values through formal principles, is not aggregative à la the Benthamite model. It is also more than a procedural account of the public interest, because Flathman's definition serves as "a reminder to decision-makers to remember moral considerations, to abide by formal principles, to employ community values as well as individual interests, and to give reasons in terms of these values for their decisions" (351).

I want to suggest that John Dewey is an important thinker in the historical development of public interest, even though he is rarely evoked in the public interest literature referenced above. I believe, in fact, that Dewey holds an intriguing notion of the public interest that is an alternative to the liberal aggregationist rendering and the classical conceptualization of the "common good." What is more, Dewey's understanding of the public interest may be seen as sharing several features with Flathman's approach, including the emphasis on the role of community values and the contextual, situationally constructed nature of the public interest. Dewey also anticipates Souraf's (and others') later association of the public interest with the democratic method of dispute resolution. Yet Dewey's work adds at least two additional critical elements to public interest theory: (1) a method of democratic social inquiry modeled after the ideal workings of the scientific community, and (2) a focus on the key role of deliberation, social learning, and interest transformation in this process.

Given these contributions, as well as the fact that Dewey is gaining increasing prominence in environmental philosophy, I devote the rest of this section to a brief discussion of his understanding of the public interest. I follow this analysis with a consideration of what a Deweyan retrieval of the public interest might have to offer environmental philosophers.

Dewey's most well-known treatment of the public interest takes place in his seminal work in political philosophy, *The Public and Its Problems* (1927). There, he describes the pressing political and intellectual challenge of the public in the age of industrial capitalism: to organize itself so it might intelligently control and attain its shared interests. According to Dewey, this proves to be a difficult task, mostly because of the fragmenting economic, technological, and social forces of modern life:

> Indirect, extensive, enduring and serious consequences of conjoint and interacting behavior call a public into existence having a common interest in controlling these consequences. But the machine age has so enormously expanded, multiplied, intensified and complicated the scope of the indirect consequences, has formed such immense and consolidated unions in action, on an impersonal rather than a community basis, that the resultant public cannot identify and distinguish itself. And this discovery is obviously an antecedent condition of any effective organization on its part. Such is our thesis regarding the eclipse which the public idea and interest have undergone. (314)

On the surface, Dewey's understanding of the public interest here sounds analogous to what we might refer to today as "market failure"—that is, the situation in which private transactions produce externalities that spill over onto nontransacting individuals, a state of affairs commonly thought to require some sort of government intervention in the private realm. Yet there is more at work in Dewey's notion of the public interest than this, and his conceptualization is not properly reducible to a purely economistic reading. Indeed, Dewey demonstrates a commitment to a strong normative notion of the public interest in his discussion of the interest of citizens in securing desirable social consequences, suggesting that where many share a particular good, an especially compelling reason exists to realize and sustain it (1927, 328). For Dewey, the common awareness of this shared interest ultimately defines the social and moral aspects of the democratic ideal, and it is through public talk and participation in the affairs of the local, face-to-face community that this consciousness is formed and solidified (368).

But how does a community go about identifying its shared good or public interest? As I discuss in the previous chapter, for Dewey, this involves experimental social inquiry into actual public problems and conflicts, a process modeled after the method of the natural and technical sciences. By holding narrower special interests up to the scrutiny of the wider community, Dewey believes, their merits could be assessed from the perspective of the emergent "more inclusive interests" of the public, identified though open discussion and free debate (1935, 56). This, in turn, would reveal the true public interest partially embedded within a particular problem solution or policy proposal. The glare of publicity would expose private interests masquerading as public ones, and through this process of debate and deliberation, the community could test alternatives, ascertain social consequences, and identify the most widely shared good among citizens. Indeed, Dewey thinks one of democracy's virtues is that it "forces a recognition that there are common interests, even though the recognition of *what* they are is confused; and the need it enforces of discussion and publicity brings out some clarification of what they are" (1927, 364).

For Dewey, effective democratic participation in the affairs of the community requires that individuals come to such public deliberations with an open mind. They must be willing to listen to others and accept the possibility that their own preferences may be misinformed or short-sighted and that they may change (perhaps dramatically) in the process of engaging in reasoned and respectful argument with their fellow citizens. As Matthew Festenstein writes, these Deweyan norms of inquiry, read off the practices of the scientific community, also condition participants to look for ways in which to establish common interests as they make meaningful personal and psychological connections with others:

> In Dewey's presentation, the epistemic virtues of tolerance and open-mindedness shade into imaginative sympathy with the travails of others. . . . The commitment to participate, to offer arguments and to hear the views of others, has the psychological corollary of leading participants to think in terms of possible criticisms and alternative views, and to conceive of their own interest is in a way which takes account of the interests and views of other participants. Traditions of shared communication tend to establish bonds of trust and sympathy and to lead individuals to identify their interests with those of the broader community. Moreover, in the process of communication, the interests of separate persons and groups are harmonized with one another. (1997, 88)

Although Dewey's notion of the public interest is partly procedural in nature, it is clear that his conceptualization is not grounded in simple utilitarian methods of preference aggregation or the mechanical balancing of individual interests. Dewey's approach also avoids the pluralist conflation of the public interest with the outcome of interest group struggle. In some situations, he concludes, conjoint activity may produce such a significant and large public interest that it requires organized intervention in and "reconstruction" of the affairs of a group (1927, 281). This is a far cry from the traditional pluralist view of the state as little more than an "umpire" among competing interest groups.

Yet neither is Dewey's understanding of the public interest premised on prepolitical or metaphysical notions of the "common good" in a classical sense. Instead, in Dewey's model, the public interest is to be discerned through the workings of social inquiry and democratic discussion and deliberation; it is thus a political, rather than an economic, construction. As I indicate above, consumer sovereignty is rejected: Individually held preferences and private interests bearing on the public good are not taken as given but are to be submitted to the test of free and open debate among citizens, a process in which they could be challenged, enlarged, and transformed as citizens engage and learn from each other in deliberative settings. Dewey defended this process in 1939:

> Democracy is the belief that even when needs and ends or consequences are different for each individual, the habit of amicable cooperation—which may include, as in sport, rivalry and competition—is itself a priceless addition to life. To take as far as possible every conflict which arises—and they are bound to arise—out of the atmosphere and medium of force, of violence as a means of settlement into that of discussion and of intelligence is to treat those who disagree—even profoundly—with us as those from whom we may learn, and in so far, as friends. A genuinely democratic faith in peace is faith in the possibility of conducting disputes, controversies and conflicts as cooperative

> undertakings in which both parties learn by giving the other a chance to express itself. (1939a, 228)

For Dewey, this educative potential of democracy and democratic deliberation in particular suggests that citizens could not only broaden their interests and moral outlooks to take in the larger public good but could also sharpen and improve the intellectual and communicative skills necessary to participate in this process over time (1927, 366).

This faith in the intellectual capacities of the common citizen and the potentially enlightening and ennobling power of education distinguishes Dewey from democratic realists, such as his colleague and frequent critic Walter Lippmann, who takes a much less sanguine view of the political and administrative capacities of the public. Whereas Lippmann memorably defines the public interest as "what men would choose if they saw clearly, thought rationally, [and] acted disinterestedly and benevolently" (1955, 40)—and comes to the elitist conclusion that citizens are intellectually incapable of effectively governing themselves in such a manner—Dewey retains an unyielding faith in the competence of citizens and their ability to develop the necessary ability and motivation to identify and secure their shared interests through democratic deliberation. As Melvin Rogers has recently pointed out, this faith is joined by the moral conviction that the public ought to be seriously engaged in those decisions that affect them:

> Dewey's argument concedes that experts possess information that citizens facing a particular problem do not. . . . Yet, and in contrast to Lippmann, recognizing the epistemic limitations of citizens need not require us to abdicate or substantially diminish the role they ought to serve. Dewey's argument is that policy for what to do, what trade-offs will be made, and where to invest economic and educational resources is an issue that falls to the public precisely because the consequences of those decisions extend beyond the realm of experts. (2008, 212–213)

Noting that such social and political knowledge is not an innate possession but rather a "function of association and communication" (Dewey 1927, 334), Dewey suggests that the institutionalization of the scientific spirit in education and public life would foster the kind of democratic diffusion of knowledge of social consequences that would allow citizens to chart their own political and policy courses. This knowledge would also promote the intelligent control and direction of economic and other social forces for the greater public benefit:

> Economic agencies produce one result when they are left to work themselves out on the merely physical level, or on that level modified only as the knowledge, skill and technique which the community has accumulated are transmitted to its members unequally and by chance. They have a different outcome in the degree in which knowledge of consequences is equitably distributed, and action is animated by an informed and lively sense of shared interest. (333)

We must remember, however, that the public is fallible in Dewey's understanding; it can be mistaken about what is in its interest at any point in time and in any given situation. Incomplete information about the causes and consequences of particular social problems and widespread commitment to beliefs that subsequent inquiry determines to be false can lead communities astray, as can more insidious forces, such as ideological bias, political secrecy, and the ubiquitous corrupting influence of economic power. Yet, like the ideal of scientific inquiry (even if it may at times fall short in practice), for Dewey, this democratic social intelligence is potentially self-correcting, progressively rooting out error by casting its epistemological net out to the broadest possible range of alternative beliefs and experiences and vigilantly maintaining its open and transparent character:

> It is of the nature of science not so much to tolerate as to welcome diversity of opinion, while it insists that inquiry brings the evidence of observed facts to bear to effect a consensus of conclusions—and even then to hold the conclusion subject to what is ascertained and made public in further new inquiries. I would not claim that any existing democracy has ever made complete or adequate use of scientific method in deciding upon its policies. But freedom of inquiry, toleration of diverse views, freedom of communication, the distribution of what is found out to every individual as the ultimate intellectual consumer, are involved in the democratic as in the scientific method. (1939b, 135)

The public interest, on Dewey's view, is thus not an absolute, universal, or ahistorical good. It is constructed in each policy and problem context as conjoint activity produces indirect social consequences that the democratic public wishes to direct into collectively identified and validated channels. It follows, then, that many "publics" will exist, just as many public interests will develop in various times and places. The designated public interest on any given policy question, that is to say, cannot be stated in advance of the democratic appraisal of causes and consequences and the contextual, cooperative search for a wider shared interest in a specific problematic situation. For Dewey, it is therefore always a good to be discovered by a public motivated to secure its shared interests as a democratic community, a commitment that ensures not only the identification and maintenance of such interests but also the development of individuals as fully self-realized and enriched citizens (1927, 328). Conflict is not ignored; rather, deliberation within the method of democratic social inquiry can promote the discovery of new courses of action and reveal underlying shared interests. In Dewey's understanding, this process could, in fact, result in the transformation of the underlying conditions that produce such conflict among individuals and groups, making it possible for a common political culture to be established and maintained (Caspary 2000, 17).

It must be said that Dewey offers no final answer or universal substantive standard for judging, once and for all, *what* is in the public interest. To do so would have gone against his historical-evolutionary view of moral and political life as well as the overall contextual nature of his epistemology and ethics. But Dewey's view of the public interest, while largely procedural, is also not the kind of thin "proceduralist liberalism" premised on the imposition of hypothetical abstracting devices, conversational constraints, or "neutralizing" conditions on the deliberative process (e.g., Rawls 1971; Ackerman 1980; Gutmann and Thompson 1996). It is instead shot through with the norms of "good" inquiry, including, as we have seen, reasonableness, openness, tolerance, and respect for other participants in common conversation and debate. As Dewey puts it in his 1920 book, *Reconstruction in Philosophy*: "Wide sympathy, keen sensitiveness, persistence in the face of the disagreeable, balance of interests enabling us to undertake the work of analysis and decision intelligently are the distinctively moral traits—the virtues or moral excellencies" (173–174).

The Public Interest and Its Promise for Environmental Ethics

In light of the preceding discussion, and given the widely acknowledged normative and rhetorical heft of public interest discourse in constitutional, administrative, and public policy circles (an influence that exists despite the lack of consensus on its descriptive meaning), I think environmental philosophers would be well advised to link environmental value claims to a pragmatic, Deweyan notion of the public interest in their scholarly and public projects. Not only would this join the specialized and fairly private discourse of environmental philosophy to a powerful public ideal, but I believe that advocacy of the pragmatic model of the public interest sketched above would also offer a potentially formidable—although not impervious—defense of environmental values and goals in the public realm.

For example, under this approach, corporate and private interests advanced as justifications for particular public policy goals (or as reasons against them) would be held up to intelligent and discriminating public scrutiny, their claims tested and weighed in the forum of public reason and judged from the vantage point of the wider public interest. Ideally, as a result of this process of open social inquiry, special interests and biases—where and when they exist—would be revealed rather than left to masquerade as bearers of the "public interest." Indeed, as proponents of such special interests advance their policy proposals in the public sphere, the logic of their arguments and the validity of their supporting evidence would be subjected to open debate and public evaluation, and they would be required to justify their claims and proposals to the democratic community in the language of the public good.

In a Deweyan search for the public interest, however, policy actors would be held publicly accountable to the preponderance of scientific evidence supporting, for example, the human role in global climate change and its likely future human and environmental impacts. This is not to say that Deweyan inquiry into such a challenge as the global climate change (GCC) problem would ignore real scientific uncertainty where it exists (such as the lack of precision in estimating the timing and magnitude of climate change, the accuracy of general circulation models, and so on). In fact, it would acknowledge and seek to identify additional areas of scientific and social ignorance and work to deliberately and efficiently reduce them over time. In some cases, this inquiry may even require the scientific community to more effectively meet the informational needs of decision makers and the public, a responsibility that may challenge historical research priorities in climate-change science (see, e.g., Pielke and Sarewitz 2002). This speaks to a linked and concurrent discussion of the role of a "public interest science," in which university and professional scientific researchers self-consciously focus on solving urgent public environmental and human health problems rather than on commercial or narrowly professional interests (Krimsky 2003). But getting back to the main point, a Deweyan, democratic search for the public interest in the GCC debate would not take corporate or various political interests at face value. It would insist on an open, deliberative process of practical reasoning over the claims of variously interested parties, including scientists, decision makers, and citizens; and it would be respectful rather than dismissive of the cumulative weight of scientific evidence in policy arguments.

This model of inquiry into the public interest in GCC policy would work to expose pernicious forms of undemocratic distortion of the results of scientific investigation through various forms of corporate media and political manipulation and other practices designed to mislead and misinform popular opinion and public understanding of climate-change science, including those of some self-described scientists (e.g., Gelbspan 2005; Oreskes and Conway 2010). Inasmuch as environmental philosophers want to ground their ethical claims for conserving or preserving parts and processes of the natural environment in the best science available, and to the degree that we want to appeal to decision makers (and the public) through well-reasoned normative arguments for specific policy goals, one would think that it would be to the field's great benefit to support such democratic scientific inquiry under the banner of the public interest in environmental policy discussions.

Of course, Lippmann has a point; citizens are not always rational, clear-thinking, or intellectually deft enough to understand all the scientific and technical nuances of environmental problems. Indeed, in a case as complex as GCC, one would need to have advanced training in atmospheric and other physical and natural sciences to possess a truly deep and comprehensive grasp of the scientific and technical nuances of the phenomenon (and even then, we can be assured that much would escape apprehension). But the alternative is to have the discussion be controlled only by scientific and technical experts or leave it to the jostling of interest-group politics or the logic of the marketplace. To my mind, one of Dewey's most significant legacies is to remind us that citizens may at times lack the knowledge and skill to conduct certain aspects of public affairs themselves, but they are always educable, and, moreover, are able to consult experts and participate in the decision-making and administrative process if given the opportunity. As Robert Westbrook writes:

> Dewey did not dispute the provision that inquiry should be left in the hands of the competent; it was an essential provision of the regulative ideal of inquiry that he shared with Peirce. But he contested the claim that most

> members of the public were not capable of competent participation in the inquiry necessary for the making of public policy. Most of the inquiries tributary to making public policy were, he agreed, best left to experts. . . . But when it came to judging "the bearing of knowledge supplied by others upon common concerns" he believed that most people possessed this capacity, and he charged that advocates of the rule of experts greatly exaggerated the intelligence and ability it took to render these kinds of judgments. (2005, 186)

In addition, a Deweyan notion of the public interest, inasmuch as it relies on the deliberative process of a reasoned public debate and discussion (a process open to a diversity of human and environmental value claims and devoted to the search for a common ground among participants), gives us a normative counterpoint to economic and utilitarian renderings of the public interest. The public interest, for Dewey, is not the default philosophy of market individualism; that is, it does not take individual preferences as given, nor does it subscribe to an aggregative logic that chains public choice to the balance of individual consumer demands or willingness to pay. It is, to sound a theme keyed earlier, a political rather than an economic concept (or a metaphysical one). As a result, arguments against proposed policy responses to the problem of anthropogenic climate change that invoke the public interest understood in narrow economic terms—for example, the argument that it is against the "public interest" for government to impose new costly environmental regulations—have in essence co-opted and misapplied a normative political concept, rendering it as nothing more than preference satisfaction. In defining *a priori* the public interest through the language of economic individualism, significant and commonly held *public values* at play in such cases—such as aesthetic, moral, and cultural goods—are left out in the cold.

Furthermore, I propose that claims made on behalf of the public interest (pragmatically understood) in GCC and other environmental policy debates would have a greater motivational effect and would carry more legitimate political clout than the typical environmental ethical argument that we *must* pursue protective environmental policies that secure nonanthropocentric values. This would be expected simply because of the widely acknowledged power and resonance of the public interest in political and administrative discourse. But it would also follow, I believe, from the strong association of the Deweyan version of the public interest with core democratic and epistemic values discussed above, commitments that elicit a wide and deep allegiance from citizens, decision makers, and scientists. Last, although the public interest is not a decision procedure in the sense that it can yield direct and detailed prescriptions for *specific* public policies (e.g., should the United States reduce carbon emissions to 7 percent below 1990 levels? Or 15 percent below? Or perhaps 30 percent?), it can direct public discussion and debate to broader policy goals (such as the general aim of reducing carbon emissions) as politically valid concerns, ones that in many cases also serve the narrower normative agendas of environmentalists.

What, then, to make of the traditional normative claims of environmental ethics—that is, that nature should be protected because it has its own moral status or intrinsic value? A turn to the administrative and policy standard of the public interest does not mean that such claims are rendered irrelevant; rather, it is that they must be placed within a wider (and more public) normative and policy context to be politically effective. Although intrinsic value arguments can be a part of the reasoning process that defines the public good in addressing serious environmental problems (though, as I discuss in the last chapter, perhaps they are less vital in discussions regarding climate change policy), they will gain more salience and policy relevance, I believe, if they are advanced within the broader framework of public interest discourse. Among other things, this speaks to environmental philosophers' adoption of a more open and accommodating stance within environmental value discussions. Environmental philosophers should also be prepared to make compelling and intelligent arguments for engaging in a truly democratic inquiry into the public interest in environmental policy debates, and these arguments should not entail an exclusivist or ideological endorsement of anthropocentrism *or* nonanthropocentrism in such debates.

The Deweyan model offers ample room for environmentally cast articulations of the public interest. For instance, environmental philosophers can inform public discussions of what is in the public interest by evoking environmental values that citizens share as a part of a common cultural inheritance and to which large numbers of the public express loyalty (e.g., Dunlap and Mertig 1992; Kempton, Boster, and Hartley 1995; Shutkin 2000; Sagoff 2007). Philosophers, that is, can substantively flesh out the public interest by articulating widely shared environmental values in deliberative contexts as constituting the legitimate public interest in specific situations. Once more, there is no reason why this process is not open to claims supporting the intrinsic value of nature, because these now are properly viewed as reasons for the public interest in a certain context or issue, with the public interest offered as a normative justification for adopting a certain environmental policy. Indeed, as I argue elsewhere (Minteer 2006), I believe this understanding of the relationship between moral regard for the environment and the wider public good may be found in the mature work of the "father" of environmental ethics, Aldo Leopold, who saw love for nature as a motivational force that would promote the health of the land and, in turn, the civic vitality of the political community.

The pragmatic, democratic view of the public interest I am defending here departs from many current environmental philosophers' presumptions that appeals to the public interest are necessarily antagonistic to the promotion of various environmentalist ends and the justification of robust environmental policy. As I discuss in the next chapter, Rolston (1998)—perhaps the most influential nonanthropocentric philosopher in the field—believes that claims to democracy and public values in environmental cases will only result in a power struggle, one that may pretend to be democratic (or in the public interest) but will ultimately be determined by bargaining power and, presumably, by unfettered economic might. Rolston's apparent adherence to the pluralist, interest-group model of democracy here renders him incapable of seeing how an alternative process of open deliberation and cooperative social inquiry can transform preferences and reveal shared public values able to justify preservationist—or, at any rate, non-exploitationist—environmental policies.

Accordingly, I suggest that environmental philosophers can greatly benefit from exposure to the work of political theorists and policy scholars who, over the course of the past three decades, have considerably expanded our understanding of the character and potential of deliberative democracy and participatory political thought and practice (e.g., Barber 1984; Fishkin 1991, 2009; Benhabib 1996; Gutmann and Thompson 1996; Bohman and Rehg 1997; Dryzek 2002; Jacobs, Cook, and Carpini 2009). Drawing from earlier foundations in the writings of Aristotle and Rousseau, and also from later thinkers, such as Dewey, the deliberative conception of democracy is, as Joshua Cohen puts it, centered firmly on the idea that shared political power is justified "on the basis of free public reasoning among equals" (1997, 412). Many of its proponents argue (as does Dewey before them) that this sort of expansive and participatory model of democratic action can produce individual self-transformation along more public-spirited lines (Warren 1992). Democratic theorist Benjamin Barber, for example, defines his approach of "Strong Democracy" around this transformative experience, writing that the strong democratic ideal is to be thought of as

> politics in the Participatory Mode where conflict is resolved in the absence of an independent ground through a participatory process of ongoing, proximate self-legislation and the creation of a political community capable of transforming dependent, private individuals into free citizens and partial and private interests into public goods. (1984, 132)

Barber's view clearly evokes Dewey's earlier insights about the function of social learning in democratic inquiry as well as the ability of public deliberation to create a more inclusive and enlightened view of the public interest. It also restates a perhaps more controversial point—that is, political life has no "independent ground," no metaphysical, preexperiential, prepolitical claim or foundation upon which we can confidently construct a robust democratic politics. There are only citizens committed to an ongoing civic dialogue and debate, one that Barber (and Dewey) is wagering on to produce a more expansive understanding of the public interest as private (e.g., consumer) interests are transformed through public talk.

In the environmental realm, a growing analytic and empirical literature has identified a range of deliberative enterprises that evoke, either explicitly or implicitly, the Deweyan/Barber model of politics. From citizens' juries and watershed councils, to focus-group discussions, community roundtables, and so on, we are gaining a clearer picture of the conceptual and institutional possibilities for increased citizen participation and deliberation in environmental problem solving and decision making (e.g., Burgess, Limb, and Harrison 1998a, 1998b; Sagoff 1998; Rippe and Schaber 1999; Aldred and Jacobs 2000; Wondolleck and Yaffee 2000; Baber and Bartlett 2005; Sabatier et al. 2005; Robinson et al. 2008). There is good reason to think that such participatory and deliberative democratic models can promote the expansion of meaningful environmental concern among citizens (see Gundersen 1995).

Yet despite the promise of these emerging models of deliberative democracy, in practice, like any other political technology, they frequently fall short of perfection. Indeed, many thoughtful observers have rightly noted that proponents of strong democracy must be attentive to a number of problems afflicting actual deliberative contexts, including the unequal possession of discursive skills and the undemocratic influence of political and economic power (Young 1996; Sanders 1997; Bohman 2000; Box 2007). These approaches may also face the additional question of legitimacy in the representation of the interests of future generations and nonhumans in deliberative contexts (O'Neill 2002). Although it is beyond the scope of the present chapter to examine these issues in sufficient detail, any defense of deliberative democratic methods must necessarily keep these concerns at the center of discussions about the prospects for deliberative democratic institutions on the ground. As Dewey himself concludes, in a remark that has become popular among political theorists celebrating his recent revival as a deliberative democrat: "The essential need . . . is the improvement of the methods and conditions of debate, discussion, and persuasion. That is *the* problem of the public" (1927, 365; emphasis original).

Conclusion

I try to show in this chapter that environmental philosophers have something to gain from a reconsideration of traditional "anthropocentric" political and philosophical thought and that doing so does not require sacrificing normative commitments to the intrinsic value of nature or support for pro-environmental policy. Although a Deweyan retrieval of the public interest can help extend the political and ethical vision of environmental pragmatism, conceptually it works at a different and more generalized level than the pragmatist theory of value. Therefore, the approach presented here is in theory open to multiple philosophical positions in environmental ethics—provided, that is, they do not seek to subvert or distort the larger process of free democratic inquiry into the public good. Although environmental ethicists (and environmentalists generally) cannot be guaranteed that our arguments will always carry the day, we should be supportive of efforts to give such claims a fair hearing and confident enough of their validity and persuasiveness that we are willing to enter into public debate and "take our chances." Likewise, we should also be willing to consider the possibility that, as difficult as it might be for a scholarly field that prides itself on "getting it right," we might sometimes be wrong.

All the same, I think there is good reason to believe that an open, deliberative search for the public interest will provide the best means for environmentalist goals to be successfully articulated in citizen debates and decision-making situations. But again, no independent assurances guarantee that the environmentalist agenda will move forward in every case. Appeals to the intrinsic value of nature, environmental rights, or various other ontological arguments about the status of natural values carry no overwhelming political weight or transcendent policy status; they certainly are not moral trumps that can silence all citizens who disagree with them. This may be a hard pill for some environmental ethicists to swallow, but I simply know of no other way to maintain a meaningful political commitment to democracy in environmental ethics, a commitment that I believe is vital for normative reasons (e.g., citizens really do "count") and more pragmatic ones (e.g., as I discuss in Chapter 2, I feel that such a model offers the best hope for a self-correcting method of social problem solving that is sorely needed in environmental policy).

I suggest in this chapter that the notion of the public interest, especially as understood in Dewey's work, provides a useful link between environmental philosophy and the policy community. It therefore promotes the further development of the field's considerable, although still largely unrealized, public potential. Despite Callicott's (2002a) claims to the contrary, and as I discuss in Chapter 1, many environmental philosophers (including nonpragmatists) are deeply concerned about the field's track record of policy irrelevance. For example, Eugene Hargrove (2003), editor of the journal *Environmental Ethics,* proposes that graduate students in public policy be required to take environmental ethics courses to counterbalance the dominating force of economics in policy programs and the willful exclusion of environmental ethical subject matter among the policy studies community. Although I am certainly all for this, I believe that this argument also needs to run in the other direction: Graduate students in environmental philosophy and ethics should receive training in public policy and political studies as well as in the field's traditional allied pursuits (i.e., the natural sciences). I hope the reconciliation of environmental ethics with the public interest—and in the process, the linking of the field with wider normative discussions in public policy and public administration—is one step in this new direction.

4
Intrinsic Value for Pragmatists

Thinking Like a Garden

One summer, when I was about ten years old, I intentionally and maliciously killed a couple of garter snakes. Growing up in a rural area of New York State, I often encountered them while playing in my backyard, particularly near a rock wall at the edge of my mother's tomato garden. The rocks were long, thin, and loosely stacked—the perfect place for the snakes to bide their time, waiting to terrify ten-year-olds stricken with an irrational, although nonetheless paralyzing, fear of them. One day, I decided that something had to be done. Because I could not bring myself to curl my fingers under the rocks to lift them up and expose the sleeping (although, to my mind, no less threatening) reptiles, I enlisted the services of my cousin, who seemed foolishly unconcerned about the risk involved in such a mission. On a beautiful summer day, then, my cousin and I set out on our murderous crusade. He lifted the rocks, and I coolly shot the snakes with my pellet gun. It was a surprisingly efficient procedure. By the second snake, we had it down pat. My cousin even had the apparently brilliant notion to collect the victims in a five-gallon bucket for disposal later (I think this was to involve a celebratory bonfire, but I cannot recall for certain).

Everything seemed to be running smoothly, but we had made a fatal error—our operation was being performed in full view of my mother standing at the kitchen window. Somewhere between the deposit of the second dead snake in the bucket and the lifting of the next rock, she appeared next to me, bringing the backyard carnage to a premature end. When she demanded to know exactly what we thought we were doing, I simply replied that I was killing snakes, figuring that the justification for ridding the garden of my tormentors was so obvious that it demanded no further explanation. She frowned and in a scolding voice said, "You shouldn't do that. They're living things. It's cruel, and it's wrong." Suddenly, despite my stony resolve and the conviction that I was acting on the unimpeachable principle of "death to all snakes," a wave of guilt washed over me. It *was* wrong, and I knew it. I knew it not because of my mother's undeniable authority (although this doubtless made it more compelling) but because clearly the snakes *were* alive, and this sort of wanton and unprovoked pellet gun killing *was* cruel. Thus the ugly affair ended, although not before my cousin pointed at me and blurted out the typical recriminations of ten-year-olds caught in the act: "It was *his* idea." Of course, he was right.

I mention this story because I think it is suggestive of a common intuition many of us have toward the value of elements of the natural world. The moral claim my mother made in the snake example is essentially an argument for the intrinsic value of nature (or, at least, reptiles), similar to the sort of "life principle" figuring in the moral projects of such philosophers as Kenneth Goodpaster, Paul Taylor, and their biocentric precursor, Albert Schweitzer. I do not believe that my mother had read Schweitzer (and she most certainly was not reading the philosophy journals), so in this case we were dealing with a much more common, public sensibility about nature rather than a carefully wrought environmental ethic. But that is perhaps beside the point. The upshot is that my mother's argument for the worth of the snakes in this situation resonated with me, as I expect it would have with many people, and it made me question and ultimately condemn the moral character of my actions on that summer afternoon. Although I admit that it is nowhere near as heroic an experience as Aldo Leopold's recollection of shooting wolves in his indelible essay "Thinking Like a Mountain" (1949), reflecting on the garter snake episode is revealing, because it reminds me—in a very personal and intellectually unadorned way—of the potential power of noninstrumental value of nature claims in daily life.

In the years since this childhood experience, environmental ethics have, of course, received considerable professional philosophical scrutiny. As we have seen, beginning with the field's early development in the 1970s, most environmental philosophers have thrown their shoulders to the wheel of intrinsic value theory and nonanthropocentric arguments for the protection of nature, believing that these positions are the only philosophical stances that can be counted on to consistently justify adequate environmental protection. Pragmatist philosophers in the field have called this charter into question, often roundly criticizing the concept of intrinsic value as it has appeared in the field's literature and raising doubts about its necessity and usefulness in promoting better environmental practices and policy. Most notably, Bryan Norton, the leading exponent of the pragmatist approach in the field, has made a series of arguments over the past twenty-five years that the metaphysical and epistemological weaknesses of the concept demand that we leave it behind as we grapple with the pressing concerns of environmental management and decision making. This rejection of intrinsic value theory by such environmental pragmatists as Norton is not unexpected, because hostility to moral absolutes and preference for instrumentalist arguments are, of course, hallmarks of the writings of Charles Sanders Peirce, William James, and John Dewey, the pillars of American pragmatism.

I certainly share Norton's concerns about the character and use of intrinsic value in the work of Holmes Rolston, J. Baird Callicott, and their fellow travelers; indeed, the ideological assertion of intrinsic value in environmental policy discussions and debates—a fixture of much environmental ethical argument—poses a considerable challenge for advocates of a more pragmatic and democratic approach to environmental ethics. Surely Dewey, the iconic antifoundationalist and "instrumentalist," has little use for doctrinaire intrinsic value theory. So it seems that the only recourse is to deny the philosophical and political credentials and therefore the utility of the concept for guiding our engagements with the natural world. Presumably, then, I should seek to elaborate and defend those broadly instrumental claims about the environment implicit and explicit in specific problems and management settings.

I want to make it clear that I *do* think more environmental philosophers should take up this task, mostly because I believe many nonanthropocentric ethicists' overriding concern with the "more than human," to use David Abram's phrase (1996), has come at the expense of neglecting the "fully human"—that is, the full span of nonconsumptive instrumental values that are capable of inspiring and effecting sound environmental protection. Norton has done the most of anyone in environmental ethics to develop this project and make it an intellectually respectable, if still the minority, position within the field (see, e.g., Norton 1984, 1991, 2005). Having said this, however, a question still remains in my mind: Does an instrumentalist reading of environmental values, even one as expansive and ostensibly nonmaterialist as Norton's, accommodate the full range of the public's everyday intuitions and sentiments regarding nonhuman nature? In other words, do instrumental arguments for environmental protection exhaust the value discussion, leaving nothing behind once the full array of "uses" of ecological components and systems are taken into account across space and time?

I think not. In fact, I suggest that, although they may be the most philosophically sound and practically effective arguments to be made for, say, sustaining ecological services or decarbonizing the global energy system, they cannot be stretched far enough to fit the kind of moral intuition that, for example, stopped me from killing the snakes in my backyard. My mother's scolding clearly included something other than instrumental claims for the value of nature, and I have to admit that it looks a lot like an ascription of intrinsic value—a justification that was undeniably effective in this particular situation. Should we not, as environmental philosophers, recognize the potential usefulness of such noninstrumental claims for motivating individuals and in warranting environmental practices and policies—at least in some situations?

But given the strong position that Norton and other pragmatist philosophers apparently staked out in the environmental ethics, especially in the field's first two decades of development (see also Weston 1985), how could we expect an environmental pragmatist, especially a Deweyan, to accommodate this intuition? In fact, as I argue shortly, I believe Norton has long recognized the existence and potential usefulness of noninstrumental value (especially its rhetorical utility in certain cases). What he has really objected to, I suggest, has been less the possibility of intrinsic natural value and more the universalist and foundationalist uses of the concept by such theorists as Callicott and Rolston. I also think that Dewey's moral philosophy incorporates a particular, although admittedly idiosyncratic, understanding of intrinsic value. Moreover, I believe this version can do the ethical and practical work in environmental philosophy required to respond to citizens' support for this value of nature that I think clearly exists, albeit in varying degrees and manifestations.

If we are truly interested in upholding our democratic values in environmental ethics (as I have argued to this point), then we need to be respectful of a range of public environmental commitments, even if as pragmatists we find some of them—such as the endorsement of intrinsic natural value positions—philosophically troubling at first blush. If nonanthropocentric philosophers, such as Callicott, Rolston, and others, often belittle instrumental values while holding certain intrinsic arguments dear, pragmatists have tended to neglect and often besmirch the worth and validity of intrinsic value claims in our enthusiastic embrace of a deep and wide instrumentalism, even if the former may at times resonate with a significant segment of the public. This absence of sympathy on both sides (as Dewey might have put it) has had the effect of locking out those citizens from the debate who choose to speak about the value of nature in ways that neither camp can philosophically abide. As a result, I think we do damage to the cause of an inclusive, public environmental philosophy while fragmenting support for sustainable and protective environmental policies. Surely, we can do better than this.

In this chapter, then, I set out in the following directions: First, I examine the criticisms of intrinsic value theory that Norton makes and see to what extent his position does indeed leave an opening for some recognition of noninstrumental environmental values. I then consider the role of intrinsic value in Dewey's moral project, particularly how it fits within his instrumentalist approach toward ethical inquiry and the overarching contextualism of his vision of moral experience. I suggest that this understanding can, in fact, capture the noninstrumentalist regard for nature held by the public in a manner that is especially effective for environmental problem solving and policy making. Lastly, I draw a few conclusions from all this regarding what I believe to be the productive and nonproductive uses of intrinsic value claims by environmental philosophers in arguments about conservation policy through a discussion of Rolston's discussion of the human-nature dilemma at Chitwan National Park in Nepal.

Norton on Noninstrumental Value

It is surely no revelation to point out that Norton has had little use for the metaphysical and epistemological freight of intrinsic value theory as it has been unpacked in environmental philosophy. It seems clear, though, that Norton's criticisms of the concept have stemmed more from his unwavering commitment to the formulation of intelligent environmental policy than from what might be thought of as more narrowly philosophical objections. I do not want to suggest that he considers the latter unimportant, especially because such a judgment would have to account for the fact that Norton (1992) has written one of the most closely argued meta-ethical critiques of intrinsic value epistemology in the field. But I think it is reasonable to conclude that Norton's reservations about noninstrumental value have been primarily motivated by his desire to speak clearly and effectively to practical matters of environmental management and problem solving, a task he believes is not well served by the tendentious ontological debates that all too often engage intrinsic value theorists' attention.

For example, in an early paper in *Environmental Ethics* that introduces his "weak anthropocentrism" to the field, Norton expresses his disagreement with the conflation of the identity of environmental ethics as a field of moral inquiry with the universal endorsement of intrinsic natural values. "I see no reason to think that, if environmental ethics is distinctive, its distinctiveness arises from the necessity of appeals to the intrinsic value of nonhuman natural objects" (1984, 139). Accordingly, Norton's stated intent is to wrest the field's unblinking attention away from the "radical, difficult-to-justify claims about the intrinsic value of nonhuman objects" (138) and turn it instead toward what he takes to be the more philosophically sound and useful consideration of a pluralistic, liberal anthropocentrism. Specifically, Norton introduces his distinction between "felt" and "considered" preferences within a human-based ontological scheme, a model that allows him to separate his approach from the crassly consumptive "strong" versions of anthropocentrism that spurred the development of the field in the first place. What emerges is a generous instrumentalism: Although we might value nature for the material goods it provides, we can also, through our reflective, considered judgments, value it as a source of inspiration and as a critical resource that can lead us toward the recognition of our moral ideals. The ascription of intrinsic value to nonhuman nature is not, therefore, required to justify our careful treatment of it.

Given this project, it would appear that Norton concludes early on that intrinsic value theory was a philosophical dead end and that a weak anthropocentric approach and a broad instrumentalism could deliver the goods (useful ones, of course) in environmental ethics. But I believe such a judgment—one held by most observers—would be wide of the mark. At certain places in his paper, for example, Norton seems to leave some degree of room for the recognition of noninstrumental values. For instance, in his discussion of Tom Regan's claim that a moral ideal governing our behavior toward an object necessarily must recognize that the object in question possesses value, Norton suggestively remarks that if Regan's understanding of "value" in this context is inclusive of intrinsic *and* instrumental value, then he concurs. If, however, Regan is speaking of intrinsic value exclusively, then Norton believes he has to disagree, because such a position clearly discounts the ability of an instrumentalist approach to do the moral work required in environmental ethics (1984, 137). This distinction suggests that Norton is not necessarily assailing the merit of noninstrumentalist views toward nature but is instead implying that those holding these views have, at the very least, some meta-ethical explaining to do and that this type of value should not be assumed to be the *only* ground for an acceptable environmental ethic.

Perhaps even more interesting is Norton's observation at the end of his essay that it would not be surprising if, "*speaking as if* nature has intrinsic value," we could effectively criticize the knee-jerk consumerism that commonly defines our immediate preferences (1984, 148; emphasis original). But he follows this remark by once again arguing that we do not *have* to make the "questionable ontological commitments" of the attribution of intrinsic value of nature to reform destructive environmental practices—such a business can be undertaken within the confines of the instrumentalist axiology in a weak anthropocentric framework. Norton's closing invocation of Occam's razor underscores the ontological conservativism driving this position.

In this early paper, then, Norton is troubled by the epistemic problems regarding the justification of intrinsic values as well as the metaphysical status of non-instrumental claims. But I argue that he is more concerned with the positive project of advancing an anthropocentric alternative to nonanthropocentric value theory in environmental ethics and with demonstrating that it can provide a sufficient philosophical defense of environmental protection than he is with refuting the notion of noninstrumental value. As his remarks above illustrate, Norton does seem to recognize that intrinsic value claims might prove useful in the practical task of value criticism and problem solving. Despite this concession, however, his ontological and epistemological misgivings about the concept lead him to endorse the instrumentalist project as the most reasonable and sound approach to take when arguing about environmental protection.

Norton's measured receptivity to the idea of intrinsic value is also evident in his 1986 paper, "Conservation and Preservation: A Conceptual Rehabilitation." In his attempt to revise our understanding of the motivational pluralism underpinning the practices of conservation and preservation on the landscape, Norton concludes that the values promoting environmental preservation might spring from a variety of sources:

> Preservationists are united by Leopold's argument and they work to set aside undisturbed ecosystems from human use. Their motives may be human and consumptive, human and nonconsumptive, or nonanthropocentric, or any combination of these categories. Given their unifying argument, reasons from any of these categories will be sufficient, and none of them individually necessary, to justify the application of preservationist policies to at least some ecosystems. Nonanthropocentrism, therefore, is sufficient, but not necessary, to support preservationism. (1986, 213–214)

Far from rejecting the usefulness of intrinsic environmental values, Norton here openly recognizes their role in preservationist arguments. He, however, simply chooses to argue differently—specifically, from a stance that requires us to conserve the full biological bequest of nature to future generations of humans. Believing that both justifications will actually lead to the same practical policy results in certain situations, Norton in this paper makes his first pitch for what he would later term the "convergence hypothesis" (see Norton 1991; Minteer 2009). But it is important to point out that, as in his earlier paper, Norton does not reject the role of intrinsic value claims in justifying environmental policy. He simply wants to emphasize that they are not the *only* resources at environmentalists' disposal and probably not the most effective or coherent in certain situations.

Norton publishes what is perhaps his strongest pragmatic critique of nonanthropocentrism and moral monism in environmental philosophy in a 1995 issue of the journal *Environmental Ethics.* Taking aim at Callicott's ecocentric approach, Norton argues in this essay that the monistic reductionism characterizing Callicott's work is especially damaging to the cause of a practical environmental philosophy—one that could contribute to real-world policy discussions and environmental problem solving. He particularly regrets Callicott's turn toward disengaged ontological and metaphysical solutions for environmental quandaries—that is, the quest to determine which entities have moral "standing"—and concludes that such approaches will not, on balance, be as effective as those appealing to "the relatively noncontroversial and intuitive idea that the use of natural resources implies an obligation to protect them for future users—a sustainability theory based in intergenerational equity—rather than exotic appeals to hitherto unnoticed inherent values in nature" (1995, 356).

Although I think Norton here exaggerates the paucity of noninstrumental environmental values in public life, his conclusion is squarely in line with his larger purpose in this essay: the vigorous defense of the validity and soundness of instrumental value justifications in supporting good environmental policy. At the end of his paper, Norton's tolerance of Callicott's nonanthropocentrism appears to have reached a breaking point. Restating his concerns that ontological and monistic responses to environmental problems will founder on the rocks of abstraction and ideological dogmatism, among other vices, Norton concludes by suggesting that we might do well to abandon the concept of intrinsic value altogether, "whether monistic and ungraded or pluralistic and graded into degrees" (1995, 358).

This remark clearly seems to rebut my contention that Norton has and continues to accept a notion of noninstrumental value. It appears, then, that either I am wrong in arguing this interpretation of his project or Norton changes his position during this time. I argue that neither is the case. Considered in context, Norton's dismissal of intrinsic value here is, I think, the result of more than a decade of work attempting to elevate pluralistic, human-based axiological approaches and to contribute to practical policy debates and decision making. With such nonanthropocentrists as Callicott continuing to pay all their philosophical attention to metaphysical founding and the quest for a universal master principle, Norton simply has had enough. Unconvinced that intrinsic value claims have been advanced in the field that manage to avoid the pitfalls he outlines, Norton concludes that nonanthropocentrists' understanding of the concept is, in the end useless, and even counterproductive. Therefore, he believes it is time to dump the rubric and its philosophical and practical liabilities and devote attention elsewhere—namely, the achievement of "policies that protect nature and natural processes according to our best scientific knowledge and reduce uncertainty and improve our knowledge for future management problems and decisions" (1995, 355). Because intrinsic value theory *as it had been employed* in environmental ethics tended to obscure this practical task, and because Norton is confident that his intergenerational humanism could promote more than adequate environmental policy, there is thus no *overriding need* for us to make intrinsic value arguments regarding the treatment of the natural world.

In other words, I do not think Norton gives up on the idea that we might, in certain situations, properly choose to value elements of the natural world noninstrumentally—he just does not believe that we should refer to this activity as recognizing something called "intrinsic value" because of the epistemic and ontological failings it has exhibited at the hands of nonanthropocentric theorists. Rather, we should pursue other, more productive valuation frames that are compatible with a fully human worldview. For example, as he writes in his 1992 critique of intrinsic value in *The Monist,* Norton argues that rather than follow something like Callicott's "monistic inherentism,"

> it seems much more reasonable, and simpler, to follow [Eugene] Hargrove, who believes that the distinction between instrumental and noninstrumental value is important, but who views it as a distinction between two types of anthropocentric values. Or, more radically, to follow me in the path of John Dewey, who rejected the idea of intrinsic value altogether. I do *not* follow Dewey in therefore assimilating all value to instrumental value. I simply choose to stop using the tainted terms. This more radical course obviates the need for hairsplitting and, more importantly, *points the way toward an exploration of anthropocentric, noninstrumental values.* (1992, 221–222; emphasis added)

We may conclude, therefore, that Norton has long recognized the existence and place of noninstrumental values in the larger axiological framework of environmental ethics. He has *not* been willing, however, to place these values in a fully blown nonanthropocentric worldview; humans "do" the valuing, which may or may not be instrumental. Further, Norton is no moral realist. In valuing natural elements noninstrumentally, he argues that we need not commit to objective moral facts or labor under the demands of monistic and universal theoretical stances. Rather, his position builds upon a relational theory of value perception that moves beyond the vestigial Cartesianism Norton diagnoses in many environmental theorists' work. So, for example, although he approves of Eugene Hargrove's own (different, but similarly labeled) "weak anthropocentrism," Norton nevertheless rejects Hargrove's insistence that a firm philosophical line be drawn between instrumental and noninstrumental values. Norton is also uncomfortable with Hargrove's understanding of intrinsic value, presumably because of his suspicion that the latter has not been able to jettison the troubling ontology and epistemology of the concept. Therefore, Norton seems to be making a careful distinction between ontological accounts of intrinsic value (which he rejects) and an anthropocentric accommodation of pragmatic noninstrumental value (which he accepts).

In more recent work, Norton appears to have warmed even more to a nondualistic and pluralistic understanding of intrinsic value. In his 2005 book, *Sustainability,* he advocates tolerance of alternative value positions, including articulations of noninstrumental value within a broader adaptive management framework. As he writes:

> The pragmatic pluralist, who recognizes that people value nature in many ways, need not deny that humans value natural objects "noninstrumentally." For example, many people value nature spiritually; this value is surely noninstrumental, and it is clearly a human value. Once we accept pluralism and a continuum of types of values, spiritual and other noninstrumental values attributed to nature can be seen as differing types of *human* value. (374; emphasis original)

All the same, Norton is skeptical of the long-term utility of intrinsic value talk in environmental discourse. As we develop better "linguistic tools" for describing and defending the values communities attach to nature, he argues, generic and experientially detached references to "intrinsic value" will give way to sharper and more specific language referring to particular biophysical indicators tracking shared commitments (i.e., place-specific values). Such terms—along with more detailed arguments for protecting certain natural features and attributes as community goods—will, Norton predicts, prove more useful in the long run than "thin" attributions of intrinsic value. Still, as a pragmatist philosopher committed to experimentalism and pluralism, it is important to emphasize that Norton remains willing to hold the intrinsic/noninstrumental value position open as a live option in environmental ethics, though he continues to reject folding such value into any sort of broader nonanthropocentric worldview.

To sum up, Norton admittedly delivers serious criticisms of intrinsic value as it has been described and defended in environmental ethics. Concerned with the various metaphilosophical problems of the concept, he also believes that intrinsic value theorists' preoccupation with ontological issues has led them astray of real-world matters of environmental practice. But Norton also stops short of denying the existence and role of noninstrumental values in fostering environmental regard and sound environmental policy; he always recognizes a specific understanding of and holds, on the best days, a kind of grudging appreciation for the usefulness of noninstrumental values in certain contexts. All the same, his is a different version of noninstrumentalism than that traditionally advanced by nonanthropocentrists. Indeed, Norton is often not willing to call such values "intrinsic" for fear of evoking the "exotic" philosophical heritage of the term. Lastly, we can see that many of his criticisms are spurred by his larger philosophical project of promoting a more pluralistic and contextual understanding of environmental values as alternatives to the ideological and foundationalist arguments of such nonanthropocentrists as Callicott.

Dewey and Intrinsic Value

If my observations above are at all on the mark, we are still left asking what we should conclude about the relationship between noninstrumental values and pragmatic environmental philosophy. Specifically, what do we make of Norton's remark that Dewey "assimilated" all value to instrumental values? Is Norton, the leading environmental pragmatist, effectively breaking ranks with the classical pragmatic camp when he admits to recognizing noninstrumental value? I do not think so, but this judgment requires some explanation. Dewey's infamous refusal to countenance "ends-in-themselves"—final goods that are not means to still further value formations—surely appears to suggest a serious disdain for noninstrumentalism. Indeed, this has been the popular view of Dewey's value theory through the years. But is this impression of Dewey's hostility toward intrinsic value entirely warranted? I am here thinking of a particularly interesting passage in his *Reconstruction in Philosophy* where Dewey, in reference to moral goods, concludes that "if the need and deficiencies of a specific situation indicate improvement of health as the end and good, then for that situation health is the ultimate and supreme good. It is no means to something else. *It is a final and intrinsic value*" (1920, 180; emphasis added). Contra Norton's statement, it certainly sounds as though Dewey here recognizes noninstrumental values of some sort. But how do we reconcile this remark with Dewey's emphatic rejection of all manner of fixed values and ends-in-themselves?

The answer, I think, is to be found in his thoroughgoing contextualism—Dewey's emphasis on the problematic situation as the "center of gravity" in moral experience (Pappas 1998). At its most fundamental level, his moral project suggests that instead of imposing any number of predefined ethical absolutes or universals on the specific difficulties that vex us, we might do better to work from the vantage point of the problematic settings themselves. In particular, Dewey argues that we need to construct the unique "good" of each situation, a good that is to be "discovered, projected, and attained on the basis of the exact defect and trouble to be rectified" (1920, 176). This argument for the significance of context places a premium on experimentation and moral deliberation; individuals must be prepared to meet each problematic situation with a willingness to engage in intelligent and creative inquiry. As Dewey succinctly puts it, "The business of reflection in determining the true good cannot be done once and for all"; rather, "it needs to be done, and done over and over and over again, in terms of the conditions of concrete situations as they arise. In short, the need for reflection and insight is perpetually recurring" (1932, 212). By rehearsing and testing "ends-in-view," or those hypothetical solutions to moral quandaries that serve as organizing forces in moral deliberation, we are able to arrive at a reconstructed phase of experience that brings inquiry and the problematic situation at hand to a terminal resolution.

According to this understanding, then, we simply cannot avoid having to puzzle out the import and relevance of the specific facts and circumstances of each problematic situation and their bearing on our evaluative judgments. This holds even if the conditions in question echo previous ethical quandaries, for although Dewey recognizes that comparable cases recur and that it is "the part of wisdom" (1920, 176) to compare them, he thinks this does not absolve us from having to decide how to "overhaul" such moral resources and apply them to the immediate difficulty in question (1932, 283). This construction of the moral good on a contextual basis thus reorients our critical attention toward specific problems and their proposed solutions rather than to abstract questions of value theory and philosophical founding. For Dewey, it simply does not make sense to engage in speculative reflections on ontological matters apart from problematic situations. "*Moral* goods and ends exist only when something has to be done," he maintains (1920, 176; emphasis original), and the intellectualist tendency to become mired in detached reasoning only creates unnecessary and potentially distracting philosophical "busy work" (1938, 112).

In light of this project, how are we to understand Dewey's remark about the "intrinsic value" of certain ends in specific situations? Clearly, much of Dewey's discomfort with the idea of intrinsic value is the result of its conflation with ends-in-themselves, moral goods that transcend cultural experience and resist appraisal and criticism. Dewey fears that such an understanding of these absolute and independent values ultimately works to preclude the need for moral deliberation altogether. On this important point, it is worth quoting him at length:

> The notion that a moral judgment merely apprehends and enunciates some predetermined end-in-itself is, in fact, but a way of denying the need for and existence of genuine moral judgments. For according to this notion there is no *situation* which is problematic. There is only a person who is in a state of subjective moral uncertainty or ignorance. His business, in that case, is not to judge the objective situation in order to determine what course of action is required in order that it may be transformed into one that is morally satisfactory and right, but simply to come into intellectual possession of a predetermined end-in-itself. Goods previously expressed assuredly are material means of reaching a judgment as to what to do. But they *are* means, not fixed ends. They are material to be surveyed and evaluated in reference to the kind of action needed in the *existing* situation. (1938, 169–170; emphasis original)

The embrace of fixed ends is thus disastrous for intelligent moral inquiry, because their *a priori*, preexperiential character undercuts real moral deliberation and clouds the empirical circumstances of the ethical context—the problematic situation. Not surprisingly, an unmistakable democratic conclusion emerges from all this: Moral deliberation rests squarely on the potential of each individual to respond creatively and responsibly to the dilemmas in which he or she finds him- or herself. This description of the standards of inquiry and debate lays bare the moral heart of Dewey's political project, where democracy is not consigned merely to governance and statecraft but is instead a "way of life," a normative vision of the role and character of the individual in the moral and political community.

Rather than ends-in-themselves—independent goods that are absolute, universal, and "injected into the situation from without" (Dewey 1920, 176)—Dewey's alternative ends-in-view are thus guides to action that help resolve our myriad ethical quandaries. As a result, they are inseparable from the real-world contexts in which they are constructed. Accordingly, noninstrumental values can enter into moral deliberations as hypothetical resources drawn upon to direct behavior toward the consummation of cooperative moral debate and an end to the problematic situation. As such, these noninstrumental values are always potential *means* able to structure ethical inquiry (as are instrumental claims). The upshot is that this model paints a strongly pluralistic, situation-based picture of noninstrumental value claims. In the environmental application, therefore, moral arguments that advance the notion of the intrinsic value of an element of nonhuman nature (e.g., a wetland threatened by suburban development) are appraised and criticized on the basis of their ability to contribute to the resolution of the specific problem in question. If moral deliberation and the "dramatic rehearsal" of the consequences flowing from such a claim lead to an effective result (sufficiently protective and democratically authentic environmental policy), then the noninstrumental claim offered in defense of *this particular wetland* moves from a contextual "end in view" to a contextual "end" or "final value." But—and this is critical—it is never an *end-in-itself.* Its philosophical status is entirely dependent upon its role in contributing to the resolution of the situation in which it was entered, its relationship to the valuations and judgments of past experience, and its contribution to still further moral deliberations in other situations awaiting future inquiry.

What does this Deweyan approach accomplish for environmental pragmatists? First, it maintains a version of noninstrumental goods that breaks free of the philosophical shackles that Norton describes. For in this view, and contrary to nonanthropocentrists' renderings, noninstrumental claims are not epistemically or metaphysically foundational. They are *contextual* and are justified in terms of their ability to contribute to the resolution of specific environmental problems. Second, as mentioned before, they are also fundamentally pluralistic: Because problematic situations differ, appropriate ends-in-view and final ends are also expected to differ. Even the same general type of landscape element—again, using the case of wetlands—varies widely in ecological features and functions (e.g., differences in habitat value, groundwater recharge ability, flood control, and so on) and social attributions (e.g., aesthetic values and recreational potential). Third, the emphasis on the relationship between values and empirical contexts suggests that the philosophical attention is, according to pragmatists, turned to all the right places—the real worlds of practice and policy making in which environmental problems are addressed and ameliorated. Fourth, such contextual noninstrumental values are also not fundamentally independent of other types of value claims. This is because, in most cases, these claims prove sufficiently effective only when joined by an array of more numerous *instrumental* arguments for environmental policies of the sort Norton consistently argues for. Finally—and I believe this is a key point—these noninstrumental values are entirely open to public criticism and revision.

If my reading of Dewey's contextualism is accurate, then I argue that environmental philosophers working in the pragmatic mode can accommodate noninstrumental values in their projects without running afoul of the metaphysical and epistemological problems that beset nonanthropocentrists' versions of intrinsic value. Although Dewey clearly rejects the universalist and foundational qualities of noninstrumental goods, he maintains a recognition of moral ends that is concrete, pluralistic, and resolutely experimental. Therefore, Norton, in supporting noninstrumental values within an anthropocentric worldview, is not working against the pragmatic grain (at least, Dewey's moral project).

But we still might ask why, even if intrinsic value can be reconstructed along these lines, pragmatists would feel compelled to go down the noninstrumentalist road at all. The answer, I believe, is that, when viewed in this fashion, noninstrumental values can play an important part in justifying good environmental policy. But the weight these values will have in public deliberations over environmental management and problem solving is different than that typically ascribed by nonanthropocentrists to intrinsic value claims. In the final section of this chapter, I suggest just what I take this role to be.

Noninstrumental Values and Conservation Policy: People and Nature at Nepal's Chitwan National Park

A revealing example of nonanthropocentrists' understanding of the place of their intrinsic value arguments in environmental policy and problem solving may be found in the writing of Rolston, a member of the pioneer generation of academic environmental ethicists and probably the most strident defender of a strong nonanthropocentric environmentalism. In a 1998 paper that is partly devoted to responding to my pragmatic critique of his work, Rolston leaves little doubt about his understanding of the character and force of intrinsic value claims in international conservation efforts. There, Rolston describes the case of Nepal's Chitwan National Park (CNP), a UNESCO World Heritage Site protecting the habitat of several endangered and threatened species, including the one-horned rhinoceros (*Rhinoceros unicornis*), and home to a large tiger population (*Panthera tigris*).

The Chitwan Valley, located in the Tarai lowland of Nepal, was sparsely populated until the 1950s due to malaria. The overthrow of the feudal Rana regime in 1951, however, paved the way for a massive (and successful) malaria-eradication program. This effort, combined with a resettlement program to reduce population pressure in the hill regions, resulted in a dramatic increase in the valley's population density throughout the 1950s and 1960s. The valley forests and wildlife habitat in the region absorbed the brunt of this transformation, with the result being that the tiger and rhino were pushed nearly to extinction in less than a decade of settlement (Gurung 1983). In response to this pressure, the government established a wildlife sanctuary to protect the rhino in the early 1960s and expanded this area to a national park (the nation's first) in 1973.

In his discussion and analysis of the conservation problem presented at CNP, Rolston laments the continuing human pressure on the park's biodiversity. While regretting the crushing poverty in the region, he nevertheless uses this case to make a strong and unabashedly nonanthropocentric argument. "I put the tigers first," he writes, and "have financially supported WWF [World Wildlife Fund] efforts to save Asian and African species, and morally approve the present policies, on grounds that tigers as a species ought not to be sacrificed on the altar of human mistake, regardless of what persons made mistakes where in the complex chain of events" (1998, 350).

In more recent writing, Rolston again underscores the significance of a nonanthropocentric ethic in meeting the conservation challenge in CNP:

> People cannot live in the park or cut grasses, graze cattle and buffalo, or timber the park at will. They are allowed to cut thatch grasses several days a year, and 30 percent of park income from tourists is given to Village Development Communities. The Royal Nepalese Army is responsible for preventing poaching, grazing, cutting grasses, pilfering timber, and permanent habitation on the land. They also do what they can to improve the lot of the people. Probably the park would not survive the local social pressures except for the tourist income, which the national government much desires. Probably, however, the park would not have come into existence and been maintained except for the nonanthropocentric concerns of groups such as World Wildlife Fund to save the endangered species there. (2009, 104–105)

Given this situation (at least, as he characterizes it), in his earlier essay, Rolston asks me what I could possibly say to those Nepalis who wish to "sacrifice the park to relieve their poverty" (1998, 350). As he writes, "If I did not believe (contra Minteer) that tigers have intrinsic value, if I did not believe that species lines are morally considerable, if I thought the values of tigers were only those that this or that culture chooses to assign to them, or not, I would not be making such efforts to protect them" (350). According to Rolston, as a pragmatist, I do not believe that the park's tigers and rhinos have intrinsic value, and because I therefore reject the claim that species are "morally considerable," I am left with precious little to offer to the philosophical defense of nature against human encroachment at CNP. By his lights, I can only appeal to the "flimsy" and "socially constrained" attitudes of my "subculture" (whatever that may be): those random values (which may or may not be environmental) that my community off-handedly chooses to adopt, "without any sure knowledge" of the natural world at all. Thus lacking a true appreciation for the objective, preexperiential intrinsic values present in the natural world, Rolston feels that projects like mine are doomed to failure.

Indeed, he believes that my pragmatic appeal to value pluralism and to open democratic deliberation over competing moral claims regarding nature, because it discards the notion of foundational ethical stances, leaves me, as he puts it, "in a muddle" (1998, 356). Although my position here might be "disguised as pragmatic [environmentalism]," in Rolston's view, the debate I desire will always end in a crass and environmentally exploitative "power struggle" (356). By surrendering what many environmental philosophers take to be their most powerful moral weapon—the political trump of some sort of foundational intrinsic value theory—

we pragmatists have effectively lost the moral and political argument about the value of nature before it even begins.

From my discussion in this chapter, however, it should be clear that I do think we can, as pragmatists, accommodate noninstrumental values in our justifications for conservation policy. Therefore, I see no problem in viewing threatened and endangered species as well worth saving, perhaps because of their connection to the Nepalis' long-term economic interests in a diverse and healthy ecosystem, their embodiment of aesthetic and cultural ideals of human-nature relationships and national identity, their ability to inspire and educate, and so forth. Contrary to Rolston's argument, my intent is not to reject the *idea* that we may value wild species and ecosystems noninstrumentally (or, for that matter, instrumentally). Rather, I reject the argument that such appeals *must* be made in every case and the corollary view that conservation efforts will fail if justified solely by appeal to human values and interests, however broad and enlightened they may be. And I reject as well the move by intrinsic value exponents in which they read their moral programs as advancing foundational principles detached from the plurality of goods present in human experience. So the upshot is that, like Rolston, I, too, think the tigers and rhinos of CNP may be valued noninstrumentally. But, unfortunately, this is probably the extent of our agreement. For *unlike* Rolston, I do not think that this admission solves the problem, and it is precisely this point that suggests to me the need to reconstruct our understanding of the use of noninstrumental justifications in conservation advocacy and environmental discourse.

Because I subscribe to a contextual and experimental approach toward intrinsic value, I cannot follow Rolston and simply decide to "put the tigers first" in Nepal because of some sort of ideological commitment to a universal nonanthropocentric ethic. For one thing, I do not think that the mere invocation of an intrinsic value argument prior to empirical moral examination and inquiry in this case will alleviate the Nepalis' pressure on the park landscape. It appears that, for Rolston, all that matters is that we recognize the objective moral foundations springing out of his strong nonanthropocentric worldview. Once we do this, our obligations become immediately obvious—we must protect the park's biological integrity at any cost, including, perhaps, the lives of the distressed citizens at its borders. This is not the place to discuss the sensitivity of Rolston's environmentalism—although his remark that being a misanthrope is better than being an "arrogant humanist" certainly gives one pause (1998, 356). (I should say here that I do not see the arrogance in wanting environmental ethics to be more culturally sensitive and democratic in its temperament.) But it *is* important to point out that Rolston sees no need here for further moral debate; we either recognize the proper environmental claim, or we do not. If we do not, and we nevertheless still insist on arguing in terms of environmental protection (e.g., the preservation of biodiversity), then we can only appeal to our shaky (nonfoundational) cultural values, which may or may not be shared by such individuals as those in the struggling communities of Nepal.

But how effective is an intrinsic value argument, particularly a foundational claim about the objective value of nonhuman nature, going to be in promoting the public resolution of this case? In truth, I doubt very much that this declaration of intrinsic value will have any real bearing on the events at CNP. I say this, because I do not think a solution delivered from the realm of moral ontology will ameliorate the particular problems here. Instead, it is clear to me that the dilemma at CNP hinges more on issues of historical and contemporary political ecology and broader institutional forces than it does on getting the "moral story" right about the intrinsic value of nature. Again, I do not mean to suggest that questions surrounding the moral status of nonhuman nature are totally irrelevant in these sorts of dilemmas. I simply believe that the range of concerns at stake here—the elements contributing to this particular problematic situation—are much more complicated than those that Rolston describes.

For example, to get at the heart of this conflict, I think we need to understand the extent to which the establishment of the park in the 1970s effectively denied locals access to the subsistence resources cordoned off within the new park's boundaries, depriving them of acreage for field cropping and cattle grazing while also prohibiting their access to firewood and timber resources. In addition, we should take into account the regrettable fact that the park authority did not make any significant attempts to communicate to the local residents why the park should be protected in the first place. Moreover, it apparently paid little regard to the loss of livelihood and the physical threats the park's wild animals posed to those living along the border. In short, the people were largely shut out of the conservation planning and implementation process, and their prior access to and use of the region's resources were sharply curtailed or banned altogether.

In light of these circumstances, it is not surprising that park researchers Sanjay Nepal and Karl Weber (1995) find that many of the resident peoples believe the park authority considers wildlife to be more valuable than people. Citizens' discontent with park policies is thus displayed through their disobedience of various regulations and their illegal grazing of livestock and timber extraction from the park. These activities clearly pose significant threats to the ecological viability of CNP, but the citizens are motivated primarily by political and human ecological conditions rather than faulty metaphysical positions regarding the moral status of nature. At the same time, though, it is important to note that many of the people maintain an appreciative view of conservation and wildlife, even in the face of their own social and economic sacrifices (McLean and Straede 2003).

Despite the apparent intractability of this dilemma, however, such observers as Nepal and Weber believe some cause for optimism is warranted. In particular, they suggest that multiple, reinforcing long-term strategies, such as the creation of a park buffer zone, the development of local community forestry, the improvement of agricultural efficiency and technology, and the stimulation of indigenous approaches toward wildlife conservation, promise to lead toward a successful resolution of the park problem that will protect the area's biodiversity while also providing for viable human communities (1995, 863–864). Proposals to spread the opening of the park for grass collection in different sections at different times of year also promise to diffuse the impact of access and human appropriation of park biomass (Straede and Helles 2000). At the center of these approaches is the recognition that the park authority needs to fashion a more inclusive administrative style that involves the community in the decision-making process as well as the day-to-day management of the biological resources in the region. Further, it is becoming increasingly clear that citizens' local environmental knowledge might be an enormous asset to the development of these more socially embedded and adaptive management strategies.

I argue that this sort of pragmatic attempt to balance the various human and ecological needs at CNP is more likely to achieve a sustainable nature-culture relationship than Rolston's rather simplistic "saving nature or feeding people" outlook and the embrace of a "fortress conservation" mentality that often runs afoul of social justice—and that, ironically, can be inimical to good conservation practice (see, e.g., Brockington 2002; Siurua 2006). As I mention briefly in Chapter 2, conservation scientists and professionals working to protect biodiversity in rural and developing areas are increasingly realizing the moral imperative of enlisting local peoples in conservation efforts because of the requirements of participatory justice in decision making and achieving a more equitable distribution of the economic benefits and burdens of nature conservation (e.g., Adams et al. 2004; Blaustein 2007). There is also the pragmatic consideration that nature protection can be more difficult without the support of resident peoples, who can often make or break conservation programs by engaging in (or refraining from) the illegal taking of wildlife and forest resources in protected areas. Although a healthy debate exists in the conservation and development communities over the strategic and conceptual aspects of integrating conservation and development goals at the project level (e.g., McShane and Wells 2004), the emerging view appears to be that nature conservation and sustainable development should not be approached as a zero-sum game (like Rolston's depiction of the tensions at CNP), but rather as complementary goals that can and should be pursued in tandem, even if conservationists and development advocates must at times make difficult choices and trade-offs in particular projects (Sunderland, Ehringhaus, and Campbell 2008; McShane et al. 2011).

Based on this more realistic assessment, the notion that voicing noninstrumental claims about the value of threatened species will single-handedly resolve what is, in fact, a tangled complex of historical, political, social, and economic forces and interests at CNP borders on academic fantasy. In the CNP case, I believe Rolston's reliance on an intrinsic value argument for the park's biotic community will actually do very little for the cause of park protection, mostly because this view refuses to countenance the legitimate human welfare and development interests that must be balanced with the needs of the tigers and rhinos. Again, this does not mean that environmentalists (whether in the form of the World Wildlife Fund [WWF] or other conservation organizations) should completely avoid making noninstrumental environmental claims in these sorts of cases. Indeed, I expect that, if communicated in a culturally sensitive and appropriate manner, such arguments could motivate at least some local residents to support environmental protection for the park, especially if the goal of nature conservation at CNP is also connected, at the project level, to their physical well-being and long-term economic and cultural interests. But I do not think that the argument for the intrinsic value of wildlife preservation and ecosystem integrity, standing alone (and fundamentally opposed to basic human interests), will suffice, especially because this approach does not get at the real sociopolitical and historical roots of the environmental conflict at CNP.

Although noninstrumental claims regarding the value of nonhuman nature can, at certain times and in particular places, be effective in promoting conservation policy goals, they can actually be counterproductive when employed as moral trumps to stifle public debate and political judgment. Unfortunately, and as I discuss in the previous chapters, I believe that many nonanthropocentric philosophers see these claims as offering a way to avoid political deliberation over competing moral positions in public life, thus violating the spirit of Dewey's understanding of contextual and democratic moral inquiry. Although intrinsic value arguments might be the most powerful and effective in certain circumstances (such as convincing children not to kill snakes in their backyards), they will not always be in others (such as resolving the conflicts at CNP). We therefore need to be much more circumspect about asserting the indispensability of such claims in public discourse and adopt a more pluralistic and experimental position toward the pragmatic efficacy of multiple environmental values in environmental decision making and policy arguments.

Conclusion

In this chapter, I argue that a pragmatic environmental ethics need not turn its back on intrinsic value arguments on behalf of wild species and ecosystems. I do so by offering a pragmatic-Deweyan reconstruction of intrinsic value that I believe avoids the metaphysical and ideological uses of the concept that many nonanthropocentric philosophers rely upon. By accepting a contextual and pragmatic model of the use of noninstrumental arguments in justifying particular conservation actions and policy decisions, we place great stock in, as Dewey puts it, the ability of public "debate, discussion and persuasion" (1927, 365) to help us arrive at democratically valid judgments and social outcomes. In response to Rolston's claim that such debates will only result in unctuous political deal making, I have to believe that the sort of democratic argument over competing environmental claims I have in mind is preferable to the assertion of foundational moral principles considered to be beyond critical public scrutiny and revision. Rolston's highly skeptical view of public deliberation threatens to decouple our environmental commitments from political life, a move that I think ultimately spells disaster for the cause of inclusive and effective conservation policy and ecologically informed democratic citizenship.

It seems clear that successful justifications for desired conservation programs and environmental policies will be those that creatively draw upon a plurality of noninstrumental *and* instrumental positions in open deliberation over policy and management alternatives. This view ultimately reinforces the important point—that Norton and others make—that these positions are complementary value claims rather than hard-and-fast ontological polarities. An experimental and pluralistic value framework that has a place for (contextual) noninstrumental value claims in conservation and environmental decision making will, I believe, enrich and improve the success of our moral arguments for conserving biodiversity and protecting landscapes over the long run. Along the way, we can also encourage intelligent public deliberation and collaborative moral inquiry into the direction of our mixed natural and human communities, including the proper reconstruction of our value inheritances from previous environmental debates as we meet the challenges of the present and the needs of the future.

Even though nonanthropocentric writers often employ them as "conversation stoppers" in ethical arguments about nature protection, a more pragmatic approach to noninstrumental value claims can reclaim them as democratically compatible and useful tools for achieving key conservation goals and policy outcomes. In rejecting many of the philosophical and political flaws, then, we need not abandon the concept altogether, especially if we can accommodate noninstrumental elements into a problem-oriented and pluralistic model of environmental ethics. In the end, what could be more pragmatic than that?

5

Natural Piety, Environmental Ethics, and Sustainability

Getting Religion in Environmental Pragmatism

In Chapter 4, I discuss how a pragmatic view of intrinsic or noninstrumental environmental value may be pursued within a situation-based or contextual framework, one that draws from John Dewey's understanding of ethical inquiry and problem solving. The discussion there is largely methodological—that is, it focuses on the *process* rather than the *content* of environmental ethical claims and arguments within environmental management and policy problems. I now want to turn to a more substantive consideration of environmental values by recovering a neglected aspect of the pragmatist tradition: Dewey's religious thought. It is a strain of pragmatist writing that has received scant attention from environmental philosophers. One might even draw the conclusion that classical and environmental pragmatists have very little to say about religious experience, presumably because the religious perspective seems to require a host of commitments—that is, supernaturalism, foundationalism, and perhaps a scholastic dogmatism—that run against the grain of the naturalism, contextualism, and antiformalism of iconic pragmatists, such as Dewey.

Although the view that pragmatism is indifferent, if not hostile, to religion is quite common, it is not correct. It is certainly true that contemporary pragmatists in environmental ethics, including myself, have traditionally neglected the religious dimensions of human-nature relations in favor of other topics (although Max Oelschlaeger's work [1994] may perhaps be read as a partial exception). The classical pragmatists, though, paid a good deal of attention to religious experience, even though they are often depicted as being soulless worshippers of science and technique over ultimate values and the transcendent (see, e.g., Diggins 1994). This reading, however, may owe more to the secondary scholarship on pragmatism than to anything written by William James or Dewey. Giles Gunn, for example, attributes much of the received opinion regarding pragmatism's incompatibility with religion to the great influence that Richard Rorty exerted on the tradition's revival in the 1980s, in which Rorty attempted to connect, in Gunn's words, "the development of pragmatism and liberalism's project of disenchanting the world religiously" (1998, 404).

At the same time, it must be said that the instrumentalism and naturalism of the classic American pragmatists—especially Dewey—conditioned their understanding of religion and the religious life, most notably belief in a supernatural being (which, as I discuss below, Dewey flatly rejects). This move was and doubtless still is unsatisfactory for theists who do not accept as "religious" any belief system that does not issue from and terminate in a divine power residing beyond the physical world. Regardless, it is undeniable that the founding generation of American pragmatists took the religious dimension of experience very seriously, even as they sought to reconstruct it to make it more agreeable to their own metaphysical and epistemological commitments.

In this chapter, I therefore begin to make amends for environmental pragmatists' neglect of religious experience, albeit in abbreviated and selective fashion. Specifically, I want to explore how a pragmatic and naturalistic understanding of religiosity—as characterized by Dewey in his frequently overlooked 1934 book on religion, *A Common Faith*—can enrich environmental pragmatists' notion of the religious as a quality that can attach to a wide array of human experiences in nature. In doing so, I hope to show that pragmatism (and Dewey's work in particular) encourages a more respectful and pious attitude toward nature than nonanthropocentric critics of environmental pragmatism (and perhaps even some of those who identify themselves as environmental pragmatists) have previously recognized.

Far from celebrating the triumph of human will and technoscientific mastery over nature, I suggest that Dewey advocates a normative attitude of humility toward natural conditions in *A Common Faith* that should resonate with environmentalists of a variety of convictions, including nonanthropocentrists. In particular, Dewey's religious notion of "natural piety" provides an important ethical constraint on human ambition and the desire to control natural forces. It is an attitude of harmonious cooperation with nature rather than conquest, an acknowledgment of the fundamental human dependence on natural forces residing outside the human self.

A retrieval of Dewey's concept of natural piety expands the philosophical and ethical range of environmental pragmatism, incorporating a respect for nature and a sense of the ideal in human environmental experience. It does so, moreover, without introducing any speculative nonanthropocentric theory of intrinsic value and without surrendering the broad instrumentalism at the core of the pragmatist understanding of value and experience. Furthermore, and as I discuss in my conclusion to this chapter, it provides a critical moral check on aggressively humanistic agendas for environmental action, including those couched in the rhetoric of progressive environmentalism and sustainability. (I should note that even though my primary focus in this chapter is Dewey's religious thought, the founding generation of pragmatist philosophers, in fact, held a diverse set of views on religion and religious experience. For example, Charles Sanders Peirce and James were much more open than Dewey to speculative arguments; James in particular had a strong personal and philosophical interest in the mystical and subjective dimensions of spirituality [see, e.g., Smith 1963, 1978]. Given the centrality of Dewey to my approach developed in this book, however, I confine the discussion here to Dewey's understanding of religious experience.)

Bringing Religion down to Earth: Dewey's *A Common Faith*

The religious aspects of Dewey's work evolved through a series of stages, a journey that mirrored the changes in his own personal religious beliefs and the development of his wider philosophical system (Rockefeller 1991). Growing up in Burlington, Vermont, in the shadow of the Civil War, Dewey was raised in the Protestant Christian tradition and was a member of the Congregational Church until age thirty-five, when he decided to leave the church and organized religion. As a college student at the University of Vermont in the late 1870s, Dewey fell under the sway of transcendentalist philosophy via the teachings of H.A.P. Torrey, who introduced Dewey to the Vermont transcendentalist tradition led by former UVM President James Marsh. Although he looked back fondly on Torrey and his studies in Burlington, Dewey wrote later that the "theological and intuitional phase" in his development did not have any lasting influence (1930a, 149).

A few years later, while a graduate student at Johns Hopkins University, Dewey absorbed another significant intellectual influence: the neo-Hegelianism of Hopkins professors G. S. Morris and T. H. Green. Hegelian ideas fulfilled what Dewey describes as a "demand for unification that was doubtless an intense emotional craving" (1930a, 153). Although he retained the Hegelian emphasis on unity in his mature work, over the course of the next forty years—a period that tracked his professional movement from Hopkins to the University of Michigan, to the University of Chicago, and finally to Columbia University—Dewey shed much of his philosophical idealism in favor of a more naturalistic and empirical philosophical system.

This evolution resulted in his displaying an increasingly powerful interest in the social dimensions of experience, especially ethics, education, and democratic life. Dewey published a wealth of material on these topics beginning in the 1910s, including such landmark volumes as *Democracy and Education* (1916), *Reconstruction in Philosophy* (1920), *Human Nature and Conduct* (1922), *The Public and Its Problems* (1927), and *Liberalism and Social Action* (1935) as well as several other long works and countless essays. Although his work and thought continued to evolve nearly until the time of his death in 1952, by the late 1920s, the mature elements of his pragmatist philosophical vision—that is, its naturalism, instrumentalism, and democratic humanism—were firmly in place (Rockefeller 1991, 22).

Despite Dewey's movement away from idealism toward a more empirical and experimental mode of philosophical analysis and his rejection of institutional religion in the 1890s, Steven Rockefeller, in his illuminating study of Dewey's religious thought, believes that religious experience was the culminating force in much of the philosopher's work and that his writing possesses a steady (although evolving) religiosity from beginning to end (1991, 539). Rockefeller's strong assertions here are somewhat arguable, especially given Dewey's own view of the matter. "Social interests and problems," Dewey wrote in 1930, "from an early period had to me the intellectual appeal and provided the intellectual sustenance that many seem to have found primarily in religious questions" (1930a, 154). In his autobiographical 1930 essay "From Absolutism to Experimentalism," Dewey attempts to explain and defend his reluctance to engage religious questions:

> I have not been able to attach much importance to religion as a philosophic problem; for the effect of that attachment seems to be in the end a subornation of candid philosophic thinking to the alleged but factitious needs of some special set of convictions. I have enough faith in the depth of the religious tendencies of men to believe that they will adapt themselves to any required intellectual change, and that it is futile (and likely to be dishonest) to forecast prematurely just what forms the religious interest will take as a final consequence of the great intellectual transformation that is going on. As I have been frequently criticized for undue reticence about the problems of religion, I insert this explanation: it seems to me that the great solicitude of many persons, professing belief in the universality of the need for religion, about the present and future of religion proves that in fact they are moved more by partisan interest in a particular religion than by interest in religious experience. (1930a, 153–154)

From these remarks alone, we can see that Dewey clearly is frustrated with the tendency for the discussion of religious problems to become ideological due to the influence of *a priori* doctrinal commitments shielded from intelligent public inquiry. Indeed, the private and allegedly unique nature of conventional religious beliefs is unacceptable to Dewey, who believes (as I discuss in Chapter 2) that knowing and valuing take place through a process of inquiry modeled after an idealized understanding of the scientific method. As he puts it, "The religious function in experience can be emancipated only through surrender of the whole notion of special truths that are religious by their own nature, together with the idea of peculiar avenues of access to such truths" (1934, 23). He intimates, however, that he is open to engaging religious questions via the medium of human experience—that is, naturalistically—in such a way that they are not constrained by doctrine or roped off from the rest of cultural experience due to their alleged special nature.

Dewey would indeed soon get more serious about "religion as a philosophic problem," although his treatment of the subject is (and doubtless remains) controversial, mostly because of this desire to ground faith and a sense of the divine in an earthly setting. Although Dewey wrote a number of essays on religion and

Christianity earlier in his philosophical career, in his short 1934 book, *A Common Faith,* Dewey provides his most detailed and thorough statement of his mature pragmatic view of religious experience. Noting that theists and atheists conflate the "religious phase of experience" with the supernatural, he writes that he seeks to "emancipate" the "genuinely religious" (4) from this traditional and deeply problematic association. In doing so, he hopes to bring the religious attitude into the realm of lived human experience, as it is an attitude he feels is regularly "displayed in art, science and good citizenship" (17).

To undertake such a project required some preliminary parsing of terms. Dewey makes a particular distinction between "religion" as the collective body of doctrines and practices considered in an institutional sense and "religious," which he argues should refer to a quality that could adhere to "every object and every proposed end or ideal" (1934, 8). The religious part of experience therefore does not operate on a different metaphysical plane from the other parts; it is a quality that can be attained in all areas of human experience where people display a powerful loyalty to ideal ends and a desire to achieve them. "Any activity pursued in behalf of an ideal end against obstacles and in spite of threats of personal loss because of conviction of its general and enduring value," he writes, "is religious in quality" (19).

This naturalistic reframing of religiosity in Dewey's work is perhaps most pronounced—and controversial—in his discussion of God. In his formulation, "God" denotes not a divine being, but rather the "unity of all ideal ends arousing us to desire and actions . . . a unification of ideal values that is essentially imaginative in origin when the imagination supervenes in conduct" (1934, 29–30). It is a semantic "reconstruction" that probably caused more trouble than it was worth. As Michael Eldridge writes, Dewey's intent in retaining the term is to allow the "unchurched secularly religious" to use the term in "good conscience," but its traditional association with a supernatural being appears to work against his attempt to ground religiosity in the social and natural conditions of experience (1998, 154; see also Rockefeller 1991). Still, retooling the term allows it to fit more comfortably within the strong naturalism of his philosophical system, even if it appears to change the subject with respect to the ultimate grounding and authority governing the religious life.

A key feature of the religious dimension of experience for Dewey involves the unification of self and its harmonization with surrounding conditions. "To achieve and realize a *whole* self is [in Dewey's view] the chief concern of the religious in experience," writes philosopher John E. Smith (1978, 188; emphasis original). Accordingly, religious faith for Dewey is the conviction that we can use the human imagination to project unifying social ideals into the world and actively realize them; it does not imply belief either in the existence of a supreme being or pre-experiential truths. By working to realize human ideals in experience—and choosing to live by their standards—we demonstrate and develop "moral faith" in the genuine religious potential of human life, a potential for the "unification of the self through allegiance to inclusive ideal ends" (Dewey 1934, 23). Furthermore, although they are products of human imagination, the aims and ideals that attract our loyalty and generate action (becoming religious in character) are not imaginary. They are "made out of the hard stuff of the world of physical and social experience," Dewey reminds us (33).

Dewey's thoroughly naturalistic conception of religious experience is clearly a dramatic departure from traditional theistic models. As Dewey scholar Raymond Boisvert observes:

> Typically, religious practices and attitudes are said to be grounded or rooted in an absolute Being who is their source and guarantor. Dewey begins rather with practice and claims that, when certain conditions are met, the experience in question can be deemed "religious." We do not start with a divinity and then derive social practices. We start with social practices and when certain of them are infused with a conviction that their meaning is linked to wider natural and social forces, we come as close as is possible to what traditional religions had as best about them. (1998, 144)

The natural and social forces that form the foundation of Dewey's understanding of the religious (and the source of the ideal as generated through the imagination) become, in turn, the proper object of the religious attitude, or what Dewey terms "natural piety." Rather than displaying reverence or awe of a divine being as the source of knowledge, value, and existence, natural piety is directed at the enabling conditions of lived experience—that is, the physical and social elements that support help shape human life. This is not a new idea for Dewey. As he wrote in 1907, "Piety is attachment to whatever in the sources of man's being also serves as the natural and historic fount of the values which make this being worth having. It is a cherishing consciousness that the human spirit is derived and responsible, having its roots in nature and in the past endeavor of society" (237).

Rejecting the notion that humans are above nature because of a special relationship with the divine and the view that the universe is hostile to the human enterprise, Dewey creates an alternative portrait of complex human dependence—and potential harmony—with the surrounding environment. Although nature is not always attuned to human ends, it is an inseparable partner in the human endeavor:

> The essentially unreligious attitude is that which attributes human achievement and purpose to man in isolation from the world of physical nature and his fellows. Our successes are dependent upon the cooperation of nature. The sense of the dignity of human nature is as religious as is the sense of awe and reverence when it rests upon a sense of human nature as a cooperating part of a larger whole. Natural piety is not of necessity either a fatalistic acquiescence in natural happenings or a romantic idealization of the world. It may rest upon a just sense of nature as the whole of which we are parts, while it also recognizes that we are parts that are marked by intelligence and purpose, having the capacity to strive by their aid to bring conditions into greater consonance with what is humanly desirable. Such piety is an inherent constituent of a just perspective in life. (Dewey 1934, 18)

Natural piety, as Dewey describes it, stands for a kind of reverence toward nature, which in his antidualistic understanding comprises both human social relations and the nonhuman environment. At its core, the concept suggests human reliance on natural and social conditions beyond the individual self, a relationship premised on the notion of a nature agreeable to human aims and interests. "A humanistic religion," Dewey argues, "if it excludes our relation to nature, is pale and thin, as it is presumptuous, when it takes humanity as an object of worship" (1934, 36).

"Natural Piety" and Environmental Philosophy

Dewey's arguments serve as a preemptive correction to the "despotic" view of human-nature relations that historian Lynn White, Jr. (1967), would later make famous in his well-known essay "The Historical Roots of Our Ecologic Crisis," which I discuss in Chapter 3. Unlike White, however, Dewey does not believe that "anthropocentrism" in general is the problem; rather, it is when humanism becomes arrogant and myopic—ignoring the human-nature dependence—that it gets into trouble. A truly enlightened or intelligent anthropocentrism does not, for Dewey, entail the view that humans were created as superior to the rest of the nonhuman world. Even though all values are human values (including nature-appreciating values), as an evolutionary naturalist, Dewey does not accept ontological anthropocentrism—that is, the position that humans are somehow privileged in a cosmic sense. "Humanity is not, as was once thought, the end for which all things were formed; it is but a slight and feeble thing, perhaps an episodic one, in the vast stretch of the universe," Dewey writes in *The Public and Its Problems* (1927, 345). While affirming that, from our own perspective, human concerns are necessarily at the center of interest, Dewey makes it clear that this observation does not preclude viewing human affairs as thoroughly wrapped up with natural conditions. The latter, he writes, are vital compositional elements of lived human experience.

Dewey repeatedly emphasizes the importance of maintaining this sense of humility toward nature and a desire for harmony with the environment by "cooperating with forces beyond those created by human choice" (Boisvert 1998, 153). His is what we might characterize as an "ecological" view of the human self in which individuals were conceived as part of a larger evolving social and natural whole. "A religious attitude," Dewey concludes, "needs the sense of a connection of man, in the way of both dependence and support, with the enveloping world that the imagination feels is a universe" (1934, 36).

In emphasizing the ideal of human-nature cooperation and the intimate connection between individuals and their wider social and natural conditions of experience, Dewey's concept of natural piety similarly highlights the normative notion of human accommodation to nature, particularly in those cases where we cannot easily or successfully adjust it to serve our purposes (1934, 12). Indeed, as Bob Pepperman Taylor observes, genuine religious experience in Dewey's model reflects a productive adaptation to the surrounding physical environment, a process that can occur only when human aims and activities are properly integrated with nature (2004, 47). Natural piety—the respectful attitude toward the environment that reminds us of our dependency on wider natural and social forces—facilitates this critical process of adaptation.

Here I think we can see an intriguing parallel between Dewey's writing on natural piety—and his ecological humanism—and the environmental thought of Liberty Hyde Bailey, a largely forgotten thinker in the American environmental tradition (see Minteer 2006, 2008). This situation is, I think, regrettable, given that Bailey was a gifted scientist and amateur philosopher who, in many respects, lit upon ideas that would later be picked up and advanced by the most influential historical figure in environmental ethics, Aldo Leopold. A man of many talents and interests, Bailey trained and worked as a horticultural scientist and university administrator (he was the first dean of Agriculture at Cornell University), but he was also a pioneering agrarian thinker, conservationist, and proto-environmental philosopher who authored a series of important books on environmental themes during the first two decades of the twentieth century. In addition, Bailey was an important figure in the Progressive-era "Country Life Movement," a reform effort aimed at improving the economic, social, and spiritual conditions of rural life. In 1908, President Theodore Roosevelt appointed him chair of the Country Life Commission, which was tasked with surveying the conditions of American country life and identifying means to achieve rural revitalization during a period of great urban and industrial growth. One of Bailey's fellow commission members was Gifford Pinchot, first head of the U.S. Forest Service and a pivotal thinker in early American conservation (Minteer 2006).

Bailey's philosophically oriented writing on nature reflects classic conservation themes of efficiency and resource sustainability, but it also sounds deeper moral and religious commitments to the Earth. In other words, his is a pluralistic form of environmental philosophy that ties together a profound reverence for the land and a more traditional Progressive concern with the civic health of rural communities and the wise use of natural resources. It is a synthesis, moreover, that displays an overarching commitment to scientific naturalism in a manner that would likely have drawn Dewey's strong assent. As Bailey writes in his landmark work, *The Holy Earth* (1915), human "dominion" over nature carries with it a moral injunction to demonstrate restraint and reverence toward the natural conditions of experience:

> One cannot receive all these privileges without bearing the obligation to react and partake, to keep, to cherish, and to cooperate. We have assumed that there is no obligation to an inanimate thing, as we consider the earth to be: but man should respect the conditions in which he is placed; the earth yields the living creature; man is a living creature; science constantly narrows the gulf between animate and inanimate, between the organized and the inorganized; evolution derives the creatures from the earth, the creation is one creation. I must accept all or reject all. (6)

The moral imperative for Bailey, as with Dewey, is not to conquer nature, but rather to recognize the seeking of harmony with natural conditions for our social and civic well-being—to adapt to and "cooperate" with nature, which for Bailey, the conservationist and agrarian, takes on the more concrete meaning of land, and especially soil health. As he puts it in *The Holy Earth*: "A good part of agriculture is to learn how to adapt one's work to nature, to fit the crop-scheme to the climate and the soil and the facilities. To live in right relations to the natural conditions is one of the first lessons that a wise farmer or any other wise man learns" (11).

Like Bailey, Dewey's attention to the process of adaptation and adjustment—a hallmark of his broader evolutionary naturalism—translates into what we might describe today as a broadly humanistic understanding of intergenerational obligations. In his vision, every generation inherits the widely shared ideals and values that are the historical products of human-nature interaction, and every generation is charged with the responsibility of taking care of these goods (and undertaking the actions they require) so they may be bequeathed to the future. Dewey's fidelity to the historical traditions of the community—a commitment that many readers of his work ignore—is an aspect of his work that has been effectively reclaimed by political theorist Melvin Rogers, who writes that respect for tradition becomes a living element in the moral life within his understanding of natural piety:

> The concern about piety, as Dewey understands, is a more general argument about the *past*, the ground upon which we stand as it has been built up by previous generations, in which institutions of religion are but one part. . . . But in Dewey's view, a past that infuses and aids one in negotiating the present is no past where that means historically antecedent and substantively irrelevant. So for him, a past that aids is what we call a living tradition or a habit. (2008, 128–129; emphasis original)

In addition to this intergenerational dimension, we also see in Dewey's concept of natural piety the unification of his religious thinking and his more well-known concern with community life and the development of a strong democratic culture. As he writes in *A Common Faith*:

> We who now live are parts of a humanity that extends into the remote past, a humanity that has interacted with nature. The things in civilization we most prize are not of ourselves. They exist by grace of the doings and sufferings of the continuous human community in which we are a link. Ours is the responsibility of conserving, transmitting, rectifying and expanding the heritage of values we have received that those who come after us may receive it more solid and secure, more widely accessible and more generously shared than we have received it. Here are all the elements for a religious faith that shall not be confined to sect, class, or race. Such a faith has always been implicitly the common faith of mankind. It remains to make it explicit and militant. (1934, 57–58)

The "heritage of values" to which Dewey refers surely includes the ideals generated by contact with the human imagination and the natural world—values reflected across the domain of human experience—that is, in the arts, the sciences, politics, and so on. The shepherding of these deeply felt sentiments and ideals across an ever-wider community (and into the future) is a religious act, a demonstration of moral faith in the potentialities of human life when it is properly enmeshed in the social and physical matrix of Dewey's "nature." Although Dewey's religious ideas and especially his notion of natural piety convey a serious respect for natural conditions and the desire to cooperate and adapt to environmental exigencies rather than dominate them, it is true that his vision is ultimately humanistic. Our solicitude toward nonhuman nature is motivated primarily by the recognition of its essential and profound role as the foundation for human experience, a crucial source for the workings of the human imagination and the realization of enduring social ideals. A sustainable relationship with natural conditions is thus a moral imperative, according to Dewey's emphasis on continually enriching and broadening human experience.

Yet even this expansive, cultural instrumentalism toward nature present in Dewey's attitude of natural piety—a stance that comes as close to ethical idealism as any other commitment in Dewey's later work—has led some observers to conclude his argument would ultimately fail to motivate an adequate environmental ethic, especially when it is compared with more transcendental expressions of natural piety, such that found in Emerson. As one observer writes:

> Dewey could offer his approval of the turn toward nature and away from supernaturalism, but Dewey regarded nature as something instrumentally valuable only. Since the instrumental value of nature was grounded on whatever proved to be instrumentally valuable to humanity, this type of natural piety could justify the displacement of not only ultimate purposes like those envisioned by Emerson but also the purposes of coexistent species. So, the natural piety of Dewey might lead to the exploitation of nature. (Wilson 1995, 344)

This reading is mistaken, for two reasons. First, I believe it fails to appreciate the strong expression of humility and sense of human dependency on natural conditions that Dewey emphasizes in the notion of natural piety; as I discuss, these sentiments are an important part of his directive to respect and cooperate with nature rather than dominate it. This view also is incorrect in assuming that one *must* hold a strong nonanthropocentric theory of natural value to justify appropriate environmental protection—that is, a stance that recognizes nature's inherent worth or intrinsic value in addition (or perhaps opposed) to instrumental value.

As I mention earlier, this is a common attitude in environmental ethics today. J. Baird Callicott provides one of the better summaries of what nonanthropocentrists believe to be at stake in their contest with humanistic environmental value claims:

> If all environmental values are anthropocentric and instrumental, then they have to compete head to head with the economic values derived from converting rain forests to lumber and pulp, savannas to cattle pasture, and so on. Environmentalists, in other words, must show that preserving biological diversity is of greater instrumental value to present and future generations

> than is lucrative timber extraction, agricultural conversion, hydroelectric empoundment, mining, and so on. For this simple reason, a persuasive philosophical case for the intrinsic value of nonhuman natural entities and nature as a whole would make a huge practical difference. (1999a, 31)

Although a narrow form of instrumentalism that considers nature as only a commodity has no doubt contributed greatly to the loss of wild species and wilderness, the wider instrumentalism of Dewey—a full-blown cultural instrumentalism that recognizes the many noncommodity and nonmaterial "uses" of nature, such as for spiritual refreshment, literary inspiration, and nourishing of the political imagination—is a far more complex and variegated axiological system. Moreover, Dewey's approach, especially in its religious phase, is qualitatively different from conceptions of economic and commercial value. One cannot encapsulate the full meaning of natural piety, for example, in standard economic notions of welfare, preference satisfaction, or "willingness to pay."

These exploitationist concerns about pragmatic instrumentalism also fail to appreciate the great importance Dewey attaches to nature (especially in his religious thought) as source of human value and experience. Yes, Dewey still views the natural world as instrumentally valuable, but the significance he places upon this particular "instrument" cannot be higher. In his classic 1920 book *Reconstruction in Philosophy,* Dewey laments the tendency to bifurcate instrumental and intrinsic values and to disparage the former as "merely instrumental" goods that lack the special worth of allegedly "final" ends. Only by removing the false division between instrumental and intrinsic values, Dewey argues, can religious, aesthetic, and moral ends be "woven into the texture of daily life and made substantial and pervasive" (1920, 178). Indeed, once this means-ends continuum is achieved and solidified in experience, we will be able to do away with the mischievous (that is, hopelessly dualistic) notion of "instrumental" and "intrinsic" values altogether. I discuss the continuity of values in Dewey's ethical system, and the key role of situational context and inquiry in his framing of means and ends, further in the next chapter. But suffice it to say here that we find in his writing on religion and social ethics an abiding resistance to efforts (such as those of contemporary nonanthropocentrists in environmental ethics) to create a deep ontological and epistemological division between intrinsic and instrumental values in experience.

The upshot is that although nature may provide the conditions to support the attainment of human ideals and promote human well-being (in its fullest sense), in Dewey's work it is not just a tool to be used carelessly and discarded. Rather, it is an elemental enabling condition and well of human ideals and meaning that deserve respect as such and require proper care so these ideals may be even more widely shared within and between generations. Rockefeller puts it this way:

> Dewey's philosophy is primarily concerned with the needs and problems of people, but as an evolutionary naturalist he had a keen sense of the interdependence of humanity and nature. In this regard, he argued that a vital religious faith, which involves a concern to unify the ideal and the real, should

> include an attitude of piety toward nature. . . . He rejected both a romantic idealization of nature's support for the human endeavor and the gloomy perspective of a despairing atheism. . . . Dewey wrote very little on the subject of conservation, but his concept of natural piety includes respect and care for the earth. (1998, 143–144)

Rockefeller concludes that this aspect of Dewey's thought makes it especially relevant to our current environmental predicament, which he suggests finds us searching for a lasting and balanced human-nature harmony in this "middle path" between flat-out nature worship and heedless materialism. It is, in short, the path to ecosocial sustainability.

On this reading, there is an interesting—and I believe heretofore unexplored—connection between the pragmatic idealist dimension of Dewey's religious thought and Bryan Norton's (1984) original formulation of "weak anthropocentrism." As I discuss in Chapter 4, Norton's argument, which may be seen as a precursor to his later and more explicitly pragmatist writing in the field (e.g., Norton 2005), is that among its many "uses," nature can serve as a source of human ideals—including ideals of human harmony with species and ecological systems—that can in turn be employed to critique those more economist, "felt preferences" of individuals that could lead to the exploitation of nature. Norton's early articulation of weak anthropocentrism features a broad, culturally oriented instrumentalism regarding nonhuman nature. Like Dewey's understanding of natural piety, this normative project enlists nature in the enterprise of long-term human improvement, a process Norton describes, in his early paper on the subject, as viewing nature as a "teacher of human values" and serving as a critical source of "inspiration in value formation" (1984, 135). Although Norton moved on to embrace a broader pragmatist philosophy of sustainability in the 1990s, Dewey's religious project provides a strong link between the human ideals of harmony with nature captured in Norton's earlier weak anthropocentrism—which combined what we might describe as the need to respect the role of nature as a "moral resource"—and the explicitly pragmatic approach he and others now advocate.

Conclusion: On Sustainability and a "Limited" Environmentalism

I believe that Dewey's religious thinking and his concept of natural piety demonstrate that philosophical pragmatism is much more amenable to the environmentalist agenda than nonanthropocentric critics have asserted. Although it stops short of attributing to nature direct moral standing, in connecting environmental conditions to lasting human ideals that demand widespread loyalty, Dewey's notion of natural piety fosters an attitude of respect toward the natural world as a critical foundation for the deepest and most powerful qualities of human experience, including the ideal unification of the human self in nature. By embracing this largely ignored religious dimension of Dewey's work, it is possible to articulate a genuine sense of awe and a meaningful appreciation of the natural world as well as sensitivity to the ideal elements of human-nature experience in a manner consistent with the historical pragmatist tradition. Collectively, I believe these sentiments come very close to the intuitions that motivate much nonanthropocentric ethical theorizing, yet they do not require one to subscribe to any metaphysical notion of intrinsic natural value shorn from the other "anthropocentric" values within human experience.

The emphasis on the virtues of humility, restraint, and cooperation in Dewey's notion of natural piety also provides an important normative check—within an ethically humanistic worldview—on more robustly anthropocentric forms of environmental action and concern, including those currently traveling under the banner of "sustainability." Although much of the academic and popular environmental community has widely embraced the sustainability agenda, it has also received a fair share of criticism since its emergence (at least, in its contemporary form) in the 1980s. Some critics, for example, have taken issue with the sustainability idea's semantic ambiguity and utilitarian ethos, arguing that its conceptual and cultural flimsiness—and its lack of a strong ecological element—undercuts its potential as a true conservation principle (e.g., Newton and Freyfogle 2005). Several prominent conservation scientists have expressed particular concern about the concept's traditional focus on the maintenance of human welfare (especially in its "sustainable development" modality), an orientation, they argue, that will ultimately undermine the protection of wild species and other critical elements of biodiversity (e.g., Robinson 1993; Terborgh 1999). Dale Jamieson well captures this line of criticism from a philosophical point of view:

> Sustainability, as it is employed in most of its guises, is primarily an economic and anthropocentric notion. The moral reorientation that is required, which involves new relationships between humans as well as with other animals and the rest of nature, is unlikely to be affected by developing ever more precise understandings of sustainability. We need a discourse that permits deeper discussion of aesthetic, spiritual, religious, cultural, political, and moral values. (1998b, 191)

Dewey's religious thought, I believe, provides one such reorientation that Jamieson alludes to, although again it is a move that does not require a turn to nonanthropocentric theories of natural value. Rather, Dewey's instrumentalist take on religious experience and natural piety demonstrates that a cooperative and appreciative attitude toward nonhuman nature can be part of an expansive and balanced environmental humanism and that such respect for the natural conditions of human experience must be an important part of any bequest to the future—and thus any complete model of ecosocial sustainability.

Dewey's view is therefore highly compatible with some overtly pragmatic framings of sustainability today, such as Norton's (2005), which rejects the narrower anthropocentric and economistic understandings of the concept in favor of a more experimental and adaptive model of identifying and safeguarding social options and opportunities into the future. Norton's project, I believe, is quite receptive to the human-nature idealism and abiding sense of moral restraint found within Dewey's notion of natural piety. In particular, Norton's articulation of the sustainability obligation as an expression of the "constitutive values" of the community—values that express the ideals of a people that are at the same time dependent upon particular ecological aspects of "place"—indirectly evokes Dewey's directive to adopt a pious attitude toward the social and natural conditions that are the source, in his words, of "ideals, of possibilities, of aspiration in their behalf, and as the eventual abode of all attained goods and excellencies" (1929, 244).

In addition, I think we can discern echoes of a Deweyan natural piety in the work of such neoagrarian writers as Wendell Berry and Wes Jackson, heirs to Bailey's philosophical tradition and well-known critics of the aggressive anthropocentrism and individualism of contemporary life that has taken a great toll on the landscape and, they argue, our moral character. Although Berry and Jackson strike a more nostalgic and communitarian tone than the liberal Dewey, and Berry in particular lacks Dewey's progressive faith in human improvement and his strong aversion to moral absolutes (see, e.g., Smith 2003), the human-nature harmony that both writers extol in the agrarian mode is quite sympathetic with Dewey's understanding of the need to display piety toward nature. The overarching humanism of these neoagrarian thinkers' work, too, is consistent with Dewey's respect for natural conditions as a source of human ideals and the collected wisdom (when "nature" is also considered in the social and institutional sense) of previous generations. Along these lines, Paul Thompson (2010) has recently developed a compelling fusion of agrarian thinking with environmental ethics, enlisting classical and contemporary agrarian ideals in the search for sustainability. Although Thompson does not explicitly evoke Dewey's religious project, it is certainly compatible with the general line of argument he pursues in this work (and with Thompson's own pragmatist leanings), providing a powerful philosophical bond among the traditions of American pragmatism, agrarian philosophy, and environmental ethics.

At the same time, I argue that philosophical pragmatism, at least as I describe it here, does *not* provide intellectual and moral support to some of the current views within the environmental community (increasingly lumped under the "sustainability" umbrella) extolling human ambition and the rejection of nature as a constraint on economic, political, and technological development. Consider, for example, the argument that Ted Nordhaus and Michael Shellenberger advance in their widely discussed "Death of Environmentalism" essay and subsequent book, *Break Through: From the Death of Environmentalism to the Politics of Possibility* (2007). They sharply criticize the American environmental movement for its persistent negativism and its reliance on a "politics of limits," which the authors believe "seeks to constrain human ambition, aspiration, and power rather than unleash and direct them" (17).

Their alternative, a self-described "pragmatic" environmentalism, is driven by a "pro-growth agenda" that strives to reframe environmental advocacy and sustainability around a vision of human power and prosperity. Theirs is a politics and worldview that leave behind traditional environmentalism's fixation on worldly constraints and its desire to protect a pure vision of "Nature" that exists independently of human culture and society. This liberation of environmentalism from any residual nonanthropocentric and human will–restricting tendencies, they suggest, may be uncomfortable for many environmentalists conditioned by the traditional discourse of natural limits, but it is simply unavoidable in light of our evolution to become the planet's dominant, environment-shaping species. "Whether we like it or not," they conclude, "humans have become the meaning of the earth" (2007, 272).

Although the authors are surely right to challenge the essentialism and dualistic tendencies of traditional nature-centered environmentalism—and to reject the overwhelming pessimism displayed at times by various strains of the movement—I think their Promethean alternative goes too far in the other direction. Despite Nordhaus and Shellenberger's claiming of the pragmatist mantle, in eschewing environmental limits and celebrating a bold and untamed view of human power and ambition, they depart from the nuanced and careful pragmatism of Dewey, the tradition's most celebrated and important thinker. What they miss is the crucial sense of moderation and care we find in Dewey's mature naturalism, the idea that human ambition must not push too far beyond the natural conditions and social traditions that have shaped the aims and aspirations of the larger culture. In my reading, the *Break Through* vision and similar "progressive" environmentalist projects display nothing resembling Deweyan piety and respect for nature as a primary enabling force of human existence and advancement. Although environmentalism's "politics of limits" is indeed suspect when premised on preexperiential, foundationalist notions of intrinsic natural value, it is prudent when motivated by the appropriate regard for nature as a source of human ideals—be they moral, aesthetic, political, or scientific in character.

It is telling that Henry David Thoreau, the philosopher-poet of Walden Pond, is treated rather harshly in *Break Through.* In Thoreau's writing, Nordhaus and Shellenberger argue, lie the origins of environmentalism's efforts to shackle the human enterprise: "Ever since Henry David Thoreau spent twenty-six months living alone at Walden Pond, environmental virtue has been equated with a kind of self-denial. Forsaking excess consumption for the sake of the nonhuman world has been seen as the ultimate test of one's ecological commitment" (2007, 124–125). Although it has become common to depict Thoreau as a staunch biocentrist and sanctimonious scold, his work is, in fact, much more engaged with the wider moral and civic health of the community than the traditional one-note environmentalist readings suggest (Taylor 1996). For example, Thoreau recognizes that unbridled ambition and supreme confidence in human power are too often destructive forces, a potentially self-immolating form of hubris that can corrupt nature and civic life. "We need to witness our own limits transgressed, and some life pasturing freely where we never wander," he cautions readers in *Walden* (1985, 575).

Thoreau's intent, in other words, is not to radically demote culture and society "for the sake of the nonhuman world"; rather, it is to employ nature's simplicity, beauty, and, in some cases, sublime power to critique and ultimately improve community life in the industrial age. Like Dewey, Thoreau seeks to remind us of our dependence on nature and the risks we assume when we push too hard and fast to slip our earthly bonds. Thoreau, of course, is a romantic and a transcendentalist; Dewey is a Progressive and a pragmatist. Still, I can think of no better summary of what Dewey's sense of natural piety can offer a truly pragmatic environmentalism in the era of sustainability.

6
Animal Rights and Environmental Ethics
A Pragmatic Reconciliation

The Trouble with Swans

On Arrowhead Mountain Lake, in northwestern Vermont, a breeding pair of mute swans established itself in 1993. The species, which evolved elsewhere (primarily in Europe and Asia), arrived in the United States around 1920, when several birds escaped from a private estate overseas. Not surprisingly, the swans are remarkably beautiful creatures, with their white plumage and long, curved necks. But despite an aesthetic ideal that endows them with an almost fairy-tale tranquility, the birds are, according to many wildlife managers and environmentalists, little more than obnoxious avian thugs. In particular, the swans are fiercely, and often violently, territorial. A single male will defend a range as large as twenty-five acres, driving out and often killing native bird species. They are also very heavy feeders, consuming eight to ten pounds of vegetation a day, which they procure, as one writer observes, by "using their feet like toilet plungers," an activity that swirls out lake substrate and degrades water quality (Williams 1997, 27). Moreover, the birds' hostility is not reserved just for their fellow waterfowl: Several accounts describe the swans' habit of attacking biologists, boaters, and waterfront homeowners. They seem to have a particular disdain for jet-skiers.

The mute swans in Vermont are part of a larger and potentially very serious concern among conservation managers and biodiversity scientists—the reduction of native biodiversity as a result of the introduction of exotic plants and animals into native ecosystems (see, e.g., Van Driesche and Van Driesche 2004). The swans on Arrowhead Mountain Lake are just one example of an exploding list of invasive species fanning out across the American landscape—from feral pigs in Hawaiian national parks and exotic trout in Yellowstone, to the zebra mussels of the Great Lakes and the notorious cheat grass in the intermountain West. When nonnative species become invasive, they can have destructive consequences for native species and the functioning of natural ecological systems. Although the *a priori* condemnation of exotic species by ecologists and managers has begun to be questioned—on scientific and philosophical grounds—in recent years (see, e.g., Burdick 2005; Sagoff 2005; Davis 2009), in the Vermont case, wildlife managers clearly viewed the swans as creating a significant conservation problem with respect to the protection of native waterfowl and ecosystem health. The Vermont dilemma, moreover, may be viewed as a microcosm of a larger "swan problem" that has bedeviled managers and conservationists in several parts of the country, including the Chesapeake Bay region (Halsey 2009).

Given these considerations, when the population of swans on Arrowhead Mountain Lake expanded to eight birds in 1997, the Vermont Fish and Wildlife Department, charged with the management of the state's native species and their habitats, decided it had to take action. After holding a number of public hearings, the department announced its plan to kill the swans, a move that resulted in an immediate public firestorm. A group of lakeshore residents, under the auspices of their "Arrowhead Mountain Lake Association," vehemently protested the department's proposed action, generating swarming media coverage (at least, by Vermont standards) and drawing the attention of national animal-rights organizations that promptly branded Vermont a "swan-killing state" (Williams 1997). In response to such increasing public pressure and scrutiny, the department decided to attempt to capture the swans so they might be shipped to a private conservation facility in Texas. This was easier said than done, however, and when the department was only able to capture two birds (at considerable effort and expense), it determined that this approach was not going to be a very practical or efficient means of handling the problem. The following summer, wildlife managers shot two of the six swans that returned to the lake, leading to greater public outcry and further straining the already hostile relationship between some members of the public and the department.

From the perspective of environmental ethics, the tension between some of the public and the state managers in the swan dispute would typically be explained in terms of a deeper, more philosophical disagreement about the value placed upon individual animals and ecological systems. Should we, for example, be solicitous of the welfare of individual swans and morally object to their "sacrifice" for the goal of protecting the biological integrity of the ecosystem? Or should we realize that the integrity of the other species and ecological processes of Arrowhead Mountain Lake has a certain priority over the pain and suffering (and even death) of individual creatures, one that effectively trumps the interests of the individual swans in this case?

Indeed, the mute swan case and others like it expose what many environmental philosophers have historically argued is a foundational rift between animal welfare and rights positions, which focus on the good or worth of individual animals, and the perspective of environmental ethics, which dwells on the significance of biological collectives (i.e., populations and species) and ecological systems (see, e.g., Callicott 1980; Sagoff 1984; Katz 1991; Hargrove 1992). The consensus view still appears to be that the two projects are in most important respects mutually exclusive, although, as I discuss below, many environmental philosophers have challenged this conclusion in one way or another in the years since the original rift was identified. Yet I think it is still safe to say that most environmental ethicists believe that, at the very least, serious tensions exist between the two bodies of theory, tensions that, especially in the founding years of the debate, have perhaps been ratcheted up by the exchange of some overheated rhetoric on both sides.

In this chapter, I want to examine how a pragmatic perspective on the animal rights/environmental ethics debate might offer a new way of framing the general philosophical question about the "moral considerability" and comparative moral significance of animals and ecological wholes (i.e., natural systems and processes). In fact, I argue that this approach implies a distinct movement *away* from the presumption that the debate is best resolved on these grounds—that is, through the articulation and defense of any particular claim based on an attribution of moral standing and significance. As I see it, part of the pragmatic legacy (and John Dewey's work in particular) is the attempt to wean us off these theoretical and methodological predilections in the search for authoritative moral standards, rules, and principles and the deduction of practical judgments and policy arguments from them.

In particular, I suggest that we should recognize the virtues of an environmental ethical approach that moves beyond attributions of considerability, one that focuses more of its attention on the experimental method of moral inquiry and dispute resolution that figures prominently in Dewey's work. I claim that this pragmatic reframing of the animal rights/environmental ethics debate not only is more philosophically sound but also opens up a number of new and significant possibilities for intelligent problem solving in specific animal-environment conflicts. Indeed, I believe this Deweyan approach makes good on the promise of environmental pragmatism as an especially useful and effective style of practical ethical reasoning, one that offers a number of advantages over its main rivals in environmental ethics.

To map out my discussion in the pages that follow, I first examine how the question of moral considerability in the animal rights/environmental ethics debate has been featured in the work of such philosophers as Peter Singer, Tom Regan, J. Baird Callicott, and Holmes Rolston. I conclude that this historical emphasis on moral standing leads to irresolvable questions that are best avoided in a pragmatic-oriented environmental ethics. In the following section, I consider a few notable and more recent attempts at reconciling environmental and animal ethics that have focused on bringing the two positions together at the level of moral principle. Although these efforts are significant in their attempt to establish normative compatibility between the two sets of positions, I do not believe they pay sufficient attention to the role of experimental moral inquiry and problem-oriented thinking in specific conflict situations.

Accordingly, in the next section, I discuss how a Deweyan reconstruction of the debate from general defenses of moral considerability to a recognition of the ethical weight of specific "problematic situations" involving practical contests between animal-rights positions and environmental commitments is a better way to conceptualize and to address the contests between them. In the final section, I make a suggestive case for the similarities shared by this Deweyan approach to ethics and some of the more well-known projects appearing in the contemporary dispute-resolution literature, and I conclude by arguing that a pragmatic recasting of environmental ethics as an applied process of dispute resolution can bring the field into a more useful relationship with the problems of environmental practice, including the conflicts between animal liberation/rights and environmental ethics considerations.

A final note on terminology: Although "the animals rights/environmental ethics debate" is the conventional way of referring to a set of specific and recognized philosophical disagreements between animal and environmental ethicists, it should be noted that "animal rights" in this broad usage also includes non-rights-based positions, such as Singer's (utilitarian) animal-welfare approach. To be more accurate, in this chapter, I employ the designation "animal ethics" when I discuss Regan's and Singer's positions outside the "debate" label. When I refer to the animal-environment debate as it has been discussed historically in the field of environmental ethics, however, I retain the "animal-rights" designation (referring to Regan's and Singer's positions) for the sake of consistency. But we should note here that important philosophical and often practical distinctions should be made between rights-based and welfare-based animal ethics approaches.

Reconsidering Moral Considerability: The Animal Rights/Environmental Ethics Debate

Although the major animal and environmental ethical approaches are familiar in the field of environmental ethics and perhaps applied philosophy more generally, it is useful to briefly review their salient features here to understand why the debate has proven to be so intractable and divisive over the years. Although "animal ethics" includes a diverse number of approaches, it is common practice to make the distinction between historically influential consequentialist (i.e., utilitarian) projects, such as that championed by Singer, and nonconsequentialist (i.e., rights-based) views, of the kind defended by Regan. In environmental ethics, the historically dominant positions reflect a general philosophical view that we may refer to as "nonanthropocentric holism" (or "ecocentrism"), in which collectives, such as species, ecosystems, and natural processes, are seen as directly morally considerable (i.e., possessing intrinsic value). Two exemplars of nonanthropocentric holism in environmental ethics are Callicott and Rolston. Both theorists (whom I discuss at several points in the preceding chapters) have contributed to the debate between animal rights/welfare theorists and environmental ethicists, as I show below.

Animal Ethics and Moral Individualism

Singer's ethic of animal liberation is primarily concerned with eliminating, or at least considerably reducing, the human infliction of suffering on those individual animals able to experience states of pleasure and pain, creatures that Singer refers to as being "sentient." Singer argues that we need to recognize that sentient animals have interests that must be considered when we form judgments or render decisions that will affect them positively or negatively. Although he does not argue that animals must in all cases be treated as literal equals to humans, Singer does claim that their interests (as beings that can be harmed or benefited) deserve equal consideration by moral agents. In doing so, Singer extends a classical hedonistic version of utilitarianism to the community of sentient nonhumans: In cases where our actions may affect the welfare of sensate animals, we must select the alternative that has the best possible consequence for the interests of the animal in question.

As Singer suggests in his landmark and widely read 1975 book *Animal Liberation,* this extensionist utilitarian effort finds a textual warrant in Jeremy Bentham's provocation regarding the criteria for granting moral status to animals. In his later and more overtly philosophical work, however, Singer (1993) articulates a more sophisticated version of preference utilitarianism to account for the cognitive abilities of higher mammals and, presumably, to respond to counter-intuitive readings of the implications of his early hedonistic version of the theory. Although Singer's animal welfarism, as a paradigmatic consequentialist project, does not rule out the use of animals in medical research or the ultimate sacrifice of animal lives in those cases where doing so is expected to produce the greatest net benefits for all individuals affected by the proposed action, his approach clearly places a heavy burden on human moral agents to demonstrate that said benefits will, in fact, result from the action under consideration and that they will also outweigh the harms suffered by the animal(s) in the situation in question.

Regan's approach to animal ethics, unlike Singer's utilitarian model, is properly referred to as a true "animal-rights" position, even though the designation is commonly used to refer to any and all ethical arguments calling for the fair treatment and protection of animals. Where Singer, at least in his earlier writing, locates the threshold for the moral consideration of an entity at sentience, Regan attempts to place the bar of moral consideration appreciably higher. For Regan, those animals that possess sufficient cognitive capacity such that they are able to form complex beliefs and desires are morally considerable, and we have *direct* duties toward them—namely, to avoid causing them unnecessary harm. According to Regan, these self-conscious beings are "experiencing subjects of a life" and are therefore "ends-in-themselves" that should not be treated as mere resources for human satisfaction. This class of individuals, according to Regan (2004), includes all mentally normal adult mammals, a more restricted group compared with Singer's fairly inclusive set of sentient creatures.

Not surprisingly, given these premises, Regan is categorically against sport hunting and trapping, animal agriculture, and the use of animals in all manner of scientific and commercial experimentation. In this sense, and on its face, his position is much more abolitionist than Singer's, because Regan's position does not permit utility maximization to trump individual rights, even if great aggregate benefit may result from subordinating such rights to the greater good in a given situation. According to Regan's neo-Kantian perspective, such activities always fail to respect individual animals as ends-in-themselves (2004).

It is not my purpose here to challenge either Singer's or Regan's criteria for moral considerability; I am simply outlining what are commonly understood to be their main identifying marks in discussions within the field of environmental ethics. But I also want to make note of a shared feature of both approaches. Despite their different moral foundations (in utilitarianism and neo-Kantian ethics/rights theory, respectively) Singer's and Regan's positions share a common structural form: Both are ethically individualistic in that each view attempts to defend the moral status of nonhuman animals, counted singly. For Singer, each individual sentient animal's positive experiences have intrinsic value, and an individual animal's pleasure is to be maximized to the extent possible in decisions facing (human) moral agents that have the potential to impact the animal's welfare. Similarly, for Regan, each individual mammalian "subject of a life" has a special dignity that demands respect from moral agents. Neither theory, in other words, is able to countenance the direct moral consideration of biological and natural collectives (e.g., species, natural/evolutionary processes, and ecosystems). They are both morally individualistic in their extension of conventional Western ethical concepts originally intended to apply to the class of human persons.

Environmental Ethics and Moral Holism

Environmental ethicists, unlike their animal ethicist counterparts, have traditionally set up normative shop in the realm of nonhuman collectives, especially at the level of ecological systems. That is, the field has in general been ethically holistic, viewing moral considerability in terms of the value or worth of ecosystems and their natural processes. More often than not, this holism has taken on an explicit and pronounced metaphysical cast. For example, Callicott, the leading expositor and most ardent defender of Leopold's land ethic, argues for a nonanthropocentric theory of intrinsic natural value, one that humans ascribe to ecological wholes as a result of what Callicott claims is an evolutionarily fixed faculty of emotional sympathy with our surrounding community. Spurred by ecologists' tearing down of the illusory barriers separating humans and their encompassing environmental systems, Callicott (1989, 1999a) expands the notion of community to encompass the biotic community of nature as well as the human social community. Callicott's commitment to this "weak" nonanthropocentric holism—weak in that it does not posit objective value in nature but rather defends the subjective projection of intrinsic value by a human valuer—led him to fire one of the first shots in the battle between environmental and animal ethicists in his now notorious 1980 paper, "Animal Liberation: A Triangular Affair." In it, Callicott writes of the philosophical incompatibilities between a sentient-based concern for animal welfare (such as that voiced by Singer) and a true nonanthropocentric holism (such as his own) and argues that animal liberation views and "ecocentric" views necessarily entail divergent management and policy goals in practice.

Rolston, another prominent nonanthropocentric holist, goes a good deal further than Callicott with respect to the disposition of intrinsic value in the environment. For Rolston, intrinsic value is a metaphysically real and objective part of the fabric of the natural world. That is, unlike Callicott's approach, Rolston's theory of environmental value does not rely on the consciousness or valuational activity/capacity of human valuers: Intrinsic value would exist in nature even if humans had never arrived on the evolutionary scene. This objectivist ontology of natural value establishes Rolston as what we may refer to as a "strong" nonanthropocentric holist in environmental ethics (relative to Callicott's weaker subjectivist nonanthropocentrism). The centerpiece of Rolston's position is his notion of systemic value or the productive and creative processes of ecosystems over time (1988, 1994). As he puts it, "Duties arise in encounter with the system that projects and protects [its member components] in biotic community" (1994, 177). According to Rolston, it subsequently follows from this premise that the "individual members" of the biotic community (e.g., nonhuman animals), while possessing "intrinsic value" in that they defend their own good, nevertheless pale in moral comparison with the systemic value that resides within ecosystemic wholes. Indeed, Rolston believes animal ethicists, such as Singer and Regan, have put the cart before the horse: "Valuing the products but not the system able to produce these products is like finding a goose that lays golden eggs and valuing the eggs but not the goose" (1994, 177).

Like Callicott, in his work Rolston directly squares off with animal-ethics approaches that adopt a more individualistic view toward moral considerability. In his contribution to a critical anthology of papers devoted to Singer's work, for example, Rolston gives an unvarnished assessment of the moral inadequacy of Singer's project:

> The trouble [with Singer's argument] is that this is not a *systemic view* of what is going on on the valuable Earth we now experience, before we experienced it. We need an account of the generation of value and valuers, not just some value that now is located in the psychology of the experiencers. Finding that value will generate an Earth Ethics, with a global sense of obligation to this whole inhabited planet. The evolution of rocks into dirt and dirt into fauna and flora is one of the great surprises of natural history, one of the rarest events in the astronomical universe. . . . At this scale of vision, if we ask what is principally to be valued, the value of life arising as a creative process on Earth seems a better description and a more comprehensive category than the pains and pleasures of a fractional percentage of its inhabitants. (1999, 266–267; emphasis added)

Rolston clearly thinks that Singer's preoccupation with the welfare of individual animals falls far short of providing an effective moral argument for the large-scale ecological processes that the former believes to be the source of all value in nature.

Responding to Rolston's criticisms, Singer denies that his position is unable to take account of the value of nonsentient parts of the environment, disagreeing in particular with Rolston's interpretation that Singer's focus on the experiences of sentient beings precludes him from expressing any concern about the condition of natural elements, such as plants and trees; biological collectives, such as species and communities; and macrolevel processes, such as those that maintain ecological resilience and integrity. On the contrary, Singer argues that he is able to morally consider these nonsentient parts and processes of the environment by assessing the degree to which their loss leads to the harm of those pleasure and pain-experiencing animals (and also humans) that depend upon them (1999, 327–332). In other words, and from an animal-welfare perspective, because the destruction of a forest ecosystem for economic development clearly harms those sentient animals that rely on this system for food and shelter, Singer can still claim that the development of the forest is ethically wrong from the sentientist position, even if he is unable to directly consider the nonsentient parts and processes of the environment that Rolston holds in such high regard.

In the revised edition of *The Case for Animal Rights,* Regan (2004) also replies to the general criticism that his animal-rights view is not able to account for the importance environmental philosophers and conservationists attach to such efforts as the protection of endangered species. The rights view, Regan reaffirms, "restricts inherent value and rights to individuals" and therefore does not apply directly to populations and species (xxxviii–xxxix). Nor does it, he writes, accord individuals of rare species any more or fewer rights than individuals from an abundant species. Yet Regan insists that the animal-rights approach can still support environmentalists' intuitions about the need to protect threatened species, a claim he defends with a two-part argument. First, Regan writes that, under the animal-rights view, we have an obligation to stop moral agents (humans) from violating the rights of animals through such actions as poaching and habitat destruction. In addition, he suggests that the rights view supports the notion of "compensatory justice," which would require us to do more for individual animals within endangered populations because of past harms (e.g., poaching, habitat destruction) that have put them at biological and ecological disadvantages. Taken together, Regan argues that these elaborations of the individualist animal-rights perspective can be employed to defend the environmentalist agenda with regard to the protection of endangered "experiencing subjects of a life."

Still, Regan is aware that this approach will not sit well with those who insist on an environmental ethic that recognizes species and ecosystems as possessing their own independent moral status:

> Environmental philosophers in general, including the most distinguished among them, will not be satisfied with the environmental implications of the rights view, whether augmented by principles of compensatory justice or not. They will say (and in fact some have said) that species have inherent value.

> And so do ecosystems and the biosphere. Which is how we should account for our obligation to save endangered species, including plants and insects, not just "fuzzy mammals." To which I can only make the following response. It is not enough to confer inherent (or intrinsic) value on species, ecosystems, or the biosphere. One wants a compelling argument for doing so. Not only has this not been done . . . I believe it cannot be done. (2004, xl–xli)

The upshot is that animal ethicists, such as Regan and Singer, and environmental philosophers, such as Callicott and Rolston, clearly disagree about what entities are morally considerable and, subsequently, what entities or natural processes should "matter" in our moral deliberations over particular decisions, actions, or policies. The debate, which hinges on the seemingly divergent foundations of moral individualism and moral holism, would appear to be irresolvable, not the least because it is difficult to imagine just what sort of evidence could be brought to bear by either side that would convince the other it had somehow erroneously conferred moral standing on its animal or environmental subject.

A Few Rapprochements

Despite these sharp lines drawn in the sand by environmental ethicists, several notable attempts have been made within the field to reconcile animal liberation/rights approaches. In fact, in later work, Callicott himself backpedals on his earlier and aggressive condemnation of animal ethics in "A Triangular Affair." Specifically, in his 1988 paper, "Animal Liberation and Environmental Ethics: Back Together Again," Callicott writes that animal-rights approaches and ecocentric projects need not be mutually exclusive, because a communitarian ethical theory—one that recognizes a series of duties and obligations to other members of our "mixed" (i.e., human and biotic/nonhuman) communities—can accommodate animal ethicists' concern for the moral considerability of individual nonhuman animals *and* holistic nonanthropocentrists' regard for ecological systems and processes (see also Callicott 1998). Callicott's "corrective" to his original position has been joined by a host of sympathetic accommodationist projects in environmental ethics that attempt to mend fences with various animal-ethics positions.

Dale Jamieson, for example, has argued that animal liberationists can subscribe to many of the same "normative views" as environmental ethicists, because both are responding to the same kinds of threats to animals, humans, and ecological systems. Moreover, and similar to Singer's argument recounted above, Jamieson (1998b) suggests that animal liberationists can value nature as habitat for sentient beings: The environment possesses a "derivative value" in the sense that it plays a significant (i.e., valuable) role in the lives of sentient animals. On another front, Rick O'Neil has argued that we need not view the two camps as being in direct conflict with one another, because animal ethicists attempt to establish the *moral standing* of sentient creatures, while environmental ethicists are actually performing a philosophically separate (and not necessarily incompatible) task of defending the *intrinsic value* of nonsentient elements of nature. O'Neil's (2000) argument, which relies on some semantic hair splitting between these two notions, is essentially an effort to create a kind of meta-ethical "zoning" that would confine both camps to their appropriate moral spheres.

Most significantly, perhaps, Gary Varner (1998) has offered an intriguing argument for the normative convergence of animal liberation/rights and environmentalist commitments in the case of "therapeutic hunting" of irruptive wildlife species (such as white-tailed deer) that have a tendency to overshoot the carrying capacity of their range (what Varner refers to as "obligatory management species"). After working through the main elements of Singer's utilitarian animal-liberation position and Regan's more stringent animal-rights position, Varner concludes that a consistent adherent to either principle would be compelled to side with environmentalists concerned with collective species viability or ecological health in the situation of wildlife population control to salvage ecological health. As Varner writes, "An individual genuinely concerned with animal welfare, and even one who attributes moral rights to nonhuman animals, can support the only kind of hunting environmentalists feel compelled to support, namely therapeutic hunting of obligatory management species" (115–116). Varner deftly shows how "thinning the herd" in such cases actually comports with animal liberationists' concern for pain and suffering, because skilled killing of animals that reduces their numbers to an environmentally sustainable level avoids greater potential painful suffering and death due to sickness and starvation. He also demonstrates how therapeutic hunting is in keeping with animal-rights proponents' desire to minimize the transgression of individual rights in situations where harm to animals is inevitable. In this case, it appears that some animals must be culled to avoid an even worse situation, one that would result in starvation and agonizing deaths for a greater number of animals over time as their habitat becomes steadily degraded.

From Moral Considerability to Problematic Situation

Although these efforts at reconciling animal and environmental ethics are conceptually significant and well-motivated, it should be noted that the emphasis of these projects has been mostly on achieving philosophical compatibility at the level of moral standing or moral principle. That is, these attempts at rapprochement between environmental ethics and animal liberation/rights have sought to resolve the conflict as if it were primarily, and most significantly, a general philosophical debate over the moral status of nonhuman animals and nature rather than a series of *practical* conflicts requiring the evaluation of competing goods and deliberation over alternative proposals and claims in specific cases requiring intelligent judgment. Even Varner's project, which does engage one particular class of contexts in which the animal-environment dispute occurs in practice (the case of "therapeutic hunting"), is concerned mostly with questions relating to moral standing and supporting normative principles in animal ethics in its attempt to justify an "environmental" judgment (i.e., to cull populations of certain irruptive species to protect ecosystem health) through a nuanced reading of the commitments of Singer's and Regan's philosophical systems.

This focus on general normative principles and broad, conceptual issues of moral standing and moral significance in efforts to harmonize animal and environmental positions is not surprising, because over the course of its short academic life, environmental ethics has been fairly consumed with these classic philosophical questions of moral considerability and ontology. And, of course, this theoretical orientation is not found only in the compatibilist approaches in environmental ethics that Callicott, Jamieson, and Varner offer; it remains the dominant form in the field and is also embraced by those environmental ethicists who remain critical of the insufficient "moral coverage" of animal ethics (as we can clearly see in Rolston's criticism of Singer in the previous section). On all these fronts, environmental ethicists are simply following the traditional approach to ethical theory more generally—namely, the investigation into the grounds for moral standing and the accompanying search for rules, standards, and principles by which to govern the relationship between moral agents (and, in this case, also between agents and moral "patients").

And, as should be clear from the above discussion, this concern with matters of moral considerability and the substantive content of moral principles in environmental ethics also characterizes much of the paradigmatic work in animal ethics. For example, the programs of Singer and Regan may be seen as seeking to extend conventional ethical concepts (respectively, utility and rights) to the previously excluded class of nonhuman animals, and Singer and Regan devote a good deal of attention to the moral standing question. In parallel fashion, environmental ethicists, especially nonanthropocentrists, often employ the language of intrinsic value as a kind of proxy for a moral rights–type claim about the standing of nonhuman nature, with supporting arguments and defenses of exactly what parts of nature "count" in a moral sense (which for nonanthropocentric holists include entire ecological systems and processes).

If animal and environmental ethics are united, then, in their shared recognition of the fundamental importance of questions of moral considerability and the critical role of general moral principles in delineating and justifying the corollary duties we have *vis-à-vis* animals and environmental systems, we may nevertheless still ask whether this kind of approach is the best way to conceptualize the ethical enterprise. In particular, we may question whether the traditional emphasis on matters of moral standing and the search for and defense of an authoritative (and usually small) set of normative principles in environmental and animal ethics provide an adequate and complete model for the kind of reflective moral inquiry required by the complex problematic situations that arise in human experience in the natural world. I do not believe it does.

The demands of plural and competing goods and claims in the moral life and the multilayered and textured normative/empirical contexts of practical problem-solving efforts in actual cases of animal-environment conflict seem to require something more than global attributions of moral considerability and the invocation of one or a few general principles. At the very least, I say that this standard approach is certainly not the *only* way to conceptualize the purpose and practice of environmental and animal ethics, just as it is not the only way to view moral reasoning and theorizing in a more general sense. Here, the pragmatic approach to environmental ethics promises to be of some help. Indeed, as I describe in various ways in the preceding chapters, the pragmatic critique in the field has opened the door for a number of alternative models serious about linking ethical theory and environmental practice, including new methodological and normative projects either inspired by or directly adapted from the work of the classic American pragmatists. Although it encompasses a good deal of philosophical diversity, as I have discussed, this pragmatic alternative in environmental ethics generally accepts, if not celebrates, value pluralism, embraces an experimental approach to ethical claims about the natural world, and focuses much more seriously on the empirical and normative contexts of moral experience than the historically dominant theoretical efforts in the field.

Of all the pragmatist insights, I argue that Dewey's understanding of ethics, especially his view of moral reasoning as an experimental activity carried out in the context of specific "problematic situations," is one of the more valuable intellectual bequests for a pragmatic environmental ethics. Dewey's reconstruction of ethics (and philosophy more generally) to focus more on the methods of inquiry, deliberation, and problem solving rather than broad notions of moral considerability and the *a priori* authority of fixed principles provides us with a way of conceptualizing the moral enterprise that engages rather than dismisses the multifaceted nature of moral problems, including the irreducible multiplicity of goods that constitute specific practical conflicts. In the following section, then, I examine these key Deweyan features in greater detail.

Dewey and the Reconstruction of Ethics as Experimental Inquiry

As I discuss in Chapter 4, Dewey repeatedly argues that philosophers' traditional method of applying general ethical claims articulated prior to reflection and investigation into the facts of and values already extant in specific problematic situations is a misguided approach to the quandaries of moral experience. This approach, in his view, does not recognize the novel demands and circumstances of each new problem situation, nor does it adopt an appropriately provisional and fallibilist attitude toward moral principles and theories possessed before inquiry into specific problem contexts. Instead, Dewey suggests that the thorny difficulties and conflicts of human experience require an experimental method of inquiry similar to that employed in the natural and technical sciences. As he writes in his landmark work, *Reconstruction in Philosophy*:

> A moral situation is one in which judgment and choice are required antecedently to overt action. The practical meaning of the situation—that is to say the action needed to satisfy it—is not self-evident. It has to be searched for. There are conflicting desires and alternative apparent goods. What is needed

> is to find the right course of action, the right good. Hence inquiry is exacted: observation of the detailed makeup of the situation; analysis into its diverse factors; clarification of what is obscure; discounting of the more insistent and vivid traits; tracing the consequences of the various modes of action that suggest themselves; regarding the decision as hypothetical and tentative until the anticipated or supposed consequences which led to its adoption have been squared with actual consequences. This inquiry is intelligence. (1927, 173)

For Dewey, the role of intelligence in ethics is defined by an individual's (and community's) ability to examine the needs of an uncertain and disrupted (i.e., "problematic") situation and to renovate the moral resources accumulated in previous experience for use in appraising and guiding present and future ethical analysis. This "unified method of inquiry," which Dewey argues could be profitably applied to facts *and* values, is most fully described in his aforementioned 1938 book, *Logic: The Theory of Inquiry.* As I describe in Chapter 2, this basic pattern of inquiry, derived from the logic of problem solving in the natural and technical sciences, is also linked, in Dewey's view, to the moral and epistemic virtues of democratic politics.

Dewey's accounting of the role of inquiry in addressing moral problems and his description of the normative character of such inquiry (i.e., a method marked by toleration, sympathy, etc.) suggests a more *procedural* view of ethics, one in which values, principles, and moral standards emerge through the method of experimentation and situational analysis rather than simply being taken "off the shelf" and imposed on specific moral problems and conflicts. This dynamic reconstruction of ethics thus redefines the business of normative reflection as a particular kind of practical problem solving, making it more akin to contemporary methods of dispute resolution than to traditional ethical theorizing (I have more to say about this correspondence in the final section).

In keeping with its robust experimental framework, Dewey's ethical system also emphasizes the traditionally discounted significance of discovery and creativity in any effective moral inquiry: "Inquiry, discovery take the same place in morals that they have come to occupy in sciences of nature. Validation, demonstration become experimental, a matter of consequences" (1927, 179). This understanding of the open-ended nature of moral experience embraces the time-tested truth of value pluralism and introduces the prospect of weighing numerous and often-competing goods in practical deliberations over right actions and judgments. Dewey's view on this matter does not signal a flat-out rejection of held moral principles and their encompassing theories so much as it endorses a more holistic model of moral reasoning, one in which the multiple values and empirical circumstances of each problematic situation are directly engaged by moral inquiry rather than dispelled by the philosophical appeal to abstract, universal principles:

> A moral philosophy which should frankly recognize the impossibility of reducing all the elements in moral situations to a single commensurable principle, which should recognize that each human being has to make the best

> adjustment he can among forces which are generally disparate, would throw light upon actual predicaments of conduct and help individuals in making a juster estimate of the force of each competing factor. All that would be lost would be the idea that theoretically there is in advance a single theoretically correct solution for every difficulty with which each and every individual is confronted. Personally I think the surrender of this idea would be a gain instead of a loss. In taking attention away from rigid rules and standards it would lead men to attend more fully to the concrete elements entering into the situations in which they have to act. (1930b, 288)

Because moral situations, in this reading, are sufficiently complex and different from one another to challenge the uncritical reliance upon any single and unmodifiable moral claim as governing inquiry into potential alternative courses of action, the search for a monolithic, universal philosophical foundation for ethical experience is doomed to failure. As he recognizes, each problematic situation, no matter how closely it may seem to resemble previously experienced dilemmas and disruptions, always presents us with something novel and unexpected. As a consequence, Dewey writes, we should not try to constrain any particular moral discussion to the language of a single principle or set of principles prior to reflective inquiry if we wish to respond intelligently and effectively to the varying dilemmas of human experience. Dewey's view clearly suggests an image of morality as an adaptive, organic process:

> In fact, situations into which change and the unexpected enter are a challenge to intelligence to create new principles. Morals must be a growing science if it is to be a science at all, not merely because all truth has not yet been appropriated by the mind of man, but because life is a moving affair in which old moral truth ceases to apply. Principles are methods of inquiry and forecast which require verification by the event; and the time honored effort to assimilate morals to mathematics is only a way of bolstering up an old dogmatic authority, or putting a new one upon the throne of the old. But the experimental character of moral judgments does not mean complete uncertainty and fluidity. Principles exist as hypotheses with which to experiment. (1922, 164–165)

For Dewey, the continual refinement of the method of inquiry, and the critical social learning that inquiry affords is participants, thus replaces the traditional philosophical loyalty to preexperimental general moral principles:

> No past decision nor old principle can ever be wholly relied upon to justify a course of action. No amount of pains taken in forming a purpose in a definite case is final; the consequences of its adoption must be carefully noted, and a purpose held only as a working hypothesis until results confirm its rightness. Mistakes are no longer either mere unavoidable accidents to be mourned or moral sins to be expiated and forgiven. They are lessons in wrong methods of using intelligence and instructions as to a better course in the

> future. They are indications of the need of revision, development, readjustment. Ends grow, standards of judgment are improved. . . . Moral life is protected from falling into formalism and rigid repetition. It is rendered flexible, vital, growing. (1927, 179–180)

Ethical theories are, in this understanding, critical tools for analyzing and interpreting particular social problems and conflicts, not fixed ends or positions to which we must accord privileged philosophical status or, worse, behavioral obedience. In the next chapter, I discuss how this rejection of the dominant method of "principle-ism" by Dewey for a more contextual and experimental alternative finds empirical support in public attitudes toward environmental management.

In sum, Dewey significantly shifts discussions of moral theory and argument away from a preoccupation with the ontological status of general moral principles and toward the refinement of the process of intelligent inquiry and the development of better and more effective methods of cooperative problem solving. In effect, ethics here becomes an explicit form of conflict resolution. It is a process of reducing disagreement among disputants through the method of "social intelligence," which for Dewey is driven by the logic of experimental inquiry and achieves its ends by transforming problematic situations into more "consummated" and stable organic arrangements.

Reframing the Debate: Environmental Ethics as Dispute Resolution

So what does the Deweyan approach to ethics have to contribute to the animal rights/environmental ethics debate? I believe this pragmatic articulation of ethics as a process of experimental inquiry suggests that, unlike the historically dominant approaches within both camps (if not applied ethics as a whole), we should address ethical conflicts like those between environmental and animal ethics as *practical disputes* requiring cooperative investigation and a deliberate method of problem solving rather than as abstract philosophical debates over questions of considerability and comparative moral significance. That is, I think Dewey's work instructs us that we would do better to turn our attention to refining specific methods of observation, moral analysis, and empirical evaluation, adopting a more experimental and case-based approach to ethics, than we would to elaborate and to defend metaphysical and moral arguments for the intrinsic value of ecosystems or the interests/rights of nonhuman animals.

The pragmatic alternative, endorsing ethical pluralism as well as the provisional and instrumental nature of moral principles, thus frames ethical inquiry as a more creative and dynamic process, one in which discovery and invention play an important part in our moral deliberations over alternative claims and proposals. These commitments certainly suggest a very different orientation to philosophical disputes than ethicists have taken in the past. Indeed, in many respects, Dewey's reconstruction of ethics as briefly outlined above issues a view of moral life as an explicit process of cooperative dispute resolution, especially in those public conflicts (like most on-the-ground animal-environment disputes) that involve multiple and competing stakeholders and seemingly entrenched disagreements about alternative values, interests, and scientific or technical issues.

It is instructive to consider the relationship between Dewey's approach and the burgeoning dispute-resolution literature that has made significant inroads in many of the policy and planning fields. In particular, general Alternative Dispute Resolution (ADR) frameworks, such as those characterized as "consensus-based" or "negotiated agreement" approaches, have gained intellectual support and administrative credibility in the past two decades as alternatives to litigation and conventional forms of adjudication between contesting parties. Common attributes of these ADR frameworks include (1) voluntary participation in the negotiation by parties in the dispute; (2) direct, active, face-to-face participation of the disputants or, in some cases, their representatives; and (3) collective agreement by the participating parties on the process of the negotiation as well as consensus on its outcome (Wondolleck and Yaffee 2000). In the environmental application, Environmental Dispute Resolution (EDR) techniques and processes have been employed in a variety of sociopolitical contexts, including policy-level conflicts, such as environmental rule making and policy dialogues in the U.S. Environmental Protection Agency, and site-level disputes, such as conflicts over the use and management of natural resources, the siting of industrial facilities, and public disputes over various land-use and pollution-control issues (O'Leary et al. 1998; O'Leary, Nabatchi, and Bingham 2004).

What explains the appeal of these approaches? For starters, EDR methods offer parties to an environmental dispute the hope that they can achieve their goals without having to resort to highly adversarial, risky, and expensive litigation. In addition, EDR supporters praise the method's attention to building healthy and enduring relationships among disputants, its general versatility and ability to respond to increasingly complex cross-sector and transboundary environmental problems, and the decentralized structure and efficiency of EDR strategies compared with traditional bureaucratic approaches (O'Leary et al. 1998; O'Leary, Nabatchi, and Bingham 2004; Wondolleck and Yaffee 2000). Although the literature on ADR and EDR methods is voluminous and expanding daily, for present purposes, we can briefly consider two influential and complementary models, projects that I believe also display an intriguing Deweyan influence. One is the "principled negotiation" approach that Roger Fisher and William Ury develop in their bestselling book, *Getting to Yes* (1991). The other is the negotiated agreement framework for resolving public disputes that Lawrence Susskind and Jeffrey Cruikshank put forth in their book, *Breaking the Impasse* (1987). It is worth outlining the core components of both models, if only in bare-bones fashion here, because I suggest that they offer interesting practical articulations of a Deweyan model of social inquiry that can prove useful in resolving problematic situations, including disputes between environmental ethical and animal rights/liberation claims.

The method of principled negotiation as set forth in *Getting to Yes* comprises four main activities designed to facilitate consensus in any situation marked by prima facie disagreement: (1) separating the people from the problem, (2) focusing on stakeholders' underlying interests rather than their stated bargaining positions, (3) searching for and inventing options for mutual gain and fulfilling shared interests, and (4) employing fair standards and principles in the negotiation chosen through a process of collective inquiry and debate. A notable feature of Fisher and Ury's approach to dispute resolution, and one that evokes Dewey's understanding of inquiry discussed above, is their attention to the creative possibilities of collaborative negotiation strategies, in which novel solutions and tactics may arise through a process of collective deliberation and specific brainstorming efforts. Likewise, their emphasis on the role of communication in identifying underlying shared interests in situations of outward conflict over held positions indirectly evokes Dewey's commitment to cooperative inquiry and his focus on harmonizing and integrating competing interests in situations of conflict. And, as item four above suggests, Fisher and Ury's process of principled negotiation places great importance on the collective search for principles by the disputants that can serve as critical standards for choosing among competing solutions to the problem under negotiation. This aspect also echoes Dewey's view of general principles as analytical and discursive tools for resolving practical disputes.

Susskind and Cruikshank's approach in *Breaking the Impasse* shares many similarities with the negotiation process described in *Getting to Yes*, including the importance of identifying options for mutual gain and the necessity of meaningful cooperation among disputants, yet it presents a somewhat more elaborated discussion of the public negotiation process and in doing so provides a fuller view of many of its underlying epistemological foundations. In their book, Susskind and Cruikshank describe "good outcomes" of negotiated settlements as those agreements that are (1) perceived as fair by all participants (a perception that hinges on the process's being open to continual revision by the parties), (2) efficient, (3) wise (in the sense that disputants should have experience with their own community and its problems so they can anticipate and work through them), and (4) stable (agreements must endure and include provisions for future renegotiations). One of the most interesting concepts presented in *Impasse* is what Susskind and Cruikshank refer to as "prospective hindsight," or the valuable problem-solving wisdom that accrues from addressing similar challenges in the community's past experience. This notion, along with Susskind and Cruikshank's emphasis on continual revision in the negotiation process and the idea that joint fact finding can significantly reduce error in the proceedings, gives the epistemological commitments of *Impasse* an unmistakable Deweyan, pragmatic drift.

Although this abbreviated treatment obviously cannot take their full measure as practical philosophical frameworks or policy tools, it should be sufficient to demonstrate some of these methods' striking similarities to Dewey's project, especially to the contours of his universal pattern of inquiry. I believe this resemblance may be seen in a number of places, including, as mentioned above, both programs' rejection of the unexamined authority of *a priori* principles and all manner of fixed positions as well as their emphasis on continual revision and adjustment of the negotiation process itself. In addition, both dispute-resolution projects' emphasis on creative ways to engage and integrate seemingly incompatible values, goals, and objectives through careful methods of reasoning, fact finding, and open deliberation clearly mirrors Dewey's logic of social inquiry. Moreover, Dewey's recognition and defense of value pluralism and his accompanying arguments for toleration of different views of the good, not to mention his commitment to cooperative inquiry and the self-correcting nature of democratic discussion, suggest further harmonies between his project and these leading contributions in the dispute-resolution literature. Last, these methods demonstrate a Deweyan faith in the self-regulating character of experience, in which standards and decisions arise from an iterative process of deliberation and hypothesis testing to meet inquirers' (disputants') needs and interests within the circumstances of the problematic situation.

Dewey scholars are also reflecting on and noticing these sympathies more. William Caspary (2000), for example, makes a compelling case that the theme of conflict resolution resounds in much of the philosopher's work. I believe Caspary is correct in emphasizing this thread in Dewey's thought, especially as it figures in his approach to ethics and his theory of public reasoning. I suggest, in fact, that contemporary methods of cooperative dispute resolution, such as those set forth in *Getting to Yes* and *Breaking the Impasse,* not only revive many Deweyan themes but also actually offer practical methodological frameworks that can give us a sharper and more concrete operationalization of Dewey's philosophy of inquiry in specific problematic situations. For these two ADR projects are good manifestations of social intelligence as Dewey understood it: the controlled, cooperative, and experimental approach to social problems, shored up by a commitment to the norms of free and open inquiry, yet always aware of the limitations presented by human fallibility and the appearance of the novel and unexpected. And their value as potential ethical resources, albeit within a reconstructed, procedural view of ethics, is just now being discovered.

Facts and Values in Animal-Environment Conflicts

One of the benefits of approaching animal-environment conflicts via the pragmatic method of conflict resolution is that it can open up possibilities for increased understanding and reconciliation at the level of practice. Disputes that appear to be mired in irresolvable philosophical disagreements about animal welfare and ecological integrity can often prove amenable to attempts to seek out policy common ground or acceptable compromises without requiring deeper philosophical assent. Often, this pragmatic reconciliation is possible because the conflict resolution framework, unlike the ethical debate, turns attention to empirical details and factors in the case that could present real opportunities for "mutual gain" among the contesting parties.

For an example of this in practice, let us return to the mute swan problem I describe at the beginning of this chapter. If we consider the mute swan case in greater detail—and avoid framing it in the terms of a philosophical dispute between normatively opposed programs in animal rights and environmental ethics—we see that some common ground between the state wildlife officials and the lakeshore residents regarding what to do about these biological "invaders" does, in fact, exist. Indeed, their comments in the local newspapers reveal that many of the members of the Arrowhead Mountain Lake Association recognized the potentially undesirable effects the swans could have on the health and integrity of the lake system. Furthermore, a number of them believed that some sort of control action might be necessary. What many contested was therefore not the ecological reality of the problem but rather the *method* of control (shooting) devised by the Fish and Wildlife Department to handle the bird situation, and, in some cases, the political authority of the state wildlife managers to control what were seen as local resources. Many lakeshore residents, for example, spoke of wanting to manage the bird problem themselves by shaking or "addling" the swans' eggs in their nests, considered by many observers to be a reasonable form of swan birth control, at least when numbers are low (Allen 1998). Ultimately, then, the goal of maintaining a healthy Arrowhead Mountain Lake was a practical end that united both camps. Yet it is easy to lose sight of these converging interests if we overemphasize the importance of conflicting ethical attachments to individual animals or ecosystems.

For another example of this kind of pragmatic resolution of animal-environment conflicts, consider the controversy surrounding the welfare impacts of ecological field research on Steller sea lions in Alaska. Composing roughly 70 percent of the entire population, the Alaska Steller sea lion population experienced a puzzling and dramatic decline in the 1970s and 1980s, with a more than 80 percent reduction in the Alaskan population recorded in the past three decades (National Research Council 2003). The Steller was listed as a federally threatened species in 1990, with the more rapidly diminishing western stock upgraded to endangered status in 1997. Even though the sea lion studies have received a comparatively massive investment of federal research dollars (more than $120 million was spent on studies during 2001–2004 alone), the exact cause of the decline remains unclear, although researchers are optimistic that the studies planned and currently underway will go a long way toward pinpointing the source of the population decline and hence inform an effective recovery and conservation effort, while at the same time shedding important light on the workings of a large and complex aquatic ecosystem (Dalton 2005b).

In 2005, the Humane Society of the United States (HSUS) sued the National Marine Fisheries Service (NMFS)—the federal agency overseeing the sea lion studies—on the grounds that it did not properly execute and monitor research on the animals. HSUS argued that NMFS granted permits allowing "intrusive, duplicative, uncoordinated and unnecessary research" on the animals. In particular, HSUS objected to marking and sampling methods that included hot branding of the lions, among other techniques (Dalton 2005a). NMFS defended the studies by arguing that the invasive techniques are standard in the field and do not pose a threat to the overall health of the sea lion population. The techniques, NMFS argued, are a reasonable means to gather data needed to understand why populations are declining and to design measures for the recovery and conservation of populations and thereby the species (Lee 2005). After a May 2006 court order essentially sided with the HSUS and shut down Steller research, the NMFS and HSUS reached a settlement agreement in June 2006 that allowed only low-impact studies of the animals (i.e., excluding hot branding, tooth extractions, etc.; Nature 2006).

Although the ethical conflict between concern for the well-being of individual animals (sea lions) and the conservation of the population/species is significant in this dispute, like the mute swan dilemma, it may also be seen to hinge on an empirical debate—in this case, disagreements about the proper design and monitoring of field research and the impacts of sampling and marking techniques on the health of the larger sea lion population. It also reflects differences of opinion about the adequacy of existing research and perhaps a dispute about the techniques and tests essential to the research program (Dalton 2005a, 2005b). These are all important considerations, but ultimately they are scientific, managerial, and technical questions, not moral ones. They do not necessarily require resolving a foundational ethical debate over the relative value of sentient beings, species conservation, ecological health, or advancing scientific knowledge. As a result, the parties are closer together than seems to be the case at first glance, suggesting that a clarification of research protocols and a more coordinated permitting system at the NMFS might alleviate some of the most serious objections of the animal-welfare proponents.

In fact, in January 2006, NMFS announced that it was preparing an Environmental Impact Statement to "analyze the potential environmental impacts of administering its grant and permit programs" for the lions and northern fur seals (*Callorhinus ursinus*). NMFS would also "evaluate measures that will improve efficiency and avoid unnecessary redundancy" in the studies and "standardize research protocols" (NOAA–National Marine Fisheries Service 2006). The final report, which was completed in the spring of 2007, concludes that the research is not likely to threaten the endangered Steller population and advocates an even more expansive research program—including approval for lethal take of small numbers of individual lions if the research application can demonstrate the action will lead to information useful to the conservation of the species (National Oceanic and Atmospheric Association 2007). Although an improved research design and increased monitoring and oversight of the Steller studies will probably not assuage all the animal-welfare concerns about the invasiveness of some of the research techniques, the deliberate elimination of unnecessary and duplicative studies should reduce the aggregate number of unavoidable harms to the animals. It should also increase the likelihood that the expected conservation benefits of the research—so critical to the justification of the controversial techniques in the first place—are realized.

This kind of pragmatic common ground between animal-rights proponents and wildlife/environmental researchers and managers is often available despite the history of conflict (e.g., protests, litigation) and lack of trust that has developed between both groups. In an interesting paper published in the journal *Conservation Biology,* Dan Perry and Gad Perry (2008) argue for greater cooperation among animal-rights supporters and wildlife conservationists, correctly noting that both groups care about animals' well-being, even if they emphasize different understandings of this good (i.e., individuals vs. populations/species). Furthermore, the authors suggest that both groups have important policy interests in common, including preventing the introduction of invasive species (thus avoiding negative ecological impacts and the need for lethal control) and regulating more stringently the international exotic pet trade, which is widely seen as a major conservation problem and a welfare issue for marketed animals, such as tigers (32).

Cases like the mute swan and sea lion disputes—and other dilemmas arising from the impacts of ecological research and management on sentient and nonsentient organisms, populations, and ecosystems—have become increasingly common in ecology and conservation biology and often require researchers and managers to make difficult ethical choices in the course of their work. I examine this situation in greater detail in Chapter 8. But for now, I can say that, despite the apparent incompatibility of animal-centered and population/species/ecosystem-centered approaches in environmental ethics, there is reason to believe that such philosophical differences do not always preclude practical accommodation and agreement at the policy and management levels. Indeed, more nuanced and anticipatory discussions of shared conservation and welfare goals among animal welfare/rights proponents and environmentalists (including the philosophical and professional variety) can help us avoid falling into philosophical stalemates over which entity—individual animals, populations, species, or ecosystems—is of "ultimate" value in situations of conflict.

Conclusion: Toward a Pragmatic Holism in Environmental Ethics

I suggest in this chapter that the historical intractability of the environmental ethics/animal rights debate is largely due to its being construed, even by those seeking to make philosophical amends, as a contest between general and competing claims of moral considerability. I argue instead that we would be better off approaching the dispute as a class of problematic situations in the Deweyan sense, concrete problems that require the application of intelligent methods of inquiry, such as those found in certain consensual dispute-resolution frameworks. That is to say, I propose that the focus in this debate should be on specific problematic cases involving environmental and animal conflicts that require cooperative inquiry and creative problem solving rather than on the (purely) philosophical question of the comparative moral status of animals and the environment and the deduction of general principles marking off our purported moral duties toward them. This does not mean that the intellectual task of defending animal interests/rights or the value of ecosystems is no longer necessary or important, for it surely is. But I do not think that this task alone gets us very far in our efforts to resolve real environment-animal conflicts. It would not have proved very useful, for example, in clarifying and reconciling the interests in either the mute swan or sea lion case described above; these dilemmas require a more pragmatic method of analysis and decision making than the traditional assertion of claims of moral standing and significance.

The reconstruction of the animal rights/environmental ethics debate as a series of practical disputes, defined by unique combinations of empirical and value conflicts in specific problematic situations rooted in time and space, moves the field of environmental ethics more squarely into the realm of environmental and social practices—in particular, the sphere of public decision making and community problem solving. In doing so, it begins to advance the well-known but often hard-to-accomplish mission of pragmatism as a praxis-oriented approach that engages the real dilemmas of human experience. In rejecting all forms of indulgent speculation and theorizing disconnected from the trials and tribulations of daily life, Dewey's thorough recasting of the traditional philosophical enterprise helps us position environmental ethics on the front lines of environmental conflict, where it may yet make some useful contributions to resolving policy disagreements and specific site-level disputes, including those hinging on the frequent tensions among the goals of animal welfare and rights, population viability, and environmental health/integrity.

Again, the pragmatic approach I am advocating by no means dismisses traditional questions of moral considerability and the search for normative principles to guide human relationships with animals and the natural environment. But it does insist on viewing these commitments as tools for problem solving and dispute resolution (embodiments of "prospective hindsight") rather than as fixed rules or directives that must be followed without question. In practice, the emphasis on fixed positions—for example, preexperiential foundations for moral standing or value—can obscure underlying shared interests and can result in turning disputants away from the kinds of compromise, concessions, and creative integrative solutions prized by Dewey and present-day conflict-resolution theorists. Instead, I argue in the preceding pages that the focus should be more on methods of cooperative inquiry and negotiated agreements, in which a variety of moral claims regarding nonhuman animals and the environment may be advanced as reasons for adopting a particular proposal or policy or choosing a particular course of action.

What I propose in this chapter, then, is not just a new tack toward the animal rights/environmental ethics debate but also an alternative approach to environmental ethics more generally, one that might be called "pragmatic" or "anthropocentric" holism. It is pragmatic in its emphasis on experimental methods of inquiry and conflict resolution; its rejection of *a priori,* preexperiential "first principles"; and its endorsement of value pluralism and dynamism. It is holistic in its focus on the *entire* problematic situation (a situation that will most certainly include identifiably discrete elements—i.e., individuals—*and* larger ecophysical processes and contexts) as well as on its accounting of the multiple goods and relevant empirical circumstances that define a particular conflict between opposing claims in specific environmental disputes (including those between advocates of environmental health and animal rights/welfare). And it is anthropocentric in the sense that it insists that all values expressed in public deliberations are human values, voiced and experienced by humans. That is, all values are understood in public negotiations not as human-independent (i.e., strong non-anthropocentric) values but rather as ways that people do indeed value animals or nature and that may act as good reasons to select specific courses of action or policies (Norton and Minteer 2002, 398–399). As I argue in Chapter 4, this approach can accommodate such claims as those declaring the intrinsic value of nature and the rights of nonhuman animals (as it can instrumental valuations), but it insists on subjecting these to the critical test of public discussion and inquiry oriented toward the goal of securing wise, efficient, and enduring agreements among stakeholders.

The field of environmental ethics needs to move beyond its historically dominant emphasis on the formulation and defense of general and universal arguments for why nonhuman nature (parts and wholes) matters. Although we can benefit from additional good work in this area, and I would not want any line of productive inquiry shut down simply because it probes the philosophical foundations of natural value, I believe that we already are flush with a wealth of principles and theories articulating the value of nonhuman individuals, populations, species, and ecosystems. I suggest instead that what we really need now—at this point in the field's development—are clear and effective frameworks for dispute resolution and problem solving that can inform and improve public negotiation and debate over the problematic situations that arise in the environmental context. This does not mean the wholesale replacement of normative environmental ethics with descriptive ethics; I am not arguing for the field to become an application of moral sociology. But it does mean working to make environmental ethics more responsive and relevant to the concrete affairs and dilemmas of human environmental experience. And it insists that its animating philosophical debates—such as the protracted dispute with animal rights philosophies—always be joined on solid ground.

7

Pluralism, Contextualism, and Natural Resource Management

Getting Empirical in Environmental Ethics

Introduction: Environmental Ethics and Social Inquiry

Given the public mission of environmental ethics—that is, to make compelling normative arguments justifying sound environmental policy and management decisions—it is surprising that the field has been so methodologically conservative over the years. One would think that this pragmatic charge would have spurred the development of a more interdisciplinary style of philosophical inquiry, especially studies that incorporate the analytical and experimental tools of the policy and management sciences. Yet, as I discuss in Chapter 3, the field has remained mostly insulated from the core discourses and methods that inform environmental public policy and management. It has emphasized instead the search for philosophical "first principles," often at the expense (as I argue) of informing intelligent and democratically accountable environmental practice and decision making.

Another way to put this is that, instead of breaking new methodological and institutional ground, and perhaps contrary to its own origins as a direct response to the "ecological crisis," environmental ethics has for the most part reflected the traditional style of mainstream academic philosophy. It has generally eschewed interdisciplinary approaches in favor of a "purer" form of intellectual inquiry, one conducted by scholars working in relative isolation from the "real world" of social problems and practices. Although some encouraging developments indicate that this may be slowly changing in academic philosophy, at least in a few inherently interdisciplinary domains, such as moral psychology (e.g., Appiah 2008), it is nevertheless still true that experimental work, even in an applied field, such as environmental ethics, remains at best a minority tradition. And even within the domain of applied ethics, moreover, other disciplines are well ahead of environmental ethics with respect to the incorporation of the empirical methods of the social sciences. For example, biomedical ethics, a close academic cousin of environmental ethics, has in recent years displayed much more openness to such methods, especially ethnographic research (see, e.g., Borry, Schotsmans, and Dierickx 2005; De Vries et al. 2007; Fox and Swazey 2008).

If environmental ethics is to have more of an impact in policy and management discussions, I believe it needs to adopt a more interdisciplinary spirit regarding the study of environmental values with respect to their structure and content and their potential roles in the public realm. As part of this process, the field could benefit greatly by integrating the methods of the experimental social sciences, particularly studies of public environmental ethics and attitudes, into its more traditional methods of theoretical analysis and argument. A more naturalistic and empirical approach to the study of environmental ethics, by breaking down some of the epistemological and ontological walls dividing the "two cultures" of the humanities and the sciences (Snow 1959), has the potential to broaden the intellectual scope of the field. It can also demonstrate its relevance to the public arena as a practical philosophical endeavor able to deepen the understanding of environmental values and attitudes within the social sciences. Public beliefs and values are in turn crucial data for assessing our assumptions about the meaning and structure of environmental ethics, including the variability of ethical beliefs regarding nature and the relationship of these commitments to policy and management choices.

In this chapter, I describe and discuss two experimental studies of public environmental ethics (performed by myself and collaborators at the University of Vermont) that I suggest can shed useful empirical light on a pair of key philosophical issues in the field as well as inform environmental ethicists and resource managers about the normative content of public environmentalism. The first study addresses a major philosophical and empirical debate in environmental ethics: the question of ethical pluralism and the degree to which the public embraces a wide array of ethical positions toward nature. The second study focuses on an important methodological question surrounding the significance of ethical principles in environmental decision making—namely, whether individuals conform to a more principle-centered or context-centered style of ethical judgment in environmental dilemmas.

I believe this sort of experimental work can open up new possibilities for a pragmatic environmental ethics that is more conversant with the environmental social sciences while also helping natural-resource managers and policy makers understand the wide range of the public's environmental ethical commitments. Additionally, it will begin to fill a hole in the empirical scholarship on public environmental ethics, a lacuna that exists not only within environmental ethics but also within the social-science literature. Although social scientists have for decades employed survey methods to understand the structure and substance of public environmental opinion (see the useful synthesis by Guber [2003]), empirical research on environmental ethics (of the sort considered in this book) remains largely absent from the literature. Public opinion studies of environmentalism have historically been concerned with either measures of general environmental values and worldviews or more narrowly construed attitudes about specific management and policy goals. The classic example of the former is the "new environmental paradigm" (NEP) research carried out by Riley Dunlap and Kent Van Liere, which measured public beliefs about such notions as the limits to growth, fragility of nature, and the need for a steady state economy (Dunlap and Van Liere 1978; see also Dunlap et al. 2000). Political scientist Lester Milbrath (1984) subsequently built upon this model by incorporating a more explicit focus on environmental values within the NEP. In the mid-1990s, a team of cognitive anthropologists contributed an important and influential study that explored environmental values within larger "cultural models" of human-environment relationships, revealing broad public support for environmentalism (Kempton, Boster, and Hartley 1996). More policy-specific empirical treatments of environmental attitudes have appeared in work investigating a great variety of subjects over the past few two decades, including views of public-land management, wildlife and endangered species, climate change, and energy policy, among other topics (see e.g., Shindler, List, and Steel 1993; Kellert 1996; Leiserowitz 2006; Nisbet and Myers 2007; Bolsen and Cook 2008).

Empirical research on environmental ethics can make an important contribution to the philosophical and social-science literatures, bringing empirical data to bear on key questions in environmental philosophy while also demonstrating the relevance of the discipline for discussions of public policy and management. This opens up new possibilities for the field, particularly with respect to its utility for environmental professionals, which in my experience are often deeply interested in and intrigued by environmental ethics but find the high theoretical tone of the discussions unappealing and the argumentation incompatible with the social-scientific approach to studying environmental values. In the rest of this chapter, I attempt to demonstrate this potential by weaving together the normative and empirical dimensions of this more naturalistic form of inquiry in environmental ethics, focusing primarily on the pluralism and contextualism questions, as mentioned above. I set up each study with a discussion of the philosophical debates on these issues to provide some background, and I then follow this with presentation of the public opinion surveys designed to investigate these questions via empirical methods.

Exploring Public Ethical Pluralism toward the Environment

Historically, the dominant axiological structure of environmental ethics has been referred to as "moral monism," a term that captures the presumption that environmental ethics must be reduced to a single theoretical-ontological type of environmental values (i.e., nonanthropocentric intrinsic value). As I discuss briefly in Chapter 4, the monistic form of much of environmental ethics has been a point of some debate in the field over the past two decades (see, e.g., Stone 1987; Callicott 1990; Varner 1991; Wenz 1993; Norton 1995; Minteer 1998; Callicott 1999b). An alternative position, "moral pluralism," soon became explicitly identified as an alternative meta-ethical option in environmental ethics (see, e.g., Stone 1987). Moral pluralists in environmental ethics reject the reductionistic move of the monists and argue instead for accommodating multiple normative principles, especially (in the case of pragmatists) the full sweep of instrumental and humanist values that nature holds for individuals and communities.

Although one need not be a pragmatist to be a moral pluralist (e.g., W. D. Ross's theory of "prima facie duties," which, while pluralistic, is wrapped in a deontological ethical approach at odds with the experimentalism of pragmatists, such as John Dewey), this position is one of the defining features of pragmatic philosophy. Given that individuals are differently situated and are shaped to a significant degree by dissimilar traditions and experiences, as well as the fact that novel ethical situations and problem contexts are always emerging, pragmatists argue that adherence to any single moral principle or rule in the face of such complexity and change is misguided. Here we see the logical connections between a pluralistic approach to moral philosophy and the pragmatist understanding of the fallibilist nature of moral and factual beliefs in lived experience (Bernstein 1989).

The desire for the simplicity of the reductionist move of moral monism is memorably described by William James, one of the founders of philosophical pragmatism and an especially strong advocate of the pluralistic position within an empirical philosophical system:

> It is curious how little countenance radical pluralism has ever had from philosophers. Whether materialistically or spiritualistically minded, philosophers have always aimed at cleaning up the litter with which the world apparently is filled. They have substituted economical and orderly conceptions for the first sensible tangle; and whether these were morally elevated or only intellectually neat, they were at any rate always aesthetically pure and definite, and aimed at ascribing to the world something clean and intellectual in the way of inner structure. As compared with all these rationalizing pictures, the pluralistic empiricism which I profess offers but a sorry appearance. It is a turbid, muddled, and gothic sort of an affair, without a sweeping outline and with little pictorial nobility. (1920, 45)

James is obviously aware of the provocative implications of his "radical" pluralism for a philosophical tradition so embedded in the search for singular truths and final, absolute goods. It is a view of the philosophical enterprise that breaks from "the quest for certainty," as Dewey puts it, and embraces instead a contingent, dynamic, and multifaceted view of human experience, including the ethical, aesthetic, and religious.

A century later, the pluralistic stance remains controversial, particularly in environmental ethics. Indeed, it has raised serious concerns among many monistic nonanthropocentrists who feel that the surrender of a universal theory of intrinsic value will court an unacceptable—and environmentally destructive—

moral relativism and that the normative inconsistency among multiple principles will, in turn, lead to unacceptably incoherent actions in practice (e.g., Callicott 1990; Rolston 1998). Yet the recognition of plural goods (and plural sources of those goods) in moral experience—and the accommodation of this pluralism in our ethical decision making—does not commit us to any unprincipled moral promiscuity.

Rather, and as I discuss in earlier chapters, it speaks to the need for social inquiry into the conflicted situation that requires moral judgment, a move that provides a contextualist anchor able to ground pluralism within the particularized environments of specific problematic cases. Ethical deliberation within problematic situations provides possibilities for reconciling alternative moral principles as well as transforming individuals' values and attitudes through public discussion, debate, and the discursive process of reason giving (see Chapter 3). And, although it is common to encounter such demands for consistency among ethical theorists, this is, at best, a weak constraint on moral principles. As Don Loeb (1996) points out, it is always possible to avoid the charge of inconsistency by making a distinction between the cases one is considering. So, for example, we could argue that wildlife preservation matters, but not as much as ensuring a level of basic human subsistence—they are simply different considerations and do not demand that we judge them with the confines of a single moral geometry.

The pluralistic position in environmental ethics, I believe, also takes a more realistic view toward the multiscalar complexity and diversity of environmental policy and management problems, a condition that renders the monistic requirement of reliance on a single and universal philosophical theory of value misguided, whether couched as intrinsic natural value or in the economic language of willingness-to-pay (see, e.g., Norton 2005). The social and ecological setting of a legally designated wilderness area is different from an urban green, which, in turn, is different from an agrarian landscape. In other words, Yellowstone is not Central Park, and this difference speaks to the existence and significance of alternative ecological, social, and, yes, ethical circumstances, factors of central importance to the justification of our commitments to the natural world. The discussion about what this variability means empirically and normatively renders the field of environmental ethics meaningful and useful as a scholarly enterprise and as a contributor to public environmental understanding and concern.

Study Design

To study public ethical pluralism regarding nature, I (with my collaborator Robert E. Manning, an environmental social scientist at the University of Vermont) devised a typology of potential environmental ethical stances, informed by a range of sources in the philosophical and historical literature. Table 7.1 presents this typology, which includes seventeen ethical positions grouped within five broad ethical categories. This is not an exhaustive set of principles, but it is, I believe, a group that captures a wide and reasonably representative array of normative positions toward nature. I also do not claim that these clusters of ethical

TABLE 7.1 Typology of environmental ethics

Normative grouping	Environmental ethics	Representative statement
Anti-environment	Threat to survival	Nature can be dangerous to human survival.
	Spiritual evil	Nature can be spiritually evil.
Benign indifference	Storehouse of raw materials	Nature is a storehouse of raw materials that should be used by humans as needed.
	Religious dualism	Humans were created as more important than the rest of nature.
	Intellectual dualism	Because humans can think, they are more important than the rest of nature.
Utilitarian conservation	Old humanitarianism	Cruelty toward animals makes people less human.
	Efficiency	The supply of goods and services provided by nature is limited.
	Quality of life	Nature adds to the quality of our lives (e.g., outdoor recreation, natural beauty).
	Ecological survival	Human survival depends on nature and natural processes.
Stewardship	Religious/spiritual duty	It is our religious responsibility to take care of nature.
	Future generations	Nature will be important to future generations.
	God's creation	Nature is God's creation.
	Mysticism	All living things are sacred.
Radical environmentalism	Humanitarianism	Animals should be free from needless pain and suffering.
	Organicism/animism	All living things are interconnected.
	Pantheism	All living things have a spirit.
	Natural rights	All living things have a moral right to exist.

positions exist as coherent categories in the minds of individuals; they are merely heuristic tools for understanding the philosophical relationships among potential environmental ethics. A representative statement for each ethical position is also included in Table 7.1. These statements, joined by others of similar phrasing, were employed as scale items in the survey. A mail-back questionnaire was constructed that included scales designed to measure the multiple environmental ethics listed in Table 7.1. An eleven-point response scale was employed to measure agreement with each ethical statement, anchored at "strongly agree" (5) and "strongly disagree" (–5), with "no opinion" (0) occupying a middle point between them. A total of forty-two environmental ethics statements were employed as scale items for the seventeen environmental ethics in the questionnaire.

The study questionnaire was administered (following standard procedures recommended by Don Dillman [1978]) to a representative sample of Vermont households chosen from telephone directories covering the state. Of a total of 1,228 deliverable questionnaires, 612 were completed and returned, yielding a response rate of 50 percent. (A telephone survey of a random sample of nonrespondents was conducted to test for nonresponse bias; on only two scale items was there a statistical difference between respondents and nonrespondents.)

Results and Discussion

Results of the measurements of agreement for each of the seventeen environmental ethics are presented in Figure 7.1. It is clear that the study sample subscribed to a number of environmental ethical positions, as is evident from the high level of agreement placed upon multiple environmental ethics. All four environmental ethics in the "Utilitarian Conservation" category—a classically anthropocentric set of principles reflecting the direct use of nature for human survival and economic well-being—received high mean agreement ratings, particularly "ecological survival" and "quality of life" ethics. "Stewardship" ethics—weaker anthropocentric principles reflecting a sense of caring for nature for future generations and out of a religious obligation—also received substantial support among respondents, especially the "future generations" ethic, which drew the highest score of all positions in the study.

In addition, a number of nonanthropocentric environmental ethics (here grouped under the label "Radical Environmentalism"), which revolve around a set of arguments for the intrinsic value of nature, was embraced by respondents, especially "organicism/animism," "humanitarianism" (i.e., animal welfare), and "natural rights." Environmental ethics in the "Benign Indifference" category, which represented views of the human-nature relationship that set nature apart from human moral and intellectual life, received an equivocal response from the study sample. Lastly, "Anti-environmental" ethics, the most strongly anthropocentric attitudes measured in the study, received the lowest agreement scores, suggesting that their currency among respondents is weak.

The study results indicate that a broad range of ethical sentiments about human-nature relationships exists, a number of which demonstrate a high degree of acceptability in public thinking. Although the study sample of the Vermont public possesses obvious geographic and demographic limitations, I believe the data provide powerful support for environmental ethical pluralism. Furthermore, even though anthropocentric positions on the whole drew greater support than nonanthropocentric principles, I want to emphasize that several positions that capture intrinsic-value-of-nature claims, including "humanitarianism" (animal welfare), "organicism" (ecocentrism), and "natural rights" (biocentrism), clearly

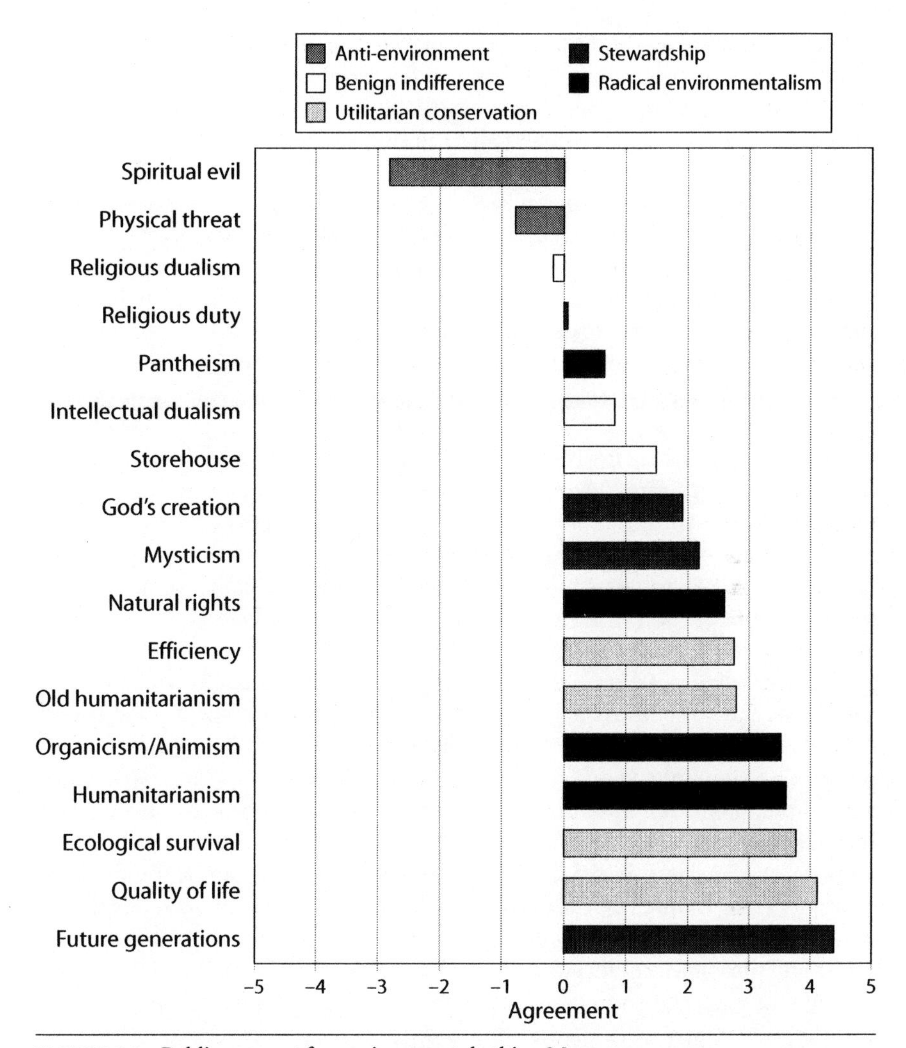

FIGURE 7.1 Public support for environmental ethics. Mean agreement scores appear on the *x*-axis: 5 = strongly agree; −5 = strongly disagree.

resonated with many of our study respondents, even if they did not occupy the top tier of principles with respect to the mean agreement scores. The study results therefore provide some empirical validation for the pluralistic stance in environmental ethics, at least to the degree that this position is motivated by the diverse normative commitments to the environment held by the public.

A study of this variety in public ethical attitudes toward nature also has important implications for environmental policy and management. For example, consider the case of public-land management in the United States. Occupying nearly one-third of the area of the country, public lands present an intriguing and often difficult set of management issues for local communities, federal land-management agencies, and the public. These issues become evident when one considers the different values associated with various land types that the federal agencies manage. A broad ethical mosaic of sorts can be seen with respect to three categories of public lands in particular: national forests, national parks, and wilderness.

National forests have been managed historically for utilitarian purposes—the provision of material benefits, such as timber, minerals, and forage, to American society. Under the canons of science, professionalism, and efficiency, national forest lands have traditionally been viewed as sources of raw materials to be managed on a "sustained-yield" basis. The national parks were born out of an aesthetic appreciation of natural wonders and the romantic association of spiritual values with nature and its elevation as a source of American cultural pride. Although the national parks, as amenity resources, share an anthropocentric foundation with the national forests, the efforts of early park advocates, such as John Muir, ensured that, from the beginning, the parks were guided by a preservationist philosophy rather than a narrow utilitarian one. Finally, legally designated wilderness on the public domain reveals an even more resolute preservationist underpinning. The passage of the Wilderness Act of 1964 provided that these lands would become the most protected and stringently managed units of the public-land system (Fox 1981; Runte 1997; Nash 2001).

What this mix of U.S. public-land types suggests is that, as a democratic society, we have attempted to "map out" our plural environmental values onto the public-land system and by doing so have fashioned a diverse, "patchy" landscape, one that admits to an array of human-nature experiences and sentiments. The mapping out has, of course, not always been successful or completely fair. Indeed, as any student of public-land history knows, this process has often been carried out under less than fully democratic conditions. Corporate interests, for example, have frequently exerted great pressure on the management of the national forests as commodity enterprises, often to the detriment of ecological values and the long-term sustainability of landscape (Hays 2006). In addition, and as land managers and conservationists have become increasingly aware in recent decades, our "maps" (i.e., institutions and policies) frequently do not provide sufficient support for critical environmental goals, such as conserving biodiversity and safeguarding ecosystem health and integrity over large scales—and across political, administrative, and legal boundaries (see, e.g., Thomas 2003; Chester 2006). This dual institutional and ecological challenge places great demands on public land management and, by extension, on our ethical deliberations about the course of human-nature relationships in such places as national forests, national parks, and wilderness (Keiter 2003).

In light of these considerations, the pragmatic and pluralistic approach to environmental ethics in management discussions would seem to hold great potential for encouraging a more inclusive and democratic approach to the public justification of land-management policies. This process, in rejecting the "one-size-fits-all" approach to ethical arguments in policy and management settings, allows for value and management trade-offs that reflect a context-sensitive approach to resource management at the landscape scale. For example, within national forests, competing demands for timber, forage, recreation, biodiversity protection, and so on may be met by tailoring forest-management programs to accentuate or deemphasize particular values and uses based on each forest's unique set of ecological properties, land-use history, and sociopolitical context. Some forest lands would be allocated to advocates of more utilitarian commodity production, while others would be set aside on ecological and aesthetic grounds, perhaps, or as areas for recreation, research, and education.

This philosophy is in keeping with the development in the United States and internationally of landscape-level conservation-planning efforts that seek to widen the scale of conservation beyond parks and protected areas to include a full mosaic of land uses (and their accompanying mix of social and conservation values), including those supporting sustainable human livelihoods and the protection of native species' ecological systems (e.g., Henson et al. 2009; Wiens 2009). It also reflects the real-world challenges of integrating the goals of nature protection and sustainable use, a complex political, institutional, and ethical challenge that requires conservation scientists and managers—if they wish to be effective—to embrace pluralism at the normative and strategic level. As conservation biologist John G. Robinson points out, this move is ultimately forced by the reality on the ground, especially the need for conservation managers and advocates to form effective partnerships with local communities, who are often critical to the long-term success of conservation projects. A key component of establishing successful partnerships, he concludes, is acknowledging that

> different stakeholders value biodiversity in different ways. Some aspire to the conservation of biodiversity for intrinsic reasons, some for its contribution to cultural integrity and social justice, others for its contribution to economic development. . . . Nature protection organizations, for instance, often seek to protect natural systems or highly valuable endangered species, but they are not necessarily insensitive to concerns of social justice of the economic well-being of residents. The primary interest of local communities might be to maintain their social and cultural integrity, and to improve their well-being and quality of life, but this does not necessarily negate their respect for the natural world. . . . In the end, conservation programs must be designed by what works in a particular context . . . not on the basis of ideological preference. (2011)

Of course, this value pluralism toward the environment can still produce intense conflict among stakeholders in policy and management debates—for example, those who view nature as a "storehouse of raw materials" clearly hold a different attitudinal and value set than those who strongly endorse nature's intrinsic value—and it is reasonable to expect these views to be in considerable tension in practice. A recent and highly visible example of this schism between alternative environmental value positions may be seen in the conflict over opening Alaska's National Wildlife Refuge for oil and gas development, a dispute that has pitted those interested in protecting the wilderness values of the refuge (often described as a "pristine" ecosystem) against those prioritizing the economic value of the region for energy development. Although such value conflicts are common and often politically challenging—they can require us to make hard choices between alternative policies that have differential outcomes for communities and the landscape—allowing for ethical pluralism and encouraging deliberation over a diverse set of environmental ethics in actual management debates can also lead to social learning and equitable forms of public compromise that allow a broad spectrum of values to be served through responsive land-management decisions. Recognizing and respecting these value differences in public planning and management discussions can importantly work to build trust and understanding among stakeholders, revealing different groups' common stake in land conservation and environmental protection, regardless of the disparate values individuals and communities attach to the environment (Wondolleck and Yaffee 2000).

As an illustration, consider the dispute over the designation and management of Grand Staircase–Escalante National Monument (GSENM) in southern Utah, which was designated by President Bill Clinton in 1996. The area became the first national monument managed by the Bureau of Land Management (BLM), an agency historically considered to be devoted to grazing and mining interests rather than wilderness values and land preservation. The designation of the area for protection under the Antiquities Act took place against the larger backdrop of the Utah BLM wilderness debate, which originated with the extension of the wilderness idea to BLM public lands (Keiter 2001). Wilderness advocates seeking preservation of the Escalante region's aesthetic, recreational, and ecogeological values squared off against state and local interests that resented federal takeover of the land, including citizens whose identification with long traditions of agriculture and resource use placed them at odds with the goals of preservationism. In addition, the region was the ancestral home of the Paiute, who sought continued access to the area's resources and a role in management decision making (Trainor 2008).

Despite the significant ethical and cultural diversity among GSENM's citizen groups, as Sarah Trainor (2006, 2008) argues, an empirical study of the public planning process reveals that the shared interest of landscape protection actually united many of the stakeholders in the case, even in the face of environmental value and cultural differences. Each group held "a deep connection to and identity with the landscape," Trainor writes, even though these identities were different and reflected distinctive cultural relationships to GSENM (2008, 354). In addition, closer examination of these diverse stakeholder groups in the planning process indicates the existence of a widely shared aesthetic appreciation of the landscape among local residents and wilderness preservationists, a sympathy that Trainor suggests may not have been uncovered if a less discursive and deliberative process had been followed that did not allow for—and validate—the expression of multiple environmental and cultural values in their own terms (2006, 18).

The empirical study of public ethical pluralism toward nature can address important questions about the substance and structure of environmental values. It also has implications for the ways in which we approach environmental policy and management challenges, especially the need to accommodate such pluralism in environmental decision making. Such examples as the GSENM case demonstrate that value diversity in environmental management debates does not preclude agreement at the level of practice, especially if this diversity is respected in public discussion and is seen as an occasion for further inquiry and learning by participants, including citizens and natural-resource managers and policy makers. Cases like GSENM, furthermore, give credence to Bryan Norton's (1991) "convergence hypothesis," which predicts that in many cases nonanthropocentric ethics and a pluralistic, noneconomistic anthropocentrism will "converge" on common environmental policy and management decisions. Although Norton's position has been criticized by some monistic environmental philosophers as incorrect (for example, J. Baird Callicott argues that it is "dead wrong" [1999a, 31]), many believe it is a reasonable prediction of the common policy goal of protecting the large ecological context that supports a wide array of human and natural values over the long run (see, e.g., Minteer 2009). In Norton's model, it is more important to get the policy or management goals right—and to develop opportunities for value expression, deliberation, and social learning—rather than to dwell on any particular moral principle regarding our duties to nature.

This brings me to the second issue I want to examine via empirical methods in environmental ethics—namely, the relative significance of ethical principles and problem context in public reasoning about environmental management. Specifically, the study I describe below explored whether a principle-driven or situation-driven/contextualist model of the role of environmental ethics in decision making was more empirically valid among the public. Following the organization of the pluralism discussion, I first describe the philosophical aspects of this question, focusing on the difference between the dominant "principle-ist" approach in environmental ethics and the contextualist alternative. I then present the results of this second empirical study of environmental ethics, this time focused on a sample of the public from the wider New England region. I conclude the chapter by discussing how the empirical approach to environmental ethics I defend avoids outmoded charges that it runs afoul of the naturalistic fallacy and reiterating its role in a more pragmatic and experimental model of environmental ethical inquiry.

Ethical Contextualism in Environmental Decision Making

Many environmental ethicists (and applied ethicists more generally) follow a deductivist or principle-centered approach to ethical reasoning, in which specific environmental policy goals and management actions are thought to be deduced from a small number of previously articulated general moral principles. This general method of deriving specific natural-resource and environmental-management decisions and policy goals directly from prior assertions of one or more normative principles can be seen in the work of many of the leading ethicists in the field. Consider, for example, Callicott's remarks about the philosophical move he believes is required if we are to protect the old-growth forests of the Pacific Northwest:

> Since old-growth forests . . . are not yet widely acknowledged to have intrinsic value, timber companies may fell them without first offering any justification whatever. If environmentalists want to stop the clear-cutting of dwindling old-growth forest on public land (to say nothing of those on privately held land) they have to go to court seeking a legal injunction. *If, on the other hand, the intrinsic value of nature were widely acknowledged and legally institutionalized,* then timber companies would have to go to court seeking permission to fell an old-growth forest—thus being burdened to offer sufficient justification—whenever they intended to do so. (1999a, 246; emphasis added)

Callicott clearly believes that the main philosophical task for environmental ethics is to *first* develop the metaphysical and moral foundations needed to support this claim and *then* work toward the subsequent application of intrinsic value to deliberations and arguments in the environmental policy realm. The adoption of a moral principle recognizing nature's intrinsic value is, for him, a necessary prior commitment if we are to arrive at technically sound and philosophically defensible environmental policy and management decisions in practice. In the logic of environmental ethics and policy argument, Callicott thinks that "reasons come first, policies second" (1999a, 32).

I believe this view of the relationship between general environmental ethical principles and specific environmental policies is widely held in the field. Consider how another nonanthropocentrist philosopher, Eric Katz, presents the urgent question surrounding the protection of biodiversity:

> The real solution to problems in environmental policy lies in a specific transformation of values—the transcendence of human-based systems of ethics and the development of an "ecological ethic." Humanity must acknowledge that moral value extends beyond the human community to the communities within natural systems. . . . *Policies that ensure the preservation of planetary biodiversity must express values derived from a nonanthropocentric moral system.* (1997, 166; emphasis added)

Like Callicott, Katz appears to believe that the correct environmental policies (i.e., "the real solution") will be attainable only after we internalize one or more nonanthropocentric principles. And, like Callicott, Katz seems to believe there is no need to inquire whether alternative ethical justifications for securing biodiversity, such as those couched in the language of human social values, are justifiable in certain circumstances or whether these might be more effective in generating widespread public and political support for protective biodiversity policies in specific situations.

Laura Westra is yet another nonanthropocentrist philosopher who appears to hold a similar view regarding the critical importance of an unyielding fidelity to principle. In her critique of Norton's aforementioned "convergence hypothesis"—that is, the assertion that we should recognize human cultural and social values as justifications for specific environmental policies, because a liberal anthropocentrism can be expected to "converge" on the same policies proscribed by a consistent nonanthropocentric position—Westra makes clear her commitment to a firm principle-ist stance, regardless of its practical implications. "Even reaching a right decision on wrong principles may not be sufficient," she writes, "if the principles are such that they would permit a morally bad decision on another occasion" (2009, 61). Westra's fear seems to be that "morally bad decisions"—that is, ones not ratified by certain nonanthropocentric principles—are the inevitable outcome of pragmatic appeals to human interests and values in environmental policy contexts. In her opinion, such ill-formed judgments will only spell disaster for the natural world by necessarily issuing exploitationist policies and underwriting destructive environmental attitudes and behaviors.

The ubiquity of this principle-ist method in nonanthropocentric environmental ethics is not that surprising, given that applied ethics is typically understood to be an attempt to bring general (and, more often than not, universal) moral standards, rules, and principles to bear on more concrete social and political problems. Even so, we may question whether this methodological approach is the best way to think about the relationship between theory and practice in environmental ethics—that is, whether it is the most effective and productive way to conceptualize moral inquiry into environmental problems and policy arguments.

Rather than beginning with the conviction that a general ethical principle—for example, one recognizing the universal duty to promote intrinsic natural values—is the only valid and defensible moral commitment and then looking to apply this principle to a specific policy or management context, we might instead begin with an inquiry into the empirical circumstances of the environmental policy context or management issue under consideration. From there, we may engage a set of moral principles—perhaps, in many cases, revising and refitting them—as we reason through and deliberate over their potential to help us resolve environmental policy and management choices. This way of thinking about the claims of environmental ethics and the method of relating these claims to natural resource and environmental policy arguments and decisions recognizes the normative and empirical weight of specific, concrete problematic situations. In turn, it moderates the influence of preexperiential moral principles when such principles are engaged apart from or before practical deliberations regarding action.

Such a shift to "contextualism," in the conceptualization of the relationship between environmental ethics and practice/policy argument, is in keeping with the pragmatic approach to moral inquiry, especially that advocated by Dewey. Even though he wrote decades before the birth of environmental ethics as an academic field, Dewey nevertheless rejects the same sort of principle-ist approach he sees as plaguing much of the Western philosophical tradition. One of these problems with this approach, at least on the pragmatic view, is the difficulty of interpreting the general principle in question in light of complex and changing experiential circumstances. As Dewey observes:

> Even if all men agreed sincerely to act upon the principle of the Golden Rule as the supreme law of conduct, we should still need inquiry and thought to arrive at even a passable conception of what the Rule means in terms of

> concrete practice under mixed and changing social conditions. Universal agreement upon the abstract principle even if it existed would be of value only as a preliminary to cooperative undertaking of investigation and thoughtful planning; as a preparation, in other words, for systematic and consistent reflection. (1932, 178)

In Dewey's thinking, moral principles should be seen as composing only one part of the process of thoughtful and reflective inquiry into specific problematic situations. Although these claims often have a presumptive force in our deliberations over the right policy or action (a force owing to their previous success in helping us adapt to previous problems), they can, at best, capture only a particular aspect or dimension of the larger, complex experiential situation in which we find ourselves engaged. Because past experience shows that these unstable and indeterminate contexts often find us struggling to harmonize disparate rights, duties, goods, virtues, and the like—each of which competes for attention and influence in our moral judgments—the selection of any one of these for special emphasis *before* contextual analysis thwarts intelligent moral inquiry.

Not only are problematic situations sufficiently dense and complex as to call into question the formalistic application of any general principle laid down in advance; they are also diverse enough to challenge the uncritical reliance upon any *single* moral claim in governing our inquiry into potential alternative courses of action. As Dewey writes:

> A genuinely reflective morals will look upon all the [moral] codes as possible *data*; it will consider the conditions under which they arose; the methods which consciously or unconsciously determined their formation and acceptance; it will inquire into their applicability in present conditions. It will neither insist dogmatically upon some of them, nor idly throw them all away as of no significance. It will treat them as a storehouse of information and possible indications of what is now right and good. (1932, 179; emphasis original)

Dewey's pluralism, combined with his experimental approach to ethical reasoning, means that there is no *a priori*, context-independent way to rank various values, duties, and goods. Such hierarchies can emerge only through the process of deliberation, which in turn is guided by the real needs and deficiencies of the troubling situation in question (Caspary 2000, 162). This strong commitment to the methodological dimensions of ethical thinking and analysis—to the operations of inquiry that allow the community to distinguish between the valued and the valuable, the desired and the desirable—thus ensures that pragmatist approaches like Dewey's do not run afoul of the naturalistic fallacy. As I say earlier, empirically held values and norms are always submitted to a process of appraisal and revision (and often replacement), an activity driven by the particularized needs and dynamics of experienced problem situations (Anderson 1998). Dewey's is by no means a purely descriptive ethics; it is a method of inquiry, justified on logical and normative grounds, by which normative claims can be appraised, challenged, and ultimately transformed in the context of a problematic context.

It is important to note that in arguing for the instrumental and experimental role of moral principles in problematic situations, Dewey does not deny the existence of such principles, nor does he reject their role within moral deliberation and decision making. He seeks only to put them in their proper place. Historically successful moral principles promoting the good and the right are not to be uncritically accepted before experimental inquiry, just as they are not to be cast aside simply because they traffic in generalities or presume to hold a universal currency. Instead, they should be understood as potentially useful resources for comprehending and ultimately transforming particular unstable and disrupted moral contexts (Dewey 1932, 330).

Dewey is well aware that his contextualist, experimental, and adaptive model of moral inquiry is a radical departure from most approaches of the Western ethical tradition and that his emphasis on the operations of "social intelligence" in moral inquiry represents a new way of conceptualizing the enterprise of ethical theory:

> The blunt assertion that every moral situation is a unique situation having its own irreplaceable good may seem not merely blunt but preposterous. For the established tradition teaches that it is precisely the irregularity of special cases which makes necessary the guidance of conduct by universals, and that the essence of the virtuous disposition is willingness to subordinate every particular case to adjudication by a fixed principle. . . . Let us, however, follow the pragmatic rule, and in order to discover the meaning of the idea ask for its consequences. Then it surprisingly turns out that the primary significance of the unique and morally ultimate character of the concrete situation is to transfer the weight and burden of morality to intelligence. It does not destroy responsibility; it only locates it. (1920, 173)

The upshot of this is that a Deweyan pragmatic and contextualist project in environmental ethics takes a much different tack than the principle-ist method that most environmental philosophers prefer. Rather than looking to argue from the basis of a privileged class of fixed philosophical principles to specific environmental-policy judgments or management decisions, the pragmatic contextualist works instead from the empirical circumstances and resources present within the problematic situation in question. Here, the contextualist finds him- or herself examining and deliberating over potential alternative courses of action and appealing to those moral values and goods determined, through a process of hypothetical testing and experimental reasoning, to best guide inquiry and able to steer it toward a resolution. In this process, such values and goods may, in fact, turn out to be citizens' assertions of nature's intrinsic value, or they may be something quite different—that is, the articulation of various human-oriented, cultural values derived from a particular environmental system (e.g., recreation and aesthetic enjoyment). Regardless, and as I discuss in Chapter 4, these claims receive their validity and legitimacy from the dynamics of the method of inquiry and open deliberation—and their ability to render problematic situations more stable and harmonious—not from their "inherent nature" or their purported claims to any special philosophical credentials.

An interesting articulation of this Deweyan understanding of the role of moral principles in decision making has emerged in biomedical ethics, where some have argued for the adoption of a "clinical pragmatism" that integrates the concerns of patient care with an explicitly pragmatic/Deweyan method of moral analysis and decision making (Miller, Fins, and Bacchetta 1996; Fins, Bacchetta, and Miller 1997). This contextual, case-based model of ethical analysis and judgment accommodates a dynamic and sophisticated understanding of challenges in patient care, combining moral evaluation with clinical assessment in a way that avoids the kind of principle-ist tendencies I describe above (and that are also prevalent in much bioethics literature; Miller, Fins, and Bacchetta 1996, 44–47). The incorporation of a similar methodological program in environmental ethics, targeted at the dilemmas of environmental decision making in practice, could give the field more traction in policy and management debates as well as the design and conduct of ecological research (the subject of the next chapter).

Study Design

Following the Vermont study of public ethical pluralism, a second survey was devised (again, with Manning and other collaborators at the University of Vermont) to further probe the relationship between general moral principles and concrete situations in environmental ethics. Specifically, this study was intended to explore citizens' environmental ethics and their attitudes regarding a particularized land- and wildlife-management problem, framed in the context of New England's White Mountain National Forest (WMNF). A mail questionnaire was constructed that contained a hypothetical wildlife-management dilemma, couched in three different forest land contexts in and around the WMNF. Although the inherent limitations of the mail-survey instrument precluded us from providing an exhaustive and fully elaborated description of the wildlife scenario, we were able to provide a basic summary of the hypothetical problem and present the respondents with a range of management responses to resolve it. The wildlife-management dilemma was presented to the respondents in the following manner:

> This question asks your opinions about a potential management issue within the White Mountain National Forest and surrounding lands. The issue concerns beavers which live in this area. Beavers cut down trees and build dams. These dams cause local flooding, which can kill more trees. Should any action be taken to control the number of beavers and their actions? We would like you to answer this question as it applies to three different locations. The first location is an official "wilderness area" within the White Mountain National Forest. The second location is a "non-wilderness area" within the White Mountain National Forest. This area has been designated by Congress to pro-

vide for multiple uses, including sustainable timber production and outdoor recreation. The third location is "private land" outside the White Mountain National Forest. This land is owned by a commercial timber company. Please indicate the extent to which you feel beavers should be managed in each of the three locations described above:

1 = The beavers should be left alone
2
3 = Beaver dams should be breached to minimize local flooding
4
5 = The beavers should be eliminated or removed

Respondents were directed to indicate, on this five-point scale, their management decisions in each of the three forest land–use contexts described in the above scenario: a wilderness area in the White Mountain National Forest, a nonwilderness location within the forest managed for "multiple use," and private forest land located outside the national forest.

In addition, to measure support for a range of general environmental ethical principles, the survey again employed a battery of seventeen ethical statements representing five distinct normative groupings (Table 7.1). As a reminder, the ethical principles ran the gamut from strongly anthropocentric environmental ethics to strongly nonanthropocentric positions (e.g., from "Anti-environmental" ethics to "Radical Environmental" ethics). The ethical statements in this study were accompanied by a six-point response scale by which respondents could indicate the importance of each environmental ethic in influencing their decisions regarding the beaver-management dilemma in the wilderness, multiple-use, and private-land contexts. The scales for the environmental ethic statements ranged from 1 ("not at all important") to 6 ("extremely important").

The sample for this study was drawn from the population of New England residents in six states. The sampling was carried out to ensure that the list of respondents contained a proportional sample of names from each of the six states. The first questionnaire was administered via mail to a representative sample of one thousand New England households. One week after the initial mailing of the survey, a postcard reminder was sent to all names on the mailing list. Then, three weeks after the initial mailing, a second copy of the questionnaire was mailed to initial nonrespondents. Out of the 1,000 questionnaires initially mailed, 16.7 percent was returned as undeliverable, which reduced the sample size to 833. Ultimately, 344 completed questionnaires were returned for a final response rate of 41.3 percent.

Study Results

Several data-analysis methods were employed for this study, including the use of contingency tables, chi-square tests, computation of gamma scores, and paired samples *t*-tests (the analysis presented in this section was performed by Elizabeth A.

Corley, a policy scientist at Arizona State University). This analysis confirmed the hypothesis that the respondents did not just draw upon general environmental ethical principles to make management decisions. Because the environmental ethics did not adequately explain the variance in beaver-management choices (i.e., the 1-to-5 scale from "the beavers should be left alone" to "the beavers should be eliminated"), we know that factors other than a respondent's environmental ethics guided his or her management decision regarding the beavers. Analysis of the data confirmed that the context of the management decision was one of the other factors that affected respondents' management decisions.

The first set of analyses explored whether the respondents' environmental ethics in each context (i.e., wilderness area, multiple-use land, or private land) influenced their beaver-management decisions within that context. To begin this analysis, a series of contingency tables was constructed, with each of the seventeen contextual environmental ethics as an independent variable (in seventeen separate analyses) and with the contextual beaver-management scenario as the dependent variable. The concern here was whether the respondents' support for each of the seventeen environmental ethics was related to their beaver-management decisions within each context. This analysis yielded seventeen contingency tables for each context (and a total of fifty-one contingency tables). One contingency table was constructed for each environmental ethic within each of the three contexts. Because this analysis yielded many contingency tables, all the results are not presented here; instead, I focus on the relationships that were deemed statistically significant using a chi-square test. Gamma values were also computed to determine the strength of any relationship between environmental ethics and management decisions without relying solely on chi-square statistics. Gamma values varied between −1 and +1, with negative values indicating a negative relationship between the independent and dependent variables and positive values indicating a positive relationship. The closer the absolute value of the gamma was to zero, the weaker the relationship.

In the wilderness context, chi-square tests indicated that only five of the seventeen environmental ethics were significantly related to the beaver-management decision in that context: "storehouse," "natural rights," "intellectual dualism," "quality of life," and "mysticism." Even though a chi-square test for these five environmental ethics indicated a significant relationship, the gamma values for these five ethics demonstrated that the relationship between the environmental ethic and beaver-management decision was weak to moderate, with four of the five gamma values below 0.30 in magnitude. The chi-square values and gamma values for all the statistically significant chi-square tests (for all three contexts) are presented in Table 7.2.

For the multiple-use land context, ten of the seventeen environmental ethics yielded significant chi-square values when their relationships with beaver-management scenarios were explored. Again, further analysis of gamma values for each of these cases indicated that none of the relationships was even moderately strong, with each gamma value being below 0.30 in magnitude. The weakest relationship between environmental ethics and the land scenarios occurred in the

TABLE 7.2 Gamma values for significant chi-square tests for relationship between environmental ethics and beaver-management scenarios

	Gamma value		
Environmental ethic	Wilderness context	Multiple-use context	Private-land context
Threat to survival	*	0.149	0.199
Spiritual evil	*	−0.016	*
Storehouse	0.279	0.231	0.158
Religious dualism	*	0.266	0.189
Intellectual dualism	0.237	0.295	*
Quality of life	*	*	−0.19
Ecological survival	*	−0.077	*
Religious duty	*	−0.048	*
Mysticism	−0.174	−0.101	−0.163
Organicism	−0.351	−0.279	*
Natural rights	−0.229	−0.239	−0.322

Note: Independent variable = environmental ethic; dependent variable = beaver-management decision. Only the statistically significant chi-square values are shown in the table. Seven environmental ethics did not yield significant chi-square values for any context, and those seven ethics are not included in this table.

* Chi-square test not statistically significant at .05 level.

case of the private-land context, with significant chi-square values for six of the seventeen environmental ethics and gamma values less than 0.20 in magnitude for all but one of those six significant ethics.

A second set of analyses focused on how participants chose to deal with the beavers in the three different contexts. Because the environmental ethics positions were not highly correlated with the contextual beaver-management decisions, a reasonable conclusion is that environmental ethics were not the main driving force for respondents' choices regarding beaver-management scenarios. The next step was to see whether context played significant roles in respondents' beaver-management decisions. This required exploring how the respondents' choices of beaver-management decisions changed across contexts. The working hypothesis here was that context would play an important role in the choice of a beaver-management decision. We tested this hypothesis by exploring whether the respondent's management choices were different across the three contexts.

Table 7.3 compares the means and median for the beaver-management decisions in each context. At first blush, one can see that the study participants showed diverse responses to the wildlife-management scenario, depending upon the land-use context of the problem (i.e., wilderness area, multiple-use land, or private land). The mean management values for the wilderness scenario, the multiple-use scenario, and the private-land scenario were 1.82, 2.66, and 2.86, respectively. The mean of 1.82 for the beaver-management scenario in the wilderness area implies that respondents were, as a whole, more willing to leave the beavers alone in the wilderness scenario than they were in the multiple-use forest or private-land scenarios. The median values in Table 7.3 demonstrate that half the respondents felt that beavers should be left alone in the wilderness scenario,

TABLE 7.3 Descriptive statistics for beaver-management scenarios, by context

Statistics for beaver-management options	Wilderness scenario	Multiple-use scenario	Private-land scenario
N	338	335	336
Mean	1.82	2.66	2.86
Median	1	3	3
Standard deviation	0.98	0.97	1.15

Note: Beaver-management options were categorized on a five-point scale: 1 = beavers should be left alone; 3 = beaver dams should be breached to minimize local flooding; 5 = beavers should be eliminated or removed.

but in the multiple-use and private-land scenarios, half the respondents thought that action should be taken that was more invasive than breaching the beaver dams to minimize flooding.

A graphical display of the different distributions for the three scenarios is shown in Figure 7.2. This figure demonstrates that the distributions of responses varied across the three land-use contexts, with the largest differences in the beaver-management distributions being exhibited between the wilderness scenario and the multiple-use/private-land scenarios. To further explore the statistical signifi-

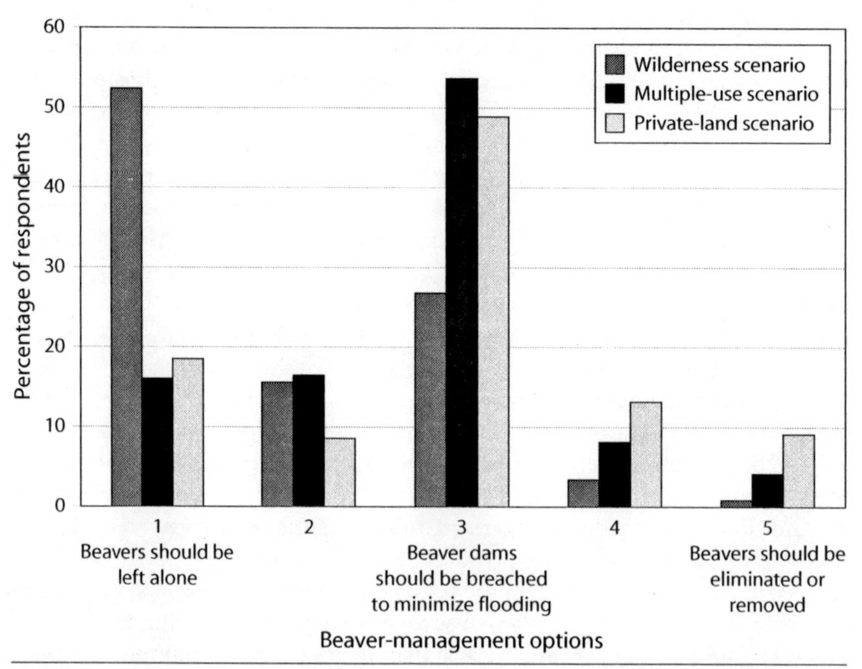

FIGURE 7.2 Beaver-management options across contexts. The *y*-axis represents the percentage of respondents selecting each management option.

TABLE 7.4 Comparison of means for beaver-management options

Comparison of scenarios	*t*-value	Degrees of freedom	Level of statistical significance
Wilderness scenario vs. multiple-use scenario	−15.188	334	**
Wilderness scenario vs. private-land scenario	−14.663	335	**
Multiple-use scenario vs. private-land scenario	−3.416	333	*

* $p < .001$; ** $p < .0001$.

cance of any difference between distributions for the three beaver-management options, paired samples *t*-tests were conducted across the three contexts.

The results of the paired samples *t*-tests are shown in Table 7.4. The mean values for the management options across all three contexts were statistically significant, with *p* values less than .001 for each comparison of means. Although all the comparisons were significantly different, the *t*-tests indicated a greater difference between the respondents' beaver-management choices when the wilderness context was compared to the other two contexts. This comparison of response distributions and calculation of paired samples *t*-values suggested that respondents' choices between the five different beaver-management scenarios were significantly different across the three contexts. Based on the analysis, we can conclude that context itself is one reason for this difference.

Discussion

These study results have several possible explanations, all of which, I believe, suggest the importance of contextual factors in shaping respondents' attitudes regarding the beaver-management problem. One conclusion that may be drawn, and the explanation that has perhaps the most radical implications for the question surrounding the significance of general moral principles in specific problematic situations, is that the land-use setting (wilderness, multiple-use, and private forest land) in the hypothetical case was simply a much more powerful factor in respondents' decision making about the beavers than any of the environmental ethics. That is, rather than relying on the ethical principles delineated in the study, the respondents might have based their management decisions on whether the beaver problem occurred on legally protected wilderness, designated multiple-use forest, or private timber-company land. In other words, their interpretation of the actions appropriate to the intertwining legal and managerial contexts of each land-use type might have been more significant in shaping their judgments about managing the beavers than the environmental ethical principles they were presented with in this case.

Yet even this interpretation of the study results does not necessarily imply that environmental ethical principles were irrelevant to the respondents' deliberations and decision making. For if we conclude that the study participants were responding to their readings of the perceived demands of the land-use context rather than their commitments to certain general environmental ethics, it is still true that the contexts themselves possess a general normative structure: "Wilderness," "multiple-use," and "private" forest land are, in fact, value-laden designations that entail, although certainly not unambiguously, a range of prima facie appropriate and acceptable uses and activities. These classifications are, in turn, partly the result of prior legal, moral, and political deliberations about issues and commitments, such as the nature of property rights, the proper extent of resource development, and the values and ends of environmental protection. Although for the purposes of this study these contexts were presented to the respondents as uncontested and fixed, in practice they are frequently the subject of intense critical scrutiny and political debate. In many cases, these land-use designations themselves become Deweyan problematic situations, which may then be transformed through social inquiry and debate (witness the heated and ongoing discussions over roadless-area designations in the U.S. national forests). Even this strong contextualist reading of the study results, then, has to acknowledge the "moral atmosphere" of the various land-use designations presented to the respondents.

A second possible explanation of the study results is that, although the environmental ethical principles might have played important roles in channeling respondents' thinking about the alternative wildlife-management options in each land-use situation, the respondents interpreted the implications of those principles differently depending on their understanding of the land-use classification in question. That is to say, the environmental ethics were not orthogonal to the respondents' deliberations in the beaver example; rather, they took on different implications depending on the respondents' interpretations of their meaning and practical requirements in the three different land-use contexts. This conclusion harkens back to Dewey's point about the necessity of inquiry into what the general principle actually means and requires in the face of the concrete situation. For example, an abstract principle promoting the "natural rights" of nonhuman nature (one of the ethics presented to the respondents) by no means makes our choice between the comparative worth of ecosystems and the "rights" of the beavers self-evident in our scenario. One possibility here is that the study respondents may have engaged in some version of "norm specification," revising the general moral principles to make them comport with the demands of particular land-use contexts so the principles took on more useful roles in their management deliberations (Richardson 1990).

A third possible explanation of the results, one that is related to the previous point, is that the moral principles were indeed important in shaping respondents' attitudes toward managing the beaver problem, but the respondents somehow *harmonized* the various ethical principles within each problematic situation, such that, after deliberation, different decisions were reached in each case, even though the respondents displayed similar patterns of importance ratings for the same principles. Here, the study participants may have been able to integrate the various ethical principles in their thinking as they reasoned back and forth from the land-use settings and management actions to the environmental ethical commitments, in the process adjusting the principles they found to be significant to make them compatible with their readings of the normative and empirical context of each forest land setting. Again, this would suggest that the principles were still important in their decision-making processes regarding the beaver problem, even if the respondents sought to balance and to harmonize them with the details and values embedded in each land-use context, a process that then lent support to different management responses in the different situations.

Regardless of which of the above interpretations is correct, land-use context seems to have played a significant mediating role between general moral principles and management decisions in this study. Although the study participants indicated that some of the ethical statements were somewhat important in guiding their thinking about the beaver-management problem, they also appeared to be responding to the specific forest land type in which the management decision was made. Whether this response entailed a significant downplaying of the environmental ethical principles in favor of more specific contextual factors or a revision and contextual adaptation of principles in deliberations over alternative management options is difficult to say with precision. Yet context clearly mattered in this case; the ethical principles themselves did not tell the whole story with respect to the wildlife-management decisions that the study respondents made.

Finally, I should note that in the present study, only *one* general empirical condition (land-use type) was manipulated in the hypothetical investigation. Future studies along these lines might explore the role of additional situational/contextual factors *vis-à-vis* environmental ethics in public attitude formation. For example, studies could investigate the influence of other biological and physical conditions; different degrees of proposed management actions; alternative historical, political, and rhetorical framings of the problematic situation; and varying administrative and managerial contexts on public normative thinking about particular environmental problems and policies. This research also points toward several complementary study methods, including interviews and focus-group investigations, that can provide more nuanced understandings of public environmental values and ethics in concrete environmental planning, policy, and management contexts (e.g., Gundersen 1995; Burgess, Limb, and Harrison 1998a, 1998b; Davies 2001; Butler and Acott 2007). Although much more work needs to be done to begin to fill out our understanding of the role of these situational factors in the relationship between public environmental ethics and natural-resource management practices, I believe the study detailed here provides a useful contribution to this new interdisciplinary enterprise and can serve as a point of departure for additional studies in this area.

Conclusion

An experimental and empirical approach to environmental ethics can greatly inform and broaden the intellectual and public impact of the field as a practical philosophical endeavor. Unfortunately, as I discuss in the introduction to this chapter, many environmental ethicists have neglected important streams of scholarship outside philosophy, work that should be treated as key to the ultimate success of field's public agenda. Callicott, for example, has frankly admitted that he and Rolston—perhaps the two most influential writers in academic environmental ethics—have "ignored" the social sciences in their work (1999b, 512). Callicott defends this disregard by making the rather odd argument that, because economic analysis and public opinion polling are already so influential in the public realm, environmental philosophers do not need to pay the social sciences any special attention. Moreover, environmental ethics is, he asserts, a *normative* enterprise; as such, it operates on a separate plane than the "descriptive" social sciences (512, 514).

This strong endorsement of the fact-value dichotomy in environmental ethics, however, is not an attractive or philosophically tenable position, especially for a field wishing to make more meaningful contributions to public discourse and environmental decision making. Among other things, it divorces ethical theory building and justification from the lived experience of individual and communities, creating a profound rift between moral principle and the social practices and institutions that environmental ethical claims are supposedly intended to inform. As Elizabeth Anderson (1998) writes, rather than driving an epistemological wedge between normative claims and empirical beliefs (à la Callicott), the pragmatist views empirically attained knowledge as *fundamental* to the justification of moral principles. Indeed, a good part of the latter's public legitimacy is derived from our real experience in living with such principles in daily life. Furthermore, this evidence is defeasible, so pragmatists do not commit the naturalistic fallacy when they propose an evidential link between facts and values (20).

The desire to separate environmental ethics from public opinion also signifies, I think, a regrettable lack of interest in and responsiveness to citizens' environmental values and policy attitudes, thus further jeopardizing the search for a more inclusive, tolerant, and democratic style of environmental ethics. Although this may satisfy those desiring greater philosophical purity and simplicity in the analysis of environmental values as parts of invented metaphysical-normative systems, the price of this remove is a disengagement with the actual values and motives that shape citizens' environmental choices and behaviors and that inform environmental decision making. Although the traditional exploration of the foundations of environmental ethics will and should continue (although perhaps not to the same degree as it has in the past), we need to pay much more attention to the field's woefully underdeveloped empirical dimensions if we are committed to making the field more pragmatically relevant and effective in the future.

This more naturalistic approach to ethical inquiry will, therefore, appreciate the contribution of the social sciences in the study of moral values and their roles in public affairs. An integrated normative-empirical approach to environmental ethics reveals many productive lines of investigation into the relationship between moral commitments and practical judgments to be developed by philosophers and social scientists independently and working together on questions of mutual concern. The distinguished cultural anthropologist Clifford Geertz makes a powerful case for the philosophical and practical benefits of this kind of inquiry:

> An approach to a theory of value which looks toward the behavior of actual people in actual societies living in terms of actual cultures for both its stimulus and its validation will turn us away from abstract and rather scholastic arguments in which a limited number of classical positions are stated again and again with little that is new to recommend them, to a process of ever-increasing insight into both what values are and how they work. Once this enterprise in the scientific analysis of values is well launched, the philosophical discussions of ethics are likely to take on more point. The process is not that of replacing moral philosophy by descriptive ethics, but of providing moral philosophy with an empirical base and a conceptual framework which is somewhat advanced over that available to Aristotle, Spinoza, or G. E. Moore. . . . [It is] to make it relevant. (1973, 141)

Geertz's remarks are especially valuable for those of us interested in understanding how citizens receive the often abstract theories and principles of professional ethicists, as well as how these principles figure into environmental deliberation and decision making in specific management and policy contexts. This empirical approach to value theory, I believe, will help put environmental ethics on the path to becoming a far more relevant and useful "public philosophy" of the environment, one that is embedded in public affairs rather than epistemologically shielded from them. By engaging rather than ignoring the tools and knowledge of key disciplinary partners in the study of environmental values and obligations in the public realm, the field will make important progress toward this larger goal and will expand the intellectual appeal and pragmatic value of environmental ethical discourse in the process.

8

A Practical Ethics for Ecologists and Biodiversity Managers

WITH JAMES P. COLLINS

A Gap in Applied Ethics

The previous chapter shows that environmental ethics has often neglected empirical methods of inquiry, featuring few projects that connect, in an effective way, the core methodologies of the humanities and the social sciences. This posture, as well as the ideological tendencies of much environmental ethics described in the first part of this book, has kept the field from reaching its full potential as branch of practical philosophy that can effectively inform sound environmental policy and management decisions. For the concepts and arguments of environmental ethics to gain greater traction in the realm of environmental policy and practice, it has been argued in this book that the field needs to adopt a more naturalistic and pluralistic strategy, one that surrenders long-standing ethical dogmas in favor of a more experimental and pragmatic view of moral principles in human environmental experience—and a more context-driven and deliberative framing of these principles in decision situations requiring ethical reflection, public discussion, and reasoned judgment.

This chapter builds from the problem-oriented and empirically tempered applications in Chapters 6 and 7 by focusing on the need for environmental ethics to contribute to resolving ethical dilemmas that emerge in the realm of the life sciences (broadly construed), particularly the domains of ecological research and conservation practice. Work in these areas can often raise complex and unique practical and philosophical problems, issues and questions that require serious attention from ethicists, not to mention scientists and professionals active in these fields. Ecological field research, for example, can involve experimental techniques with the potential to harm sentient and nonsentient organisms as well as affect the structure and function of higher levels of organization, such as populations and ecosystems. The management of biological resources in zoos, aquaria, botanical gardens, and natural areas can likewise involve decisions and practices that raise a variety of ethical concerns regarding the welfare or good of nonhuman individuals, populations, and ecosystems.

Yet in general, ethicists have not focused on how ecological research and conservation management efforts can raise ethical concerns about these activities' impact on wild populations and ecosystems. This is true even though environmental ethicists frequently draw upon concepts and principles from ecology and conservation biology when making normative arguments for protecting those very same species and systems. For good reason, most environmental ethicists, when they conceptualize and discuss environmental threats, have been much more concerned with primary and more widely recognized environmental insults, such as industrial pollution, resource overexploitation and overconsumption, urban and suburban sprawl, overpopulation, and, most recently, the ecological and human consequences of extracting and burning fossil fuels. Although these issues rightly remain at the core of ethical concerns about human impacts on the environment, it is increasingly clear that ecological research and management activities themselves can have significant consequences for the well-being or integrity of animals, plants, and ecosystems and thus are deserving of explicit ethical scrutiny. But because environmental ethicists' attention has traditionally been placed elsewhere, and because the field has also developed largely as a theoretical discipline focused on the foundations of environmental values rather than as a practical discipline devoted to value clarification and trade-offs in ecological decision making, a considerable gulf runs between academic environmental ethics and the real-world dilemmas and issues that often confront practicing ecologists and conservation managers.

This gap, moreover, further highlights the greater success of bioethics *vis-à-vis* environmental ethics as a branch of applied philosophy. Biomedical researchers and clinicians, when they confront difficult ethical questions in their work, can turn to bioethicists and their literature for scholarly insight and practical guidance. Bioethics has a strong institutional presence in hospitals and research centers; scientists and clinicians often can and sometimes must consult directly with ethics committees or qualified bioethical personnel in their home institutions. Bioethics is embedded within these research and clinical communities, providing a recognized forum for the discussion of ethical issues, an established scholarly area of research yielding new research findings, and a support network to assist researchers and clinicians in making practical ethical decisions.

No analogous subfield of applied or practical ethics, however, is devoted expressly to investigating the special kind of ethical issues raised within ecological research and conservation management contexts. Environmental ethics certainly comes closest to filling this need, but, as stated above, it has not developed any special focus on the design and conduct of ecological field and laboratory experiments or (with a few notable exceptions) paid much attention to the ethical quandaries that often plague decision making in biodiversity management. And although the emergence of a more pragmatic alternative in the field has been encouraging, it has tended to concentrate more on general environmental policy questions rather than the specific and unique ethical issues presented by ecological research and management.

There is therefore a need for a novel approach within practical ethics that does not seem capable of being met by simply stretching the current disciplinary boundaries of bioethics or environmental ethics as some have argued (e.g., Ehrlich 2003). Specifically, experimental ecologists and biodiversity managers need networks and ethical support systems analogous to the ones linking bioethics with biomedical scientists and clinicians. There have been increasing pleas over the past two decades for scientists to play more active roles in environmental policy discussions and to be more responsive to citizens' interests in maintaining biologically diverse, healthy, and productive ecosystems (e.g., Lélé and Norgaard 1996; Lubchenco 1998; Norton 1998; Ehrenfeld 2000; Wilson 2002; Palmer et al. 2004). These arguments are not entirely new, but their increasing frequency and moral seriousness suggest that, more than ever, ecologists are being asked to provide citizens and policy makers with the knowledge and tools for conserving biological resources and for planning sustainable development paths. In attempting to meet their ends of this "social contract," ecologists and conservation scientists confront an expanding set of ethical challenges that are in part a function of their field's growing technical acumen and increasing, although by no means complete or infallible, predictive power. Indeed, designing and conducting ecological research and managing biological resources often raise ethical considerations relating not only to a researcher's or manager's responsibilities to public welfare and the scientific community but also to his or her obligations to wild animals, species, and ecosystems. As a result, it can be difficult to reconcile conflicting ethical responsibilities and values in these complex situations. Even value conflicts within a particular domain, such as species conservation, can become quite difficult to reason through and resolve effectively.

A Few Examples

Consider the following case: Six of the Channel Islands of California have endemic subspecies of the island fox (*Urocyon littoralis*), an endangered species, and feral pig (*Sus scrofa*) populations. Golden eagles (*Aquila chrysaetos*), a federally protected species, recently colonized the islands and drove two fox subspecies extinct while reducing a third to less than one hundred animals (Courchamp, Woodroffe, and Roemer 2003). Eradicating pigs was planned for early 2004, but population models demonstrate that eagles will then feed more heavily on foxes and trigger their extinction. Translocation alone will not eradicate the eagles, so lethal removal is suggested as the way to save the fox. What values and priorities should guide the decision regarding the appropriate conservation target in this case? Should both species be saved at any cost? If not, why does one species deserve to be saved and not the other? Is there a principled way to resolve these questions?

Or how about the hypothetical (but representative) case of a forest manager choosing to undertake a prescribed burn, a practice intended to restore a particular natural disturbance regime to the ecosystem (perhaps one in which wildfires have been suppressed for some time). The manager is here following a practical management philosophy shaped by a respect for historical ecological processes and structure—in short, a preference for a more "natural" forest ecosystem. This move, which reflects the value judgment that fire belongs in the forest (and thus itself embodies a particular ecological ethic), can, however, lead to further management and ethical dilemmas as the landscape responds in complex ways to the burning. For instance, the restoration of fire to systems in which it was previously excluded, by elevating nutrient levels, creating a more open forest canopy, and so on, can in some cases promote the recruitment of nonnative (i.e., exotic) plant species into the burn area, a scenario that can present a raft of new management problems and pose significant challenges for forest and natural-area managers and restorationists (see D'Antonio 2000; Merriam, McGinnis, and Keeley 2004; Keeley 2006). In such cases, managers would appear to confront a difficult normative question: Should they seek to restore "natural" fire regimes regardless of their impact on the spread of exotic species, or is it better to restore modified fire regimes that have been adjusted to favor native over exotic species? Doing so obviously shades the meaning of "natural" in certain ways, with the managerial or operational understanding of "natural" admitting of degrees to account for changes in the biotic conditions of the land over time.

The ethical, scientific, and management issues raised within the restoration-exotic/invasive species relationship are especially knotty, making this an exemplary class of problems. Indeed, environmental restorationists motivated by the desire to return a landscape to a more natural, "pre-invasion" state can run into further complications in cases where the eradication of invasive species results in surprising (i.e., negative) impacts on native biodiversity, the protection of which is often a primary conservation goal. One of the more infamous cases of this is the spread of invasive salt cedar, tamarisk (*Tamarix* spp.), an old-world shrub that has taken hold in western U.S. riparian systems. Salt cedar has been blamed for a litany of ecological problems, including the elevation of soil salinity and the displacement of native plant communities in the west, the degradation of wildlife habitat, and the physical modification and clogging of stream channels (Dudley et al. 2000). The wrinkle here is that the shrub has become a significant nesting habitat for the endangered southwestern willow flycatcher (*Empidonax traillii extimus*), because the bird's historical nesting habitat—in riparian cottonwood (*Populus* spp.) and willow (*Salix* spp.) stands—has been degraded by development, agriculture, and water diversion. Conservationists and managers are concerned that even controlled removal of salt cedar would be problematic for the flycatcher, because the invader has altered the soil salinity such that some areas may not be able to support replanted native vegetation (Zavaleta, Hobbs, and Mooney 2001).

Like the fire-exotic species example, the salt cedar–flycatcher case raises a number of intriguing ethical questions: Is it right for managers and restorationists to always try to restore landscapes to historical, pre-invasion conditions, even if doing so runs the risk of undermining threatened or endangered species that have adapted to the altered landscape composition and structure? Does the decision to favor certain native species require the acceptance of nonnatives in cases where the latter provide an important habitat function or whose removal would otherwise cause significant problems for some native species (but not others)? In other words, should restorationists, who are often motivated by the goal of eliminating exotic species from the land, be compelled to take a broader, more ecosystemic view of exotic species management, including not just more cautious removal decisions but also an appreciative view of certain exotic species in restoration efforts? This may involve recognizing the habitat and landscape connections described above as well as appreciating the use of (noninvasive) exotic species in biological control, such as to manage invasive exotic species that are causing recognized ecological and economic harm. But, of course, this can raise even further difficulties and questions, as introduced exotic "natural enemies" may do unpredictable things in the environment, including negatively impacting nontarget species and thus carrying additional risks for managers and restorationists (Hoddle 2004). Assessing the risks and ethical dimensions of these sorts of activities as well as evaluating the broader management and restoration goals in question (and increasingly vexed terms, such as "natural," "integrity," and "exotic") is one area where a more practical and pragmatic environmental ethics could provide a great service to environmental scientists and conservationists.

As we mention above, ecological scientists, biodiversity managers, and practical ethicists have for the most part devoted little systematic effort to exploring these sorts of issues. Exceptions include a handful of researchers who have investigated the social roles and ethical responsibilities of conservation biologists, including their obligations to ecological systems (e.g., Shrader-Frechette and McCoy 1999; Potvin, Kraenzel, and Seutin 2001; Odenbaugh 2003; Lodge and Shrader-Frechette 2003) and related discussions regarding the ethical context of ecological restoration (e.g., Light and Higgs 1996; Gobster and Hull 2000). Still others have considered some of the animal and environmental ethical questions raised by zoo-conservation strategies and techniques (Norton et al. 1995), the conceptual and moral considerations surrounding in situ and ex situ conservation of plants (Rolston 2004), and the ethical obligations of scientists who study wildlife in the field (Bekoff and Jamieson 1996; Monamy and Gott 2001; Swart 2004).

Especially relevant is the small number of papers within this literature that has stretched the scientific research ethics discussion to include recognizing the field and laboratory researcher's responsibilities to ecological systems. These include general duties in biological field research (Farnsworth and Rosovsky 1993), specific obligations to avoid harming protected areas in field research (Marsh and Eros 1999; Marsh and Kenchington 2004), the interplay of animal welfare and ecological obligations in ecological research (Vucetich and Nelson 2007), and duties to the environment as part of the decision-making process within conservation biology (Shrader-Frechette and McCoy 1999). Finally, an important body of work examines the general relationship between ecological science, ethics, and conservation policy (e.g., Norton 1987, 2005; Shrader-Frechette and McCoy 1993; Dallmeyer 2003; Sarkar 2005).

Although we can point to these and related attempts to focus more intently on the moral dimensions of ecological research and management, this work has not been coordinated in such a manner that it forms a self-conscious intellectual community with an explicit research agenda. Consequently, a more concerted attempt to organize and integrate the discussion across the sciences, humanities, and conservation professions needs to be made. We are not the first to call for this kind of effort. Writing in the journal *Conservation Biology* some years ago, Elizabeth Farnsworth and Judy Rosovsky (1993) advocate a multidisciplinary dialogue among field biologists and philosophers that would address some of the ethical questions we have identified. Our reading and experience, however, suggest that this dialogue has still not happened (see also Marsh and Kenchington 2004).

Some examples bring ethical considerations into ecological and management practice, but more development is needed. The Ecological Society of America (ESA), for example, has a code of ethics, but the code's principles are general statements covering issues mostly within the boundaries of conventional professional and research ethics (e.g., avoiding scientific misconduct, conflicts of interest). Only one principle in the ESA code speaks directly to concerns about avoiding or minimizing "adverse environmental effects" by suggesting that ecologists comply with "legal requirements for protection of researchers, human subjects, or research organisms and systems" (www.esa.org/careers_certification/code.ethics.php). "Adverse environmental effects" are not defined clearly, and the reasons these effects are undesirable in an ethical sense are not specified. Appealing to legal requirements in such a code is also not a substitute for ethical reflection, especially because legal codes may lag the practical ethical dilemmas encountered in ecological research (Angulo and Cooke 2002). For example, sometimes an action, such as bioprospecting (the search for organic compounds in nature for commercial development), may be legal but still raises serious moral questions (Dalton 2004). Rapid developments in science and technology, such as the increasing reach of genetic modification and the application of new technologies to studying and collecting biological material in the field, suggest the need for scientists to get ahead of the ethical questions that ecological research raises.

In philosophical ethics, the situation is not much more evolved than it is within ecological science. Although the field of environmental ethics has and continues to make important contributions to our understanding of a host of conceptual issues regarding the nature of environmental values and the duties these impose, for the most part (with the exceptions noted above), as discussed throughout this book, it has not been as successful in addressing in a comprehensive and sustained manner the more concrete ethical concerns encountered in environmental practice. Furthermore, and with respect to ecological research, traditional research ethics approaches, while covering duties to animal subjects in experimental studies, fail to consider the ecological dimension of "responsible conduct" and especially the trade-offs that often need to be made among animal welfare and environmental responsibility in field studies. We therefore need to find ways to use environmental ethics and other ethical theory more effectively to inform decision making in practical contexts, such as designing and conducting ecological field and laboratory experiments and making biodiversity management decisions in problematic situations.

Scientists, managers, and ethicists can all learn by studying jointly the ethical issues confronting practicing ecologists and biodiversity managers. Doing so will help ecologists respond more effectively to the ethical challenges encountered in their research and help them lead discussions of proper research design and management rather than waiting for more slow-moving, ambiguous, and often unwieldy legal guidelines and prohibitions to point the way (Angulo and Cooke 2002). In the rest of this chapter we offer a few exemplary cases in ecological research and biodiversity management and discuss some of the specific ethical considerations they raise for scientists and managers. We also provide a preliminary taxonomy of ethical issues raised by specific research and management practices, and outline the relevant literatures in theoretical and applied ethics that speak to the duties and responsibilities of practicing ecologists and conservationists. We end the chapter with a call for the collaborative development of a pluralistic ethical framework for making research and management decisions, one that will be a heuristic and analytical instrument informed by multiple domains within theoretical and applied ethics.

Ethical Dilemmas in Ecology and Conservation Biology: A Taxonomic Approach

As a first step in the process of developing a more practical ethics targeted at ecological research and conservation management, it is useful to identify and begin to organize the complex of practices and normative issues that emerge in the study and protection of organisms, populations, and ecosystems. The discussion below focuses on five general issues or situations in ethical decision making in ecological research and biodiversity management, each of which is illustrated by a case example. The first case is presented here in the greatest detail and comes closest to providing a full sense of the multilayered nature of these ethical dilemmas. The other cases provide brief glimpses of the various types of ethical questions that arise in ecological research and management contexts. Following this sampling of cases, we present a larger taxonomy of ethical issues in ecological research and biodiversity management and then move on, in the next section, to a discussion of how we might begin to approach these questions via the development of pragmatic methodologies for ecological decision making.

Scientific Uncertainty in Ecological Research and Conservation

Case Example: Since the late 1980s, many amphibian populations have declined, and some species have gone missing and are likely extinct (Collins and Storfer 2003; Stuart et al. 2004; Collins and Crump 2009). The losses are worldwide, but especially large in Central and South America and eastern Australia. Increasing evidence suggests a lethal fungal pathogen is spreading through some amphibian communities in Australia and the Americas. Thirty years of records on amphibian declines and extinctions extending from Colorado through Arizona, Mexico, Honduras, Costa Rica, and western Panama led to the prediction in 2003 that there is an unknown, but finite, probability that tropical-forest sites in central Panama would experience amphibian declines and likely extinctions when the lethal fungal pathogen reached the area (Lips, Reeve, and Witters 2003).

The pathogen may not act alone and may need just the right environmental conditions to be lethal. And it may not cause an epidemic in the years ahead. How, therefore, do we plan under such uncertain conditions? How do the various types and degrees of uncertainty surrounding the spread of the pathogen and its impact on sites in central Panama bear on the ethical questions surrounding this case? For example, in what ways are the obligations and responsibilities of the researchers, government officials, zoo curators, and conservation community strengthened or weakened by the range of predictive uncertainty in this case? How might different "infection and extinction" scenarios change or qualify the ethical obligations of the stakeholders and decision makers? How do we identify various obligations and responsibilities, and how can we construct and introduce clear and consistent ethical principles and frameworks to provide ethical guidance for making decisions in such cases?

The possible loss of the amphibian fauna in central Panama is a case study for conserving biodiversity under conditions in which decisions must be made under uncertainty. Expected amphibian declines in Panama raise ethical, legal, and social issues worth studying, because they include general properties that apply to a wide range of cases in ecology and conservation biology. What are the appropriate responses of the scientific, conservation, and policy communities? What should be their reactions to the expected decline and possible extinction of all or part of this fauna? Predicting extinction often has a major component of "decision making under uncertainty," and without the guidance of a framework for moving forward, the default decision follows from the precautionary principle: "In order to protect the environment, the precautionary approach shall be widely applied by States according to their capabilities. Where there are threats of serious or irreversible damage, lack of full scientific certainty shall not be used as a reason for postponing cost-effective measures to prevent environmental degradation" (Principle 15 of the Rio Declaration made at the 1992 Earth Summit; see Groombridge and Jenkins 2002). Ideally, we should have an ethical, positive basis for acting as opposed to not acting when the way forward is not clear (*Nature* 2004).

Given that we anticipate the pathogen will infect central Panamanian amphibian communities, the following are selected elements of the case related to stakeholder values and research questions that confront ecologists and biodiversity managers today. The list is not exhaustive but indicates the kinds of ethical challenges being encountered.

1. *Scientific community:* What is the scientific community's role and responsibility given the possible imminent extinction of dozens of species? For example, should an effort be made to capture animals to breed,

if possible, in zoos and perhaps in the pet trade? Do we first save species with the greatest probability of breeding successfully? Or should we save the rarest species, even if we know nothing about their breeding habits? What happens to "excess" animals from successful captive breeding? If the hope is to reintroduce frogs into native habitats, what happens if we cannot ensure their welfare in habitats that are now infected by the pathogen? If some species become extinct locally, should rescued animals from zoo populations be reintroduced if new species of competitors and predators are now in their habitat? Fundamentally, are there, or should there be, ethical concerns about the potentially dramatic "intervention" of scientists and conservationists in the workings of the ecological community? That is, does respecting "wild" nature always entail a hands-off approach to ecosystems? If so, what if following this principle leads to species' decline and extinction? If not, do the potential commercial implications and private nature of a conservation effort involving the pet trade degrade the value or integrity of the animals and ecosystem in an ethical sense? Or is preserving a species' lineage a value that trumps all other such considerations? What are the consequences of collecting animals for the research of investigators and their students working in the area? Is this even a consideration, or, again, does the possible extinction of species supersede such concerns?

2. *Conservation community:* What is the conservation community's role and responsibility? Which elements of the national and international conservation community should be involved in this case? Are there likely to be different conservation agendas and different justifying values for any action taken in Panama?

3. *Zoo community:* What is the zoo community's role and responsibility regarding animal husbandry? What species should be collected, and why? How many of each species should be collected, and when should they be collected? Several frog species likely to become extinct in the wild are held in zoos and breed successfully to the point that surplus animals are killed, but these institutions are reluctant to provide animals for research on what might have driven the frogs to extinction for fear of the ramifications with donors and conservationists. Does the research community have a privileged position regarding excess animals for research if it could prevent further extinctions? What is the best way forward?

4. *Policy makers/administration/public sector:* What are the administrative and policy communities' roles and responsibilities in this case? For example, should the government close and isolate the central Panamanian forest reserves with endangered frog species for fear that people may transmit the pathogen? What are the social, economic, and political impacts of doing so? Is closure justified when it is unknown how the pathogen moves among sites of infection? What is the role for the Panamanian public? What is known of their attitudes toward amphibians, conservation, and the possible management responses? What is their

place in the decision-making process? How and when do foreign-policy makers and government officials get involved? Would Panamanian officials allow collection and export of animals to zoos in other countries? Would they facilitate such exports? What intellectual property rights must be considered relative to research that might uncover economically valuable products in the course of seeking ways to protect the animals? Can Panamanian zoos handle the protection and breeding of these animals? If so, is this the best choice since the pathogen is in the country? Should zoo conservation be a priority if we can learn enough about the animals to protect them in the future?

5. *Commercial sector:* Should help be sought from the pet-trade community to develop protocols for housing and breeding animals? Should this be allowed only if frogs could be reclaimed and released back into their natural habitats? Should an ecologist working on threatened populations raise an alarm about fear of extinction from a cause like a pathogen? Doing so might expose the populations to commercial exploitation, because species are more valuable commercially if threatened. If collectors were to acquire animals during an epidemic, the risk of spreading the pathogen globally develops. Spix's Macaw (*Cyanopsitta spixii*) was driven to extinction by unsustainable collecting and habitat destruction (one male is alive in the wild). In what sense are we conserving biodiversity if a species lives only in captivity?

Postscript: In spring 2006, researchers in the El Valle region of Panama found the first dead frogs infected with the virus. Two American conservationists (from Zoo Atlanta and the Atlanta Botanical Garden) worked with colleagues in Central America and the United States to move a number of threatened frogs to ex situ conservation facilities in the United States (Collins and Crump 2009, 186). Planning efforts began for the first ex situ facility in Panama around the same time, which received its initial amphibian transfers in 2007 (www.amphibianrescue.org). Conservationists are currently exploring a suite of options to mitigate the threat of the virus to amphibian populations, including the use of probiotics and treating the organisms with antifungal drugs (Rex 2010; Lubick 2010). These interventionist efforts—and the implications of eventually returning populations from ex situ facilities to the wild—raise additional ethical questions that will require further attention and discussion in the amphibian conservation community.

Controlling Research Resources

Case Example: Exotic species are an increasing concern because of their effects on natural communities of plants, animals, and local economies. Various strategies, such as natural predators, poisons, or pathogens, are used to control common invaders (e.g., insects and plants). Recently, several exotic frog species became established in Hawaii. The coqui frog (*Eleutherodactylus coqui*) is so common now that noise from its nocturnal singing reduces home resale values and forces hotels to avoid using some rooms near the forest (www.hear.org/AlienSpeciesInHawaii/species/frogs). Hawaiians would like to eliminate the frog, and some wildlife managers are considering releasing the amphibian pathogen just discussed in the Panama case to kill the introduced species. Ironically, as some investigators study the fungal pathogen with the goal of conserving amphibian species, others want to use it for amphibian elimination. Researchers have not provided the pathogenic cultures, even for trials. But the investigators, in the course of publishing and being members of a research community, must eventually place the pathogens in a type culture collection where anyone can withdraw samples for legitimate scientific reasons. Eventually, then, resource managers where the frog is also a problem can go to the type collection for cultures. How long should a researcher with the original pathogenic cultures control access to collections, given that he or she cannot be assured that another investigator would not give away the cultures? Can it be a condition of giving the cultures that they not be released for management? Should publishing results be delayed to avoid placing the culture in a collection?

Controlling Invasive Species

Case Example: European wild rabbits (*Oryctolagus cuniculus*) from southwestern Europe are widely introduced into other countries worldwide and can be pests. Elena Angulo and Brian Cooke (2002) summarize a case with complexities that extend beyond those usually associated with deliberate release of genetically modified organisms (GMOs). Rabbits native to Europe support predators, including endangered imperial eagle (*Aquila adalberti*) and Iberian lynx (*Lynx pardinus*) populations. In the last fifty years, rabbit populations have declined mainly because of the viral myxomatosis and rabbit hemorrhagic diseases. One solution being pursued is developing a genetically modified virus based on an attenuated myxoma (MV) strain that protects against both viruses. Only a few rabbits must be vaccinated to immunize the larger population, because the strain can be transmitted horizontally among rabbits in the field. The same rabbit species is an Australian pest. Managers have considered releasing a genetically modified MV that reduces rabbit fertility through transmissible (virally vectored) immunocontraception; in other words, an introduced contagious virus would disseminate a contraceptive agent through the exotic populations of rabbits. This is not a solitary case; opossums, foxes, cats, and rodents are also candidates for control by virally vectored immunocontraception (Angulo and Cooke 2002). Some regulations focus on research and release of genetically modified organisms, but few agreements specifically address safe research, handling, and release of these organisms internationally (Angulo and Cooke 2002). Lack of regulation is a concern, but feasibility of executing these strategies and regulations aside, what ethical issues should be addressed before releasing such organisms? What are the human, animal, and ecological consequences of releasing genetically modified MV? Is it wise to genetically modify viruses for conservation and pest control? C. H. Tyndale-Biscoe (1994) considers some of the ethical implications of this practice, but, in general, what are we to make of an applied research program for rabbit management with opposing goals: conserving a declining species in Europe and killing the same species in Australia?

Specimen Marking and Monitoring Techniques

Case Example: Toe clipping is an established technique for identifying amphibians in mark-recapture field studies. Yet this practice, which involves the removal of a distinctive combination of digits (or parts of them), has been reported to result in a number of adverse effects on the animals, including inflammation and infection of the feet and limbs (Reaser and Dexter 1996). A study by Michael McCarthy and Kirsten Parris (2004) suggests that toe clipping may also negatively affect the return rate of marked frogs, thus presumably compromising ecological researchers' main objectives. Although the animal-welfare concerns raised by toe clipping are perhaps the most obvious ethical issues relevant to this case (May 2004), the McCarthy and Parris study also poses additional questions about ecological research design and conservation efforts. Put simply, is the pain and suffering endured by the animal justifiable on "advance-of-scientific-knowledge" grounds if toe clipping negatively affects animal-survival rates, ultimately undercutting the research findings? Is it morally worse to practice this marking technique on an endangered amphibian species? If it turns out that the negative effect on return rate has been overstated, is toe clipping still an acceptable practice in ecological and behavioral field studies?

Research in Pristine or Protected Ecosystems

Case Example: Russian researchers have for years been attempting to drill into Lake Vostok, a subglacial Antarctic lake buried under thousands of meters of ice. The lake, thought to have been isolated for twenty million years, might contain unique ecosystems and organisms that could greatly contribute to our understanding of Earth's climate history as well as that of early life on the planet. It may also tell us something about the possibility of life on other planets with icy environments. In the past, environmental groups have opposed proposals to drill into Vostok's pristine ecosystems, but in recent years the drilling plan has drawn criticism from other researchers in the international scientific community who are concerned that the Russian scientists' equipment will expose the lake to "unacceptable" levels of contamination (Gavaghan 2002; Giles 2004). The situation is further complicated by the fact that Antarctica is not a sovereign state but is rather a territory loosely governed by international treaties and scientific conventions. As a result, controlling regulations are often ambiguous and difficult to enforce. The Vostok drilling case raises many ethical questions, among them: Who (or what institutions/parties) should decide whether it is right to sample such pristine—perhaps unique—ecosystems? How do we gauge the risks of contamination by the researchers against the potential knowledge gained by their research? What values and standards should guide the choice of an "acceptable" level of contamination by research instruments? More generally, should ethical (in addition to technical and economic) restraints be placed on the scope and reach of ecological investigation—that is, are there some places where we should not "boldly go" for fear of irreversibly harming or contaminating remote, fragile, or pristine ecological systems? Does such a notion run completely counter to the progressive spirit of human scientific enterprise? After a series of technical setbacks, drilling into the lake by a Russian team is expected to happen at the end of 2011, with subsequent exploration planned by British and American scientists (Schiermeier 2010).

In addition to the five general issues in ecological research and biodiversity management listed above, many other research and management practices clearly provoke difficult ethical questions for scientists and conservationists. Table 8.1 presents a preliminary classification of ethical issues in ecology and conserva-

TABLE 8.1 Ethical concerns in ecology and conservation management

Research and conservation practices	Ethical issues (examples)
Specimen marking and monitoring techniques	Harm to sentient creatures; potential compromise of research results resulting from poor or harmful techniques
Field observation of wildlife	Harm to sentient creatures (disruption of breeding and migration patterns, increased physiological stress, etc.)
Sampling techniques (animal tissue, plants, etc.)	Harm to sentient creatures; increased extinction risk imposed on endangered populations
Culling animal specimens	Justification of killing living beings; evaluating harm to individual specimens vs. expected scientific and conservation benefits
Relocation of research specimens	Harm to sentient creatures; risks of negative biological and ecological impacts in new environment
Research in pristine or protected ecosystems	Disturbing ecological integrity (via experimental manipulation, waste-disposal practices, etc.); potential encouragement of environmentally destructive forms of commercialization/tourism
Bioprospecting; commercialization of ecological research and conservation	Degrading nature's dignity/autonomy via commercialization; extinction risks posed by overcollection; violations of intellectual property rights
Research on threatened and endangered species	Animal welfare vs. conservation ethics; increased extinction risks posed by invasive research etc.
Scientific uncertainty in ecological research and conservation	Obligation to act in the face of scientific uncertainty; risks of acting to conserve species or ecosystems in uncertain conditions
Wildlife population control (e.g., culling, biological control, sterilization, translocation)	Harm to sentient creatures; evaluating lethal vs. nonlethal control techniques

tion management, including a list of various research and management practices and a sampling of the specific ethical issues they pose to researchers and practitioners. We do not pretend that this is an exhaustive cataloging of ecological ethics issues but rather offer it as a point of departure—and a stimulus to further discussion about the ethical dilemmas that ecologists, field biologists, and conservationists encounter in their work.

Several observations can be made about this early classification. First, although they can be separated for analytical purposes, it is important to note that many of these practices and ethical issues can and do overlap in practice (controlling invasive species and ecological-restoration techniques, research in pristine systems and on threatened species, etc.). This underscores the value of identifying and clarifying the ethical dimensions of research and management practices, because professionals engaging in these activities may be sensitive to one type of

TABLE 8.1 *Continued*

Research and conservation practices	Ethical issues (examples)
Choosing conservation targets	Justifying differential valuation of species (e.g., abundant vs. endangered); value conflicts between ecosystem integrity and animal welfare etc.
Zoo conservation (e.g., collection, captive breeding, and habitat enrichment)	Harm to sentient creatures, respecting the dignity and wildness of captive animals; conservation vs. animal-welfare values
Release/reintroduction of captive-born or confiscated animals into the wild	Harm to sentient creatures; issues of human agency/ intervention in reintroductions
Management for the "sustainable use" of biological resources	Harm to sentient creatures; environmental risks of over-exploitation; objections to the commoditization of nature
Treating wildlife disease	Interference in the dynamics of wild populations; risks of unforeseen consequences of treatment; positive duties to promote wildlife health through treatment interventions
Ecological restoration strategies and techniques	Risks to native species and systems of using nonnative species in restoration projects; ethical objections to technological intervention in natural systems
Controlling invasive species	Harm to sentient animals; risk of unanticipated consequences of eradication on native species and ecosystem health
Management of protected areas	Obligations to protect ecological integrity and wild species; conflicts with human use and encroachment
Ecological research and conservation advocacy	Responsibility to scientific norms of objectivity; duties to promote the public good alongside conservation goals
Research design and administration	Positive duty to practice good research design and administration; negative duty to avoid duplicative or unnecessary research that negatively impacts study specimens, populations, or natural systems

ethical issue raised by their work but not to others. We should note, too, that although we include practices and issues typically covered under the rubric of "research ethics"—for example, matters of scientific objectivity and advocacy, responsibility to the public good, the proper treatment of animal subjects, and so forth—we do so in a way that highlights the linkages between these activities and commitments and the specific substantive domain of ecological science and conservation practice.

In addition to the overlapping nature of ecological ethics issues, it is clear that many of the ethical considerations captured in Table 8.1 revolve around two axes of normative tension. The first is between animal-welfare considerations in ecological research/management and what we might refer to as "higher-level" (in a scalar sense) ecological values, such as the treatment and conservation of populations, species, or ecosystems; the philosophical dimensions of this conflict are discussed in Chapter 6. As we mention above, such conflicts—when they are engaged within a traditional environmental ethics framework—are often treated reductively, with animal-welfare considerations trumped *a priori* by more holistic ecological (i.e., species or ecosystem conservation) ethical imperatives. Again, however, this is an unsatisfactory move, because animal-welfare values are important considerations in ecological research and conservation practice and will enter into scientists' and managers' practical deliberations either through their own normative force or through interest-group advocacy (as we see below). The general animal welfare–conservation conflict is, we believe, increasingly common in ecological research and conservation practice, and the fairly one-sided approach taken by many environmental ethicists (i.e., simply favoring ecological considerations over animal-ethics claims as a matter of principle) is thus not very helpful. A more pluralistic and integrative—rather than reductionistic—approach is required.

A second major conflict running through many of the ecological ethics issues designated in Table 8.1 surrounds the moral question of the intervention of researchers and managers in autonomous wildlife populations or ecosystems for conservation-relevant research and management—that is, the problem of human agency and interference in natural processes to achieve scientific or conservation goals. This issue, when combined with complicating factors, such as the pervasive epistemic condition of scientific uncertainty in environmental decision making, becomes quite difficult to manage. For example, should an ecologist studying an endangered wildlife population advocate "heroic intervention" to save a species if he or she has reason to believe—to some degree of certainty—that the population will collapse without such intervention? Given that human intervention in these cases also carries risks to the population—now and in the future (e.g., stress of translocation on the animals and the possibility of subsequent commercial exploitation of the animals in captivity)—it is not always clear that conservation intervention is the best course of action. Furthermore, global climate change is radically transforming our understanding of "appropriate" intervention in biological populations and systems; this issue is taken up again in Chapter 9.

Ethical Tools for Ecological Problem Solving

Ecological researchers and biodiversity managers need to be able to seek appropriate guidance in answering questions such as those posed above. In particular, they need to be able to identify and employ relevant ethical principles and related considerations in problematic situations. Following the pragmatic insights of John Dewey, and as the previous two chapters emphasize, we hold the view that moral principles are best understood as tools for practical problem solving. The various expressions of value, duty, and obligation in these areas of ethical theory, that is, will prove useful in revealing the moral responsibilities in specific decision contexts and may be used as deliberative resources in the process of determining what should be done in concrete research and management situations. As we have seen, this pragmatic approach places much greater emphasis on the process of moral reasoning and moral deliberation—the experimental rehearsal, testing, and revision of principles and decision scenarios in the imagination and public debate—than it does on the adherence to any single principle that might be thought of as uniquely authoritative or privileged in moral reflection.

Four primary domains of theoretical and applied ethics are the most relevant to the ethical questions raised by work in ecology and conservation management (Table 8.2): (traditional) normative ethical theory, research ethics, animal ethics, and environmental ethics. Each domain and its constituent principles may contribute to our understanding of the moral responsibilities of the ecological researcher and biodiversity manager to the public good, to the scientific and professional community, and to individual plants, animals, and ecosystems. In our view, however, each tradition is limited to the extent that it typically highlights only a particular dimension of the moral situation.

For example, the discussion in environmental ethics focuses largely on establishing the moral standing of parts or processes of nature (e.g., nonhuman individuals, species, and ecosystems). Although this focus may help identify general obligations and responsibilities to natural parts and wholes in ecological research and biodiversity management, scientific researchers and biodiversity managers also have significant obligations beyond the duties they may be said to owe to species and ecosystems. These include obligations to uphold scientific integrity and avoid conflicts of interest and responsibilities to the greater public good or welfare. These latter obligations may entail "negative" duties—such as refraining from any activities that may produce social harms—and more "positive" ones, such as the protection and promotion of biological diversity and environmental quality for an array of human cultural values. In addition to traditional environmental ethical considerations, then, these other responsibilities may also figure prominently in the deliberations in reaching an ethical judgment about what should be done in a particular research or management context.

We believe that a pluralistic and integrative ethical framework is therefore the best and most effective way to conceive of the moral resources that practicing researchers and managers require. The primary task of creating this pluralistic

TABLE 8.2 A pluralistic ethical framework for ecologists and conservation managers

Ethical domain	Subject matter/prescriptions	Representative works
1. ***Normative ethical theory***	Doing right, promoting the good, and being virtuous in the human community	
Consequentialist ethics (e.g., Utilitarianism)	Choose that action or rule that produces the best consequences for all those affected	Goodin (1995), Bentham (1996), Hooker (2000), Mill (2002)
Deontological ethics	Uphold one's moral duties	Ross (1930), O'Neill (1989), Kant (1998), Hill (2000)
Virtue ethics	Internalize and display the traits of good character	Foot (2002), MacIntyre (2007), Aristotle (1998)
2. ***Research ethics***	Responsible conduct of research	
	Uphold norms of scientific integrity, avoid research misconduct, respect human and animal subjects	Shrader-Frechette (1994), Elliott and Stern (1997), Shamoo and Resnik (2009)
3. ***Animal ethics***	Value of and duties to nonhuman animals	
Animal welfare	Reduce unnecessary animal suffering, consider the interests of all sentient beings in decision making that affects them	Singer (1993, 2002a)
Animal rights	Respect the dignity or moral/legal rights of animals	Wise (2000, 2003), Regan (2004)
4. ***Environmental ethics***	Value of and duties to the natural environment	
Weak anthropocentrism/ environmental pragmatism	Conserve nature for multiple nonconsumptive societal ends (e.g., recreation, spiritual fulfillment, education, cultural value), now and in the future	Norton (1987, 1991, 2005), Minteer and Manning (1999, 2000), Norton and Minteer (2002)
Biocentrism	Protect individual living organisms for their inherent worth/intrinsic values	Goodpaster (1978), Taylor (1986), Agar (2001)
Ecocentrism	Protect whole ecological systems and processes for their "systemic" or intrinsic values	Rolston (1988, 1994), Callicott (1989, 1999a)

framework lies with the identification and organization of the practical ethical principles across the theoretical and applied ethics literatures in ways that will help ecologists and biodiversity managers delineate the moral aspects of specific research and management dilemmas. The framework would distill from this work multiple sets of moral principles—rendered in the form of clear prescriptive statements—relevant to ecological research and biodiversity management in the lab and field. Such statements should include traditional normative ethical principles speaking to ecologists' and biodiversity managers' duties to avoid social harms or promote the general public good (now and in the future), principles relating to their obligations to the scientific or professional community, and ethical principles speaking to their responsibilities to organisms, species, and ecosystems.

The best way to go about creating this framework, and following the arguments of the early chapters of this book, is to form and cultivate a "deliberative community" of academic researchers and managers that can give shape to this new conceptual and practical tool kit. This community should be interdisciplinary: It should include ethicists, social scientists, research ecologists, and biodiversity managers tasked with exploring and debating the ethical dimensions of ecological research and biological conservation practices. The group would perform the creative functions of identifying and assembling a comprehensive ethical framework relevant to ecological research and biodiversity management and fulfill the critical role of providing peer review of this framework as a tool to aid moral deliberation and practical problem solving.

At this stage of development, we think it is best to be as inclusive as possible, so we do not wish to advocate here any particular substantive philosophical position about environmental value beyond a "thin" or procedural pragmatism. In other words, we want to borrow pragmatism's practical and experimental spirit, focusing more on the method of analysis and the aim of improving ecological and managerial problem solving. We therefore hold open the possibility that any number of principles in conventional normative ethical theory, research ethics, and animal and environmental ethics (including intrinsic value of nature positions) may prove relevant to understanding and resolving the problematic situations that ecological researchers and managers confront in their work. The proviso is that no single ethical position trumps any other position *a priori*; each is instead to be considered a potential resource for ethical analysis and decision making rather than an ideological commitment requiring universal application and devotion.

Furthermore, we wish to emphasize the contextual and situational dimension of ethical integration and decision making within problematic research and management situations rather than the more conceptual aspects of this process. Ethical integration is not only a theoretical or intellectual activity—that is, the philosophical assimilation of multiple values, duties, and interests—but also a form of practical reasoning, one performed by conflicted moral agents in complex and often morally and empirically ambiguous situations. We believe the most important "integrative" tasks in any sound model of ethical analysis are therefore action oriented and methodological in nature, improving individuals' sensitivity to the ethical context of specific practices (and their awareness of the relevant moral principles that bear on these practices) and facilitating the sharpening of individuals' imaginative and analytical skills so they may learn to take more reflective, creative, and systematic approaches to moral problems.

As Chapter 7 argues, this more pragmatic and "particularist" approach to ethics does not deny the role of general principles in ethical problem solving so much as it attempts to place them within a larger experimental process of moral deliberation and inquiry, a process that can also lead to the transformation of values as inquirers rehearse potential courses of action and also share information and trade arguments with others over "what should be done" in specific environmental research and management contexts (Wallace 1996; Norton and Steinemann 2001). Of course, such pluralistic and dynamic moral models are notoriously messy; principles can and do often come into significant conflict, despite our best attempts to achieve either conceptual or pragmatic integration. In such cases, hard decisions will undoubtedly have to be made. At the same time, however, we should remember that there are often opportunities for moral deliberation to settle on practical actions and decisions that reflect the convergence rather than the divergence of different interests and values (Norton 1991; Minteer 2009).

The ethical framework we envision will not produce absolute and definitive answers to the specific moral quandaries encountered in environmental research and management settings, but it would provide an important service by offering an instrument for clarifying and reasoning through the relevant principles and values that bear on problematic research and management situations. Still, one of the great difficulties that haunts any pluralistic model of ethics is the challenge of developing a method of integrating multiple principles or, alternatively, of articulating one or more rules to direct the selection and application of one or more principles in particular situations. Along these lines, other interdisciplinary teams of scholars have made some important attempts to identify and integrate, mainly on a conceptual level, various environmental and social values and duties in conservation contexts. One example of this work is Kristin Shrader-Frechette and Earl McCoy's (1999) "two-tier" method of moral decision making in conservation biology (incorporating general utilitarian and deontological principles), which they argue can enhance the "ethical rationality" of scientific decision making in ecology and conservation biology.

The employment of more explicit decision-making techniques, too, may prove highly valuable to researchers and managers seeking to choose between alternative courses of action, choices that often require difficult ethical and value comparisons. One of us (Ben Minteer) has recently collaborated with a team of ecologists and decision scientists to explore the use of such tools for making rational decisions among competing ethical positions in the case of sampling techniques in field studies (see Parris et al. 2010). Specifically, the study demonstrates how formal decision-analysis methods can help researchers evaluative ethical trade-offs in the case of the use of DNA-sampling methods on frogs, methods that result in welfare losses (and in some cases, death) of individuals (recall the toe-clipping discussion above). By comparing individual-level and species-level welfare in a hypothetical (yet empirically grounded) decision process, the research team was able to conclude that toe-clipping techniques for sampling were clearly inferior to other methods (e.g., collecting tadpoles, buccal swabbing, and tail tipping), although the evaluation of these other methods was contingent upon how one defined individual welfare (i.e., as suffering or as suffering plus loss of future life) and species welfare. The value of this approach is that it allows for the comparison of multiple ethical concerns in the design of field experiments and provides an explicit and useful framework for helping ecologists make nonarbitrary decisions with respect to ethical trade-offs in studies that impact nonhuman individuals and populations.

Finally, in addition to creating a multivocal normative framework for ecologists and conservationists, our proposed project would lead to the preparation of a wide-ranging set of case studies in ecological research and biodiversity management (such as more developed versions of the kinds of cases presented above) that would become a useful database for scientists, managers, and students interested in learning how ethical questions emerge in the course of field and laboratory practices and about the moral claims that may be placed on them in a given situation (e.g., Dubycha and Geedey 2003). As we have witnessed with the rapid growth of the field of bioethics, such a case database can be an important educational and analytical tool, sharpening our understanding of ethical issues and our critical thinking and problem-solving skills (e.g., Murphy 2004; Pence 2007; Veatch, Haddad, and English 2009). The development of a similarly detailed and organized case literature would allow scientists, managers, and students to compare a variety of ethical, research, and managerial issues across experiential and value contexts and would provide them with an opportunity to learn from the specific differences and similarities of the issues and cases. Such cases, developed as full educational modules complete with discussion questions, background readings, and supporting materials, could then be housed on a Web site that would serve as an integrative focus for interdisciplinary work and dialogue in this new area of practical ethics, which we might call "ecological ethics" to distinguish it from the more traditional and often highly theoretical work in environmental ethics.

Conclusion

A new approach in practical ethics and a new conceptual and analytical tool kit for ecologists and biodiversity managers are needed to help them deal with the ethical questions their work raises. These questions have to date not been addressed in a systematic fashion within the established areas of applied ethics, including environmental ethics. A comprehensive ethical framework and case-study database is therefore needed to help research scientists and biodiversity managers better understand and respond to the ethical issues they face in their research and conservation activities. These tools will not only provide critical assistance to researchers and managers as they deliberate within specific decision-making contexts but will also ultimately help create a larger and necessary forum for discussion of the complex ethical dimensions of ecological research and conservation practices.

The development of these resources—and a willingness to acknowledge and to deliberate over ethical concerns in their work—will help ecological researchers and managers respond more effectively to these challenges. The emergence of a more practical "ecological ethics" for ecologists and biodiversity managers would therefore make an important contribution to applied ethics as well as provide an opportunity for some of the philosophical arguments in environmental ethics (and other relevant areas) to be taken up more effectively, and in a more anticipatory way, by the ecological research and conservation communities. Ethical challenges, such as those we describe in this chapter, will only continue to surface with the development of more powerful tools and techniques to study and manage the planet's biota and with our growing understanding of the impact of these tools and techniques on the very wildlife, plants, and landscapes that are the subject of vital research and conservation efforts.

9
Conservation after Preservation

Shades of Green

In December 2007, a couple in northern California were convicted of violating the "Solar Shade Control Act," a little-known 1978 state law, because their trees were shading a neighbor's rooftop solar panels. Although the offending flora were planted several years before the photovoltaic panels were installed, the judge in the case ordered the owners to ensure that no more than 10 percent of their neighbor's solar panels was shaded, a decision that required either cutting down some of the illicit foliage or pruning extensively to put the trees back on the right side of the law. The case was drenched with irony; the offending trees were redwoods, an iconic species in the history of American environmental activism and one that conjures up the images of wilderness preservationists John Muir and David Brower—figures usually not evoked in discussions of environmental nuisances. Not surprisingly, this twenty-first-century litigious twist on the "save the redwoods" story drew national media attention in the spring of 2008 (e.g., Fox 2008; Barringer 2008a). The extensive coverage—and, presumably, the widely held sentiment that it was somewhat perverse to legally declare redwood trees an environmental irritant—prompted quick action from California lawmakers. In July that same year, Governor Arnold Schwarzenegger signed into law a bill that protected trees planted before the installation of solar panels in such cases, although this setback did not stop the panel owners from taking their case to civil court to seek redress for their losses (Barringer 2008a).

On one level, the redwoods–solar panels case is emblematic of an emerging tension within environmental planning in the era of sustainability—namely, the conflict between various aspects of renewable or "clean" energy technology and nature protection in land use decision making. Although there may be no inherent incompatibility between the installation of clean energy technology and other environmental goals, such as wilderness preservation and the conservation of biodiversity, it has become clear that these ends may nevertheless collide at the landscape level. Recent high-profile conflicts over the ecological and aesthetic impacts of siting of a wind farm off Cape Cod and a large solar-energy project in California's Mojave Desert have vividly exposed the challenges of accommodating multiple environmental values on the landscape and the need for us to come to grips with some very difficult value trade-offs in land-use planning and policy for a more sustainable society (see, e.g., Barringer 2009, 2010; Seelye 2010).

Yet such cases also suggest, I believe, a deeper philosophical transformation in the legal, policy, and management regimes for nature conservation and environmental protection in the twenty-first century. Specifically, I think we may be witnessing the measured movement away from the traditional preservationist worldview and value system underpinning conservation policy and practice and toward a more dynamic, activist, and transformative vision of the human-nature relationship. Although this change is complex and heterogeneous—and is being actively resisted in many quarters (including within the scientific and environmental advocacy communities)—it is nevertheless manifest in a number of areas of conservation management and policy today.

The ability of global climate change (GCC; and rapid environmental change more generally) to redefine conservation targets, and with them the underlying values motivating nature conservation and environmental management, is nothing short of profound. It already has and will continue to yield significant implications for the philosophical rationalization and justification of key areas of conservation and environmental policy in the coming decades. GCC and its synergies with other major forces of environmental change—notably habitat fragmentation, the spread of invasive species, emerging infectious diseases, and so forth—are now recognized by many observers as posing a fundamental challenge to our conventional policies and practices targeted at conserving species and managing ecosystems. In doing so, it challenges as well the traditional environmental ethical arguments and norms that have supported these policy and management goals in the past.

Conserving Nature in a Changing World

The basic science behind the "greenhouse effect"—that is, the physical process in which the accumulation of greenhouse gases, such as carbon and methane, in the atmosphere produces a warming effect on the earth's climate by trapping solar energy—has been known since the nineteenth century (Weart 2008). Although skeptical views of climate change, including the human role in driving global warming, continue to draw a degree of public attention (the late novelist Michael Crichton was an especially visible and tireless critic), such stances are increasingly marginal to an informed scientific discussion of the issue. In an important paper published in the magazine *Science,* Naomi Oreskes (2004) describes the results of an extensive review of the peer-reviewed literature on climate change. Her results confirm the overwhelming scientific agreement on the reality of human-caused climate change; none of the more than nine hundred papers examined disagrees with the consensus position. Although a good deal of uncertainty remains regarding the timing and magnitude of GCC—including the existence of climate thresholds, the role of nonlinear climate feedbacks, and, of course, the nature and efficacy of the human response (e.g., Alley et al. 2003; Keller, Yohe, and Schlesinger 2008; Lenton et al. 2008)—the international scientific community has unambiguously affirmed climate change's reality as an atmospheric phenomenon over the years.

Even though scientists have long understood the fundamental physics of the greenhouse effect and its relation to human activities, anthropogenic climate change did not appear on the public agenda until the 1980s, a lag owing to the complexities of climate-change science and to the political dynamics of the science-policy process (Brown 2002). In 1989, the U.N. Environment Program and the World Meteorological Organization created the Intergovernmental Panel on Climate Change (IPCC), an organization designed to report the state of climate-change science (produced by thousands of scientists around the globe) to the community of policy makers. The IPCC's most recent Assessment Report, published in 2007, states that warming of the global climate system is "unequivocal" and that this warming is "very likely" (90 percent confidence) due to the increase of greenhouse gas (GHG) concentrations stemming from human activities, such as the burning of fossil fuels, deforestation, and agriculture. Furthermore, global CO2 emissions grew by approximately 80 percent between 1970 and 2004, suggesting a rapidly accelerating trend in recent decades. Depending on the present and future societal and policy response to trends in GHG emissions, the IPCC predicts that the average surface temperature of the earth may increase by 3.2 to 7.2°F and perhaps as many as 11.5°F over the next century. Physical evidence of planetary warming, moreover, is already apparent, including the decline of mountain glaciers and snow cover, which are in turn linked to rising sea levels (IPCC 2007). These latter projections, moreover, appear to have been too conservative; after the release of the 2007 IPCC report, revised analyses suggest that projections of sea level rise and polar ice melt are significantly underestimated (Pew Center for Global Climate Change 2009).

Much of the public discussion of GCC impacts focuses on human concerns, for understandable reasons. Global warming and accompanying changes in the Earth's physical and biotic systems are predicted to result in a suite of human health and economic impacts, including greater malnutrition and mortality (due to increased heat waves, floods, and droughts); increased prevalence of vector-borne diseases; and the disruption of key ecological services (IPCC 2007; Millennium Ecosystem Assessment 2005). For example, warming and acidifying oceans are predicted to have highly negative implications for coral reef production, which in turn will impact subsistence-dependent communities and regional economies reliant on them for coastal protection, fisheries, and tourism (Hoegh-Guldberg et al. 2007). Although the impacts of GCC on human physical, social, and economic well-being will be geographically variable, the overarching concern among many climate policy advocates is that they have the potential to severely harm present and future generations, especially those most vulnerable to abrupt environmental changes—that is, those communities and nations that lack the ability to adapt to rapid environmental transformations or are most directly dependent upon sensitive ecosystem services for their livelihood (Adger et al. 2006; Stern 2007; Mearns and Norton 2009)

From a more traditional conservation perspective, GCC has emerged as a significant threat to the health of ecological systems and the viability of plant and animal species in this century (Sala et al. 2000; Parmesan and Yohe 2003; Thomas et al. 2004). Coastal systems, for instance, face increased erosion and wetland loss, while marine systems will be impacted by the aforementioned acidification of oceans and coral bleaching (Rosenzweig et al. 2007). GCC is also seen as a progressively serious impediment to many species' survival, having been tied to a broad range of biotic impacts, including physiological, phenological, and distributional changes (Root and Hughes 2005; Parmesan 2006). It is, moreover, a hazard that combines with more traditional threats to biodiversity, including habitat destruction, landscape fragmentation, and the proliferation of invasive species (Hannah et al. 2002; Root et al. 2003; Root and Schneider 2006; Barnosky 2009). In tandem with the spread of emerging infectious diseases, GCC has already been linked to recent amphibian extinctions, although the relationship is complicated (e.g., Pounds et al. 2006; Collins and Crump 2009). Still, according to one influential review (Thomas et al. 2004), depending on the rate and magnitude of planetary warming, up to a third of the world's species could be on a path to climate-driven extinction.

Confounding the conservation policy and management response to this situation is the complexity, unpredictability, and unprecedented nature of GCC, including its frequently nonlinear character. As Milly et al. have pointed out, GCC challenges the prevailing assumption of "stationarity" in natural systems—that is, the idea that ecological systems "fluctuate within an unchanging envelope of variability" (2008, 573). In fact, GCC may be so dramatically altering the baseline ecological conditions we operate from that we are moving out of the realm of "natural variability" in ecological systems to what some observers have described as a "no analogue" future: a new ecological reality with little relationship to historical systems and the changes within them (Williams and Jackson 2007).

If "stationarity is dead" at the hands of GCC, it will need to be replaced by more dynamic and accurate models and protocols that capture the "nonstationarity" of environmental systems to optimize and sustain planning, policy, and management efforts (see, e.g., Craig 2010). These models will need to account for the "new normal" imposed by GCC's operating in concert with other forces by recognizing that natural dynamism, which is difficult enough to predict and manage for, has been outstripped. The changing degree of variation and unpredictability imposed on natural and physical systems by a shifting global climate, in producing a deep rupture in the "normal" historical processes of environmental fluctuation and change, is thus producing a difference in kind that many are now arguing requires a new way of thinking in conservation law, policy, and management (and, as I propose in the following section, will require a new outlook in environmental ethics).

What seem to be emerging from these discussions are the broad outlines of a more flexible and anticipatory style of conservation action, one that is more proactive and interventionist in nature than the traditional nature-preservationist approaches that have long dominated species and landscape protection (e.g., Hobbs and Cramer 2008). Yet this shift to a more dynamic and elastic legal and policy regime will not come easily, especially given the pace of GCC and the traditionally static character of environmental and natural-resources law. Generally resistant to change and premised on notions of stationarity, such laws either attempt to preserve an ecosystem in a desired "natural" state (a goal found within the wetlands provisions of the Clean Water Act and the overall protective philosophy of the Endangered Species Act) or seek to reverse anthropogenic changes affecting species or ecosystems by returning them to what is seen as a "natural" environmental baseline (Craig 2010, 32–34). As natural-resources law scholar Holly Doremus writes, however, these traditional goals may no longer be realistic in the era of rapid environmental change:

> The reality of climate change untethers conservation goals from history. It simply will not be possible to protect the world that has been. Not all species can be saved from extinction in a rapidly-changing world, even with strong regulatory restrictions and expensive restoration measures. . . . We need standards that better match a world in transition, which means we need standards that can change to reflect new realities. (2010, 63, 84)

Instead of fooling ourselves that we can preserve species or systems within historically defined conditions and ranges of variability—or restore landscapes to their "predisturbance" past—we will likely have to accept the fact that GCC imposes such a high level of unpredictability and promises such dynamic and novel ecological circumstances that these models are no longer as useful as they once were. As a result, many are beginning to argue that we must take a more adaptive approach to conservation law and policy, focusing on moving environmental-policy targets, such as "adaptive capacity" and "ecological resilience," rather than the conventional preservationist and restorationist visions that have dominated conservation law and policy in the past (Craig 2010). The objective is to increase the ability of species, ecosystems, and societies to cope with rapid environmental change (resilience) while also improving the capacity of these systems to continue to deliver goods and services that are critical to human social, physical, and economic well-being (e.g., Adger et al. 2005). Yet this shift to a more adaptive, flexible, and anticipatory approach in conservation policy, in breaking with the commitment to historical ecosystems and other preservationist commitments (e.g., viewing human intervention as inherently destructive), faces a number of obstacles, including critical views originating from within the ecology and conservation-science communities.

Consider the challenge of species conservation under GCC, a subject that, as I mention above, has recently drawn much attention as we have become more aware of the increased extinction risks tied to a warming planet. As species begin to alter their ranges in response to climate shifts—generally moving upslope and to higher latitudes—they encounter many formidable physical barriers to dispersal, including mountains, waterways, cities, office parks, and highways. This situation, along with the growing recognition that traditional conservation strategies, such as the establishment of protected areas, may not be enough to save species that GCC imperils (e.g., Hannah et al. 2007; Collins and Crump 2009), has prompted some scientists and conservationists to consider moving species to more suitable locations ahead of predicted change (McLachlan, Hellmann, and Schwartz 2007; Marris 2008; Hoegh-Guldberg et al. 2008). Termed "assisted migration," "assisted colonization," or "managed relocation," the idea has proved controversial, mostly because of its potential to lead to biological invasions in the recipient systems. Despite this, some conservation advocates are already relocating species, such as *Torreya taxifolia* (a conifer with a shrinking range in the Florida panhandle), in an attempt to save them from climate-driven stresses (www.torreyguardians.org).

Although the scientific community is in widespread agreement that GCC poses a significant threat of extinction to many plant and animal species, that species are valuable (economically, culturally, or intrinsically) and worthy of conservation concern, and that drastic efforts may be required to save them, many ecologists and conservation biologists feel that managed relocation (MR) is far too risky to endorse as a conservation strategy (see, e.g., Davidson and Simkanin 2008; Huang 2008; Ricciardi and Simberloff 2009a, 2009b; Seddon et al. 2009). In response, cautious supporters have suggested that risk protocols and decision frameworks can be developed to reduce the potential for harmful ecological impacts of climate-driven relocations (e.g., Hoegh-Guldberg et al. 2008; Richardson et al. 2009), and that predictions of relocated species causing ecological damage to their new habitats is exaggerated (Sax, Smith, and Thompson 2009; Schlaepfer et al. 2009). Key domestic and international conservation agencies and organizations, such as the U.S. Fish and Wildlife Service and the International Union for Conservation of Nature (IUCN), are currently exploring MR and related adaptive measures to secure conservation goals in the face of predicted climate change impacts. Despite the growing attention to MR within the conservation community, many observers remain deeply skeptical of the practice. In particular, some critics do not believe that we have the ability to accurately predict many species' invasion potential (and subsequent impacts) and conclude that this ignorance sinks MR as a conservation practice. For these observers, MR becomes a high-stakes game of "ecological roulette" (Ricciardi and Simberloff 2009b, 252). MR clearly also exposes a larger question of value trade-offs in conservation policy and practice under GCC, as many of the debaters are aware. For example, Dov Sax, Katherine Smith, and Andrew Thompson (2009) argue that, because extinctions are irreversible, using MR to save species at the cost of an impact on the recipient ecosystem's composition and function is a choice that some biodiversity managers can defend. Conversely, even if species extinction is seen as ethically deplorable, a natural-area manager could still conclude that it is not worth sacrificing the biotic and evolutionary integrity of an ecological system, which is another environmental value, under MR to avoid losing a particular species. This may be especially true if one believes that MR may ultimately fail to save the target species, given the spotty history of past translocations and the fact that relocated species may be particularly vulnerable to other threats, especially if the population size is low (Huang 2008).

Finally, it is clear that MR reflects a dramatic break with the legal, policy, and managerial norm of fidelity to evolutionary history, as mentioned above. Among other things, the disjunction between MR and conventional methods of in situ conservation of plants and animals—and the heavy human hand required for MR, with possible destructive meddling in ecological systems—opens it up to familiar criticisms of human arrogance, especially by those who place a premium on ecological integrity as a policy goal. Under this view, MR is incompatible with prevailing models of wilderness preservation, given its acceptance of the significant human manipulation of ecological processes (Barnosky 2009). Furthermore, Ronald Sandler (2010) argues that in most cases, MR proposals would not meet the burden of ethical justification in light of the expected ecological risk of translocation to receiving systems and the fact that many of our reasons for caring about species—from their intrinsic to their instrumental value—are simply not strong enough to justify moving them outside their native ranges.

Yet, once again, in a rapidly changing world with moving ecological baselines, we may find ourselves with little choice but to come to grips with the inevitable ecological "reshuffling" forced by GCC, a condition that requires relaxing, at least in some cases, our commitments to past assemblages and notions of historical integrity (Fox 2007). For example, some ecologists and conservationists have begun to recognize the value of "novel" or "emerging" ecosystems—that is, those systems that reflect a significant degree of human modification yet are able to function without continual management (Hobbs et al. 2006; Hobbs, Higgs, and Harris 2009; Marris 2009). Such human-modified systems (e.g., a "secondary" tropical forest that has regrown after intensive harvesting of the primary forest) could play critical roles in the provision of ecosystem services, such as water purification, nutrient cycling, and carbon sequestration. They could also provide new habitats for the plants and animals we may introduce for conservation purposes in anticipation of harmful changes in their "native" ecosystems.

Still, a number of important questions remain, especially given the concern that permitting (or encouraging) species relocation and valorizing novel systems and heavily modified landscapes will draw resources and attention away from traditional conservation approaches (e.g., the protection of species in their native ranges, the preservation of historical ecological conditions, native biodiversity, and so on). There is also the fear of establishing legal and policy precedents that would allow unnecessary or inadvisable relocations that would produce unanticipated consequences for the target species and for the recipient systems. Such radical efforts to protect species under GCC, furthermore, display an atomistic focus—that is, the conservation target is generally focused on a single species of interest. As a consequence, it is an approach that would seem to be out of step with more holistic conservation models and strategies oriented toward biological communities and ecological processes. For these and other reasons, such proposals as MR force us to ask hard questions about what we are willing to do to conserve species under GCC in the twenty-first century (see Camacho et al. 2010).

Yet many conservationists argue that such practices have now become necessary and that they will only become more prevalent at the planet warms and changes in the decades to come. Indeed, the activist and preemptive mode of species conservation under GCC signified by MR will likely be increasingly ubiquitous, even within in situ conservation and restoration projects that attempt to significantly augment ecological resilience of ecological systems to help protect species in their native ranges. A good illustration of this growing trend may be seen in the Alligator River Climate Change Adaptation Project in coastal North Carolina, recently described by Joshua Lawler et al. (2010). The project is a coordinated multiorganizational effort that covers more than 220,000 hectares, most of which are under conservation ownership (e.g., lands owned by the U.S. Fish and Wildlife Service, the U.S. Air Force, and the Nature Conservancy, among others). The largest conservation holding in the area is the Alligator River National Wildlife Refuge, which provides critical habitats for the endangered red wolf (*Canis rufus*) as well as the red-cockaded woodpecker (*Picoides borealis*) and the American alligator (*Alligator mississippiensis*). Adaptive conservation management of the region is currently being pursued to address uncertainties surrounding current and projected sea-level rise due to GCC, which could devastate these populations given the low elevation of the refuge. Current and planned restoration and management activities include installing tide gates to prevent saltwater intrusion, protecting additional upslope habitat to permit natural dispersal, creating oyster reefs and sea-grass beds along the coast to protect the area from storms, and planting bald cypress on upslope lands to stabilize the soil, among other actions (Lawler et al. 2010, 41).

These and many similar examples suggest that GCC is transforming the management and policy landscape in addition to the biophysical one, putting enormous pressure on the underlying assumptions and policy and management strategies for protecting species and systems in an era of rapid environmental change. Developing legal regimes and policy frameworks for dealing more effectively with a poststationary natural environment will be a daunting task in the coming decades. In terms of conservation planning and goal setting, it will require making difficult trade-offs, such as the substitution (in some instances) of the traditional management criteria of resilience and adaptive capacity for ecological integrity and autonomy (see, e.g., Hobbs et al. 2010). In other cases, it will entail the shift away from conventional conservation targets, such as "natural" systems and native species assemblages, to an acceptance of the value of novel systems and a more dynamic and pluralistic conservation agenda.

Furthermore, although the time-honored protected-area approach to species conservation will likely remain the preferred strategy of safeguarding biodiversity in the coming decades, projected GCC trends are exposing the inadequacy of the global reserve system as species begin to shift their ranges in response to changing environmental conditions (Hannah et al. 2007). Increasing landscape connectivity and creating migratory corridors between reserves remains an option for enhancing the conservation effectiveness of some areas. Yet in other places, we will likely find ourselves considering new, perhaps even radical, conservation strategies (such as managed relocation) to save species imperiled by a rapidly changing environment. What ultimately may be required is the creation of entirely new protected areas that are planned in anticipation of species' needs under future climate shifts, an ambitious undertaking that will require considerable investment in predictive conservation science and reserve acquisition.

Along these lines, paleoecologist Anthony Barnosky (2009) has recently proposed an intriguing (and doubtless controversial) strategy for protecting wilderness values and species in the era of climate change, one that acknowledges the limitations of the older preservationist ideals yet seeks to maintain our strong societal commitment to species and wilderness conservation in the face of rapidly transforming ecological systems. Specifically, Barnosky envisions a dual system of nature reserves: One type would be actively managed for species conservation, which could include relocated species and novel assemblages, and the other would comprise wildland reserves managed to sustain ecological processes that are mostly protected from significant human modification (but that would still experience considerable ecological change). The species-oriented reserves, according to Barnosky, would require intensive human management, including such activities as managed relocation, reintroductions, and other conservation interventions, and would essentially serve as enclaves to protect plants and wildlife from extirpation and extinction by any means deemed necessary. Wildland reserves, in contrast, would be less intensively managed so as to comport with a range of wilderness values—that is, those experiential and ecological values typically not available in heavily modified landscapes. Such areas, however, would not remain a frozen ecological state; species in the proposed wildland reserves would be expected to continually change in abundance (including in some cases, extinctions) as the various forces of natural change and anthropogenic climate change operated on them. In addition to their importance as sources of wilderness experiences (and in a manner similar to Aldo Leopold's writings in the 1940s), Barnosky suggests that these wildland reserves could become key experimental "laboratories" able to help us better understand the evolution of ecosystems that are not under significant human control (2009, 207–208; see also Leopold 1949).

Although this major revisioning of natural areas policy would be difficult, even comparatively less-radical proposals to deal with the anticipated effects of GCC in protected area planning pose significant technical and managerial challenges. For example, one strategy gaining some attention of late is the notion of "moveable" protected areas that track dynamic objects of conservation interest (e.g., regenerating trees or marine species); such models would adopt temporal or spatial variations that parallel the predicted seasonal and geographical movements of the target variables (Soto 2001; Pressey et al. 2007). As Lee Hannah (2008) reminds us, however, even these novel efforts will not be enough if we do not also move forward with an aggressive climate-mitigation strategy that seeks to significantly reduce future GHG emissions.

And that, of course, is the rub: Any serious GHG mitigation policy will be dependent upon the collective will of citizens and policy makers to push it forward, a will that continues to be undermined by an inertial combination of political calculation and presentist economic analyses as well as by the public's considerable lack of basic knowledge regarding GCC. On this last point, a recently released Yale study of U.S. citizens' understanding of climate-change science is especially troubling (Leiserowitz, Smith, and Marlon 2010). Among the study results is the finding that only 50 percent of Americans believe that global warming is caused primarily by human activities, while only 45 percent know that carbon dioxide traps heat on the planet's surface. The Yale researchers also find that just 25 percent of respondents had heard of ocean acidification and oral bleaching, suggesting a widespread ignorance of GCC's ecological impacts. To make matters even worse, the study reveals that a significant portion of the public believes that banning aerosols and rocket launches is a viable solution to global warming. In all, the Yale study paints a disquieting portrait of public knowledge regarding GCC. It is sobering to consider what this failure of scientific literacy might portend for citizens' support for the bold and proactive conservation policies—and novel environmental management efforts—that will be increasingly necessary to address new ecological realities under GCC.

Conservation on a rapidly changing planet, in sum, will likely require a more flexible, innovative, preemptive approach to safeguarding species and maintaining ecosystem health in the twenty-first century, one that responds to rapid environmental change and uncertainty by enhancing ecological resilience and the capacity of systems to absorb such changes without negative consequences for the delivery of key products and services. In so doing, it will, in many instances, demand from us a more activist and "hands-on" style of species protection and ecological management and a simultaneous shift away from more traditional preservationist assumptions within key areas of conservation law and policy. I believe it will also require a parallel transformation in our ethical views justifying these assumptions.

Paradigm Shifts in Environmental Ethics

The reality of rapid and global environmental change—including GCC and its interaction with other environmentally transformative forces, such as accelerating urbanization and pollution, the spread of invasive species, and emerging infectious diseases—will ultimately compel us to come to grips with a new philosophical and ethical paradigm for species conservation and ecological management in this century, one in which conventional normative standards for nature protection (e.g., "pristine," "natural," "native") give way in many cases to more dynamic and relativist descriptive and value categories. From managed relocation of species outside their native ranges, to the emergence of novel systems as valued targets of ecological management, to the turn (in some cases) toward engineered or "invented" ecological systems for providing ecosystem services (e.g., Palmer et al. 2004), these shifts not only reflect revised judgments about the acceptability of the human modification of nature to achieve nature conservation and sustainable development goals but also speak to a deeper philosophical reorganization of the dominant ecological-policy and management worldview.

The emerging paradigm of conservation and ecological management under planetary change signals a significant departure from the traditional preservationist agenda of academic environmental ethics. Since its origins in the 1970s, environmental ethics has generally sought to provide arguments to protect nature from human influence and, especially, manipulation; in most cases, this has supported an unequivocal "hands-off" attitude toward wild nature. Indeed, the field's overwhelming focus on establishing nature's moral standing via arguments for intrinsic value (and parallel defenses of nonanthropocentric worldviews) were primarily motivated by the desire to condemn human environmental impacts and protect the human-independent integrity of species and ecosystems. Deriving historical justification and philosophical inspiration from environmentalist icons, such as Muir (and, more objectionably, Leopold), many environmental ethicists developed a presumptive anti-interventionist posture toward human-nature relationship. This perspective may be found in much of the early and canonical nonanthropocentric literature, such as Paul Taylor's influential case for biocentrism, *Respect for Nature* (1986). Among other things, Taylor's text may be read as an elegant defense of autonomous, wild nature against all forms of human manipulation and encroachment.

The preservationist, anti-interventionist position in environmental ethics, however, was not only directed at the traditional destroyers of nature's integrity (i.e., land developers, polluters, poachers, etc.). It would also be deployed by some philosophers to condemn activities pursued under the banner of conservation. Nonanthropocentric writers, such as Robert Elliot (1997) and Eric Katz (1997, 2009), for example, emphatically object to the growing practice of ecological restoration—an effort requiring significant human design and, often, technological prowess—for destroying natural value and effecting human control over the natural world. The preservationist view would also dominate, not surprisingly, in ruminations on the ethics of wilderness protection, where ecocentric writers, such as Holmes Rolston, vigorously defend the "untrammeled" and universalized wilderness ideal against its deconstructionist critics—including those "friendly," pro-conservation writers within environmental ethics and environmental history (e.g., Rolston 1991; Lemons 2007; Nelson and Callicott 2008).

Yet in a poststationary world, the resolute preservationist stance, especially in its anti-interventionist modality, is no longer practicable. As we have seen, shifting ecological baselines forced by a rapidly changing climate will render attempts to strictly preserve native species assemblages and historical wilderness characteristics extremely difficult, if not impossible, in a significant number of cases. Even though postequilibrium models in ecology—and the implications of natural dynamism and flux for environmental management—have been recognized for decades now (e.g., Botkin 1992; Wu and Loucks 1995), GCC is widely predicted to impose conditions that will mark a dramatic break with even these accounts of natural variability. What this entails for the traditional nature-preservationist agenda within environmental-ethics and conservation-advocacy circles is not the relinquishing of our ethical commitment to species and wilderness protection, but rather the revising of our understanding of and normative attitude toward the requirements of species conservation and wilderness protection on a rapidly changing planet. As I argue above, it will likely demand the acceptance of more activist and anticipatory strategies for saving species from the consequences of climate change and related large-scale, transformative forces. These efforts will involve a heavier human hand and, in many contexts, the ethical sanction of aggressive conservation interventions as well as the relaxation (to varying degrees) of the longstanding commitment to ecological history in biological conservation.

Whatever the configuration of the various strategies that will come to dominate nature conservation in this next century, it seems clear that what will be needed from environmental ethicists to support and assess these efforts are not arguments for protecting an untouched nature from human modification but rather pragmatic evaluative frameworks able to guide adaptive and effective managerial and conservation interventions. A refounded and constructive environmental ethics, that is, will need to engage the novel challenges—and especially the difficult policy and management trade-offs—of conserving species and ecosystems under global change without retreating to a simplistic form of preservationism that views the human manipulation of nature as inherently destructive and ethically repugnant. This new ethical paradigm will necessarily be pluralistic and contextual in form; it will operate within a larger scientific, philosophical, and policy model focused on the policy goals of enhancing ecological resilience and adaptive capacity in the face of rapidly emerging and unprecedented environmental transformations. It will also require ethical principles for avoiding potentially destructive interventions in ecological systems, norms reflecting a sense of restraint, responsibility, and significant community engagement with natural systems as they evolve and change (Higgs and Hobbs 2010).

Whether we like it or not, anticipatory intervention in biological populations, communities, and ecosystems will likely prove ever more necessary for conservation purposes and for the maintenance of increasingly stressed ecological services. What this ultimately spells for nature protection, I believe, is the reconstruction of conservation philosophy and action that moves us away from the ideal of preserving species and systems in historical systems and insulating them from all manner of human impacts to a model of directing ecological change in sustainable and desirable ways that promotes species persistence and ecosocial sustainability (albeit with different emphases, depending on the conservation and managerial context). Although this may strike many ethicists and conservationists as signifying a radical departure from hard-won preservationist standards, there is no reason to assume that this dynamic, activist, and proactive approach will jeopardize the strong tradition, in the United States and elsewhere, of protecting species from extinction and natural areas from degradation. Indeed, these emerging environmental-management and conservation-policy pathways under global change should reflect our commitment to species and ecological protection in addition to ensuring the provision of goods and services necessary for human survival and cultural integrity. Justifying this mission within a reorganized conservation enterprise—while simultaneously supporting serious efforts focused on climate change mitigation—is a critically important task for a postpreservationist and policy-minded environmental ethics.

A refounded, pragmatic environmental ethics that embraces ethical pluralism and assumes an experimental stance toward ecological decision making—while recognizing the need to address environmental problems via methods that seek practical accommodation of disparate stakeholder values—can be an important player in nature conservation in the era of global environmental change. This is especially true to the degree that the eclipse of historical baselines for conservation will require new modes of public dialogue among scientists, managers, and citizens with a common stake in shaping intelligent and principled policy and management goals on a rapidly changing planet. These deliberations will necessarily reflect new and dynamic standards that emerge from a more balanced interchange between ecological and social values as older preservationist and restorationist paradigms recede and we look to new conservation approaches and policy objectives more appropriate for safeguarding species and managing ecosystems under GCC.

The moral hazards we will face in this effort, however, are real. There is a genuine danger, for example, that the embrace of our responsibility for directing sustainable ecological change and the turn away from traditional preservationist norms for conservation will simply become another step toward the destructive domination of wild species and landscapes—that is, another biological power grab by humans in the era of the "Anthropocene" (see Zalasiewicz et al. 2010). Although this risk should be of great concern to all of us who care about wild species and nature, I believe it is naive to think that assuming increasingly outmoded preservationist positions in debates over conservation law and policy will significantly reduce it. Rather, the real moral challenges now facing us seem to be of the following sort: Can we become adaptive and careful stewards of species and systems as the world changes in unpredictable and unprecedented ways around us, or will we continue to push planetary biodiversity to the precipice—and into the chasm of extinction? Can we help species and natural areas adapt to rapidly changing environmental conditions without undercutting efforts to simultaneously address the societal drivers of anthropogenic climate change, pollution, and habitat conversion? Can we learn to demonstrate sufficient humility and precaution in planetary management so as to avoid creating further problems with our technological "fixes" (see, e.g., geoengineering the planet)?

These are haunting questions, in part because they are unanswerable in the present. The answers, however, will ultimately define much of our character as a people, in terms of our ethical relations with wild species and our ecological and cultural bequest to those who will come along after us. They also point the way toward a new and critically important agenda for a pragmatic environmental ethics in the coming decades.

Writing more than eighty years ago, Leopold cut to the heart of this challenge in a particularly unforgettable passage (even for him), one that I shall let close this chapter and this book:

> If there be, indeed, a special nobility inherent in the human race—a special cosmic value, distinctive from and superior to all other life—by what token shall it be manifest? By a society decently respectful of its own and all other life, capable of inhabiting the earth without defiling it? Or by a society like that of John Burroughs' potato bug, which exterminated the potato, and thereby exterminated itself? As one or the other shall we be judged in "the derisive silence of eternity." ([1923] 1991, 97)

References

Abram, David. 1996. *The spell of the sensuous: Perception and language in a more-than-human world.* New York: Pantheon.
Ackerman, Bruce A. 1980. *Social justice and the liberal state.* New Haven, CT: Yale University Press.
Adams, W. M., R. Aveling, D. Brockington, B. Dickson, J. Elliott, J. Hutton, D. Roe, B. Vira, and W. Wolmer. 2004. Biodiversity conservation and the eradication of poverty. *Science* 306: 1146–1148.
Adger, W. Neil, Terry P. Hughes, Carl Folke, Stephen R. Carpenter, and Johan Rockström. 2005. Social-ecological resilience to coastal disasters. *Science* 309: 1036–1039.
Adger, W. Neil, Jouni Paavola, Saleemul Huq, and M. J. Mace, eds. 2006. *Fairness in adaptation to climate change.* Cambridge, MA: MIT Press.
Agar, Nicholas. 2001. *Life's intrinsic value: Science, ethics, and nature.* New York: Columbia University Press.
Aldred, Jonathan, and Michael Jacobs. 2000. Citizens and wetlands: Evaluating the Ely Citizens' Jury. *Ecological Economics* 34: 217–232.
Allen, Anne. 1998. Group protests swan kill. *Burlington Free Press.* April 10.
Alley, R. B., J. Marotzke, W. D. Nordhaus, J. T. Overpeck, D. M. Peteet, R. A. Pielke, Jr., R. T. Pierrehumbert, P. B. Rhines, T. F. Stocker, L. D. Talley, and J. M. Wallace. 2003. Abrupt climate change. *Science* 299: 2005–2010.
Anderson, Elizabeth. 1998. Pragmatism, science, and moral inquiry. In *In face of the facts: Moral inquiry in American scholarship,* edited by Richard W. Fox and Robert B. Westbrook, 10–39. Washington, DC: Woodrow Wilson Center and Cambridge University Press.
Angulo, E., and B. Cooke. 2002. First synthesize new viruses then regulate their release? The case of the wild rabbit. *Molecular Ecology* 11: 2703–2709.
Anonymous. 2006. Court settlement puts sea lions back under scrutiny. *Nature* 442: 121.
Appiah, Kwame Anthony. 2008. *Experiments in ethics.* Cambridge, MA: Harvard University Press.

Aristotle. 1998. *The Nicomachean ethics.* Reissue edition. Oxford, UK: Oxford University Press.

Baber, Walter F., and Robert V. Bartlett. 2005. *Deliberative environmental politics: Democracy and ecological rationality.* Cambridge, MA: MIT Press.

Bailey, L. H. 1915. *The holy Earth.* New York: Charles Scribner's Sons.

Barber, Benjamin R. 1984. *Strong democracy: Participatory politics for a new age.* Berkeley: University of California Press.

Barnosky, Anthony D. 2009. *Heatstroke: Nature in an age of global warming.* Washington, DC: Shearwater/Island Press.

Barringer, Felicity. 2008a. In California neighbors' dispute, officials find it's time to speak for the trees. *New York Times.* July 23, 2008.

———. 2008b. Trees block solar panels, and a feud ends in court. *New York Times.* April 7.

———. 2009. Environmentalists in a clash of goals. *New York Times.* March 24.

———. 2010. Solar power plants to rise on U.S. land. *New York Times.* October 5.

Barry, Brian. 1965. *Political argument.* New York: Humanities Press.

Beatley, Timothy. 1994. *Ethical land use: Principles of policy and planning.* Baltimore: Johns Hopkins University Press.

Bekoff, Marc, and Dale Jamieson. 1996. Ethics and the study of carnivores: Doing science while respecting animals. In *Carnivore behavior, ecology, and evolution,* volume 2, edited by John L. Gittleman, 15–45. Ithaca, NY: Cornell University Press.

Benditt, Theodore M. 1973. The public interest. *Philosophy and Public Affairs* 2: 291–311.

Benhabib, Seyla, ed. 1996. *Democracy and difference.* Princeton, NJ: Princeton University Press.

Bentham, Jeremy. 1996. *An introduction to the principles of morals and legislation. The collected works of Jeremy Bentham.* Revised edition. New York: Oxford University Press.

Bentley, Arthur F. 1908. *The process of government.* Chicago: University of Chicago Press.

Bernstein, Richard J. 1989. Pragmatism, pluralism, and the healing of wounds. *Proceedings and Addresses of the American Philosophical Association* 63: 5–18.

Blaustein, Richard J. 2007. Protected areas and equity concerns. *BioScience* 57: 216–221.

Bohman, James. 2000. *Public deliberation: Pluralism, complexity, and democracy.* Cambridge, MA: MIT Press.

Bohman, James, and William Rehg, eds. 1997. *Deliberative democracy: Essays on reason and politics.* Cambridge, MA: MIT Press.

Boisvert, Raymond D. 1998. *John Dewey: Rethinking our time.* Albany, NY: SUNY Press.

Bolsen, Toby, and Fay Lomax Cook. 2008. The polls—trends. Public opinion on energy policy: 1974–2006. *Public Opinion Quarterly* 72: 364–388.

Borry, Pascal, Paul Schotsmans, and Kris Dierickx. 2005. The birth of the empirical turn in bioethics. *Bioethics* 19: 49–71.

Botkin, Daniel B. 1992. *Discordant harmonies: A new ecology for the twenty-first century.* New York: Oxford University Press.

Box, Richard C. 2007. Redescribing the public interest. *Social Science Journal* 44: 585–598.

Brint, Michael, and William Weaver, eds. 1991. *Pragmatism in law and society.* Boulder, CO: Westview Press.

Brockington, Dan. 2002. *Fortress conservation: The preservation of the Mkomazi Game Reserve.* Bloomington: Indiana University Press.

Bromley, Daniel W. 2006. *Sufficient reason: Volitional pragmatism and the meaning of economic institutions.* Princeton, NJ: Princeton University Press.

Broome, John. 2008. The ethics of climate change. *Scientific American* 298: 96–102.

Brown, Donald A. 2002. *American heat: Ethical problems with the United States' response to global warming.* Lanham, MD: Rowman and Littlefield.

———. 2009. The importance of creating an applied environmental ethics: Lessons learned from climate change. In *Nature in common? Environmental ethics and the contested foundations of environmental policy*, edited by Ben A. Minteer, 215–227. Philadelphia: Temple University Press.

Buck, Susan J. 1997. Forum on the role of environmental ethics in restructuring environmental policy and law for the next century. *Policy Currents* 7: 1–13.

Burdick, Alan. 2005. *Out of Eden: An odyssey of ecological invasion.* New York: Farrar, Straus and Giroux.

Burgess, J., M. Limb, and C. Harrison. 1998a. Exploring environmental values through the medium of focus groups. 1. Theory and practice. *Environment and Planning A,* 20: 309–326.

———. 1998b. Exploring environmental values through the medium of focus groups. 2. Illustrations of a group at work. *Environment and Planning A,* 20: 457–476.

Butler, W. F., and T. G. Acott. 2007. An inquiry concerning the acceptance of intrinsic value theories of nature. *Environmental Values* 16: 149–168.

Callicott, J. Baird. 1980. Animal liberation: A triangular affair. *Environmental Ethics* 2: 311–338.

———. 1988. Animal liberation and environmental ethics: Back together again. *Between the Species* 4: 163–169.

———. 1989. *In defense of the land ethic: Essays in environmental philosophy.* Albany, NY: SUNY Press.

———. 1990. The case against moral pluralism. *Environmental Ethics* 12: 99–124.

———. 1998. "Back together again" again. *Environmental Values* 7: 461–475.

———. 1999a. *Beyond the land ethic: More essays in environmental philosophy.* Albany, NY: SUNY Press.

———. 1999b. Silencing philosophers: Minteer and the foundations of anti-foundationalism. *Environmental Values* 8: 499–516.

———. 2002a. The power and promise of theoretical environmental ethics: Forging a new discourse. *Environmental Values* 11: 3–25.

———. 2002b. Reply to Bowersox, Minteer, and Norton. In *Democracy and the claims of nature: Critical perspectives for a new century*, edited by Ben A. Minteer and Bob Pepperman Taylor, 105–114. Lanham, MD: Rowman and Littlefield.

———. 2009. The convergence hypothesis falsified: Implicit intrinsic value, operational rights, and de facto standing in the Endangered Species Act. In *Nature in common? Environmental ethics and the contested foundations of environmental policy*, edited by Ben A. Minteer, 142–166. Philadelphia: Temple University Press.

Camacho, Alejandro E., Holly Doremus, Jason S. McLachlan, and Ben A. Minteer. 2010. Reassessing conservation goals in a changing climate. *Issues in Science and Technology* 26: 21–26.

Campagna, Claudio, and Teresita Fernández. 2007. A comparative analysis of the vision and mission statements of international environmental organisations. *Environmental Values* 16: 369–398.

Campbell, James. 1992. *The community reconstructs: The meaning of pragmatic social thought.* Champaign: University of Illinois Press.

Caspary, William R. 2000. *Dewey on democracy.* Ithaca, NY: Cornell University Press.

Cassinelli, C. W. 1958. Some reflections on the concept of the public interest. *Ethics* 69: 48–61.

Chester, Charles C. 2006. *Conservation across borders: Biodiversity in an interdependent world.* Washington, DC: Island Press.

Cochran, Clarke E. 1974. Political science and "the public interest." *Journal of Politics* 36: 327–355.

Cohen, Joshua. 1997. Procedure and substance in deliberative democracy. In *Deliberative democracy: Essays on reason in politics,* edited by James Bohman and William Rehg, 407–437. Cambridge, MA: MIT Press.

Cohen, Steven. 2006. *Understanding environmental policy.* New York: Columbia University Press.

Collins, James P., and Martha L. Crump. 2009. *Extinction in our times: Global amphibian decline.* Oxford, UK: Oxford University Press.

Collins, James P., and Andrew Storfer. 2003. Global amphibian declines: Sorting the hypotheses. *Diversity and Distributions* 9: 89–98.

Commoner, Barry. 1971. *The closing circle: Nature, man, and technology.* New York: Knopf.

Courchamp, Frank, Rosie Woodroffe, and Gary Roemer. 2003. Removing protected populations to save endangered species. *Science* 302: 1532.

Craig, Robin Kundis. 2010. "Stationarity is dead"—long live transformation: Five principles for climate change adaptation law. *Harvard Environmental Law Review* 34: 9–73.

Dallmeyer, Dorinda G., ed. 2003. *Values at sea: Ethics for the marine environment.* Athens: University of Georgia Press.

Dalton, Rex. 2004. Natural resources: Bioprospects less than golden. *Nature* 429: 598–600.

———. 2005a. Animal-rights group sues over "disturbing" work on sea lions. *Nature* 436: 315.

———. 2005b. Is this any way to save a species? *Nature* 436: 14–16.

D'Antonio, Carla M. 2000. Fire, plant invasions, and global changes. In *Invasive species in a changing world,* edited by Harold A. Mooney and Richard J. Hobbs, 65–93. Washington, DC: Island Press.

Davidson, Ian, and Christina Simkanin. 2008. Skeptical of assisted colonization. *Science* 322: 1048–1049.

Davies, Anna. 2001. What silence knows—planning, public participation, and environmental values. *Environmental Values* 10: 77–102.

Davis, Mark A. 2009. *Invasion biology.* Oxford, UK: Oxford University Press.

De Vries, Raymond G., Leigh Turner, Kristina Orfali, and Charles Bosk, eds. 2007. *The view from here: Bioethics and the social sciences.* Malden, MA: Blackwell.

Dewey, John. 1907. Review of *The life of reason, or the phases of human progress,* by George Santayana. In Volume 4 of *The middle works of John Dewey, 1899–1924,* edited by Jo Ann Boydston. Carbondale: Southern Illinois University Press, 1977.

———. 1917. The need for a recovery of philosophy. In Volume 10 of *The middle works of John Dewey, 1899–1924,* edited by Jo Ann Boydston. Carbondale: Southern Illinois University Press, 1980.

———. 1920. *Reconstruction in philosophy.* In Volume 12 of *The middle works of John Dewey, 1899–1924,* edited by Jo Ann Boydston. Carbondale: Southern Illinois University Press, 1982.

———. 1922. *Human nature and conduct: An introduction to social psychology.* In Volume 14 of *The middle works of John Dewey, 1899–1924,* edited by Jo Ann Boydston. Carbondale: Southern Illinois University Press, 1983.

———. 1927. *The public and its problems.* In Volume 2 of *John Dewey: The later works, 1925–1953,* edited by Jo Ann Boydston. Carbondale: Southern Illinois University Press, 1984.

———. 1929. *The quest for certainty.* In Volume 4 of *John Dewey: The later works, 1925–1953,* edited by Jo Ann Boydston. Carbondale: Southern Illinois University Press, 1984.

———. 1930a. From absolutism to experimentalism. In Volume 5 of *John Dewey: The later works, 1925–1953,* edited by Jo Ann Boydston. Carbondale: Southern Illinois University Press, 1984.

———. 1930b. Three independent factors in morals. In Volume 5 of *John Dewey: The later works, 1925–1953,* edited by Jo Ann Boydston. Carbondale: Southern Illinois University Press, 1984.

———. 1932. *Ethics.* In Volume 7 of *John Dewey: The later works, 1925–1953,* edited by Jo Ann Boydston. Carbondale: Southern Illinois University Press, 1985.

———. 1934. *A common faith.* In Volume 9 of *John Dewey: The later works, 1925–1953,* edited by Jo Ann Boydston. Carbondale: Southern Illinois University Press, 1986.

———. 1935. *Liberalism and social action.* In Volume 11 of *John Dewey: The later works, 1925–1953,* edited by Jo Ann Boydston. Carbondale: Southern Illinois University Press, 1987.

———. 1938. *Logic: The theory of inquiry.* In Volume 12 of *John Dewey: The later works, 1925–1953,* edited by Jo Ann Boydston. Carbondale: Southern Illinois University Press, 1986.

———. 1939a. Creative democracy—the task before us. In Volume 14 of *John Dewey: The later works, 1925–1953,* edited by Jo Ann Boydston. Carbondale: Southern Illinois University Press, 1991.

———. 1939b. *Freedom and culture.* In Volume 13 of *John Dewey: The later works, 1925–1953,* edited by Jo Ann Boydston. Carbondale: Southern Illinois University Press, 1988

Diggins, John Patrick. 1994. *The promise of pragmatism: Modernism and the crisis of knowledge and authority.* Chicago: University of Chicago Press.

Diggs, B. J. 1973. The common good as reason for political action. *Ethics* 83: 283–293.

Dillman, Don A. 1978. *Mail and telephone surveys: The total design method.* New York: John Wiley and Sons.

Doremus, Holly. 2010. Adapting to climate change through law that bends without breaking. *San Diego Journal of Climate and Energy Law* 2: 45–85.

Douglass, Bruce. 1980. The common good and the public interest. *Political Theory* 8: 103–117.

Dowie, Mark. 2009. *Conservation refugees: The hundred-year conflict between global conservation and native peoples.* Cambridge, MA: MIT Press.

Dryzek, John. 2002. *Deliberative democracy and beyond: Liberals, critics, contestations.* Oxford, UK: Oxford University Press.

Dubycha, Jeffrey L., and C. Kevin Geedey. 2003. Adventures of the mad scientist: Fostering science ethics in ecology with case studies. *Frontiers in Ecology and the Environment* 1: 330–333.

Dudley, Tom L., C. Jack DeLoach, Jeffrey E. Lovich, and Raymond I. Carruthers. 2000. Saltcedar invasion of western riparian areas: Impacts and new prospects for control. In *Transactions of the Sixty-Fifth North American Wildlife and Natural Resource Conference,* edited by R. E. McCabe and S. E. Loos, 345–381. Washington, DC: Wildlife Management Institute.

Dunlap, R. E., and A. G. Mertig, eds. 1992. *American environmentalism: The U.S. environmental movement, 1970–1990.* Washington, DC: Taylor and Francis.

Dunlap, R. E., and K. D. Van Liere. 1978. The new environmental paradigm. *Journal of Environmental Education* 9: 10–19.

Dunlap, R. E., K. D. Van Liere, A. G. Mertig, and R. E. Jones. 2000. New trends in measuring environmental attitudes: Measuring endorsement of the new ecological paradigm: A revised NEP scale. *Journal of Social Issues* 56: 425–442.

Eckersley, Robyn. 2002. Environmental pragmatism, ecocentrism, and deliberative democracy: Between problem-solving and fundamental critique. In *Democracy and the claims of nature: Critical perspectives for a new century,* edited by Ben A. Minteer and Bob Pepperman Taylor, 49–69. Lanham, MD: Rowman and Littlefield.

Ehrenfeld, David. 2000. War and peace and conservation biology. *Conservation Biology* 14: 105–112.
Ehrlich, Paul R. 1968. *The population bomb.* New York: Ballantine.
———. 2003. Bioethics: Are our priorities right? *BioScience* 53: 1207–1216.
Eldridge, Michael. 1998. *Transforming experience: John Dewey's cultural instrumentalism.* Nashville, TN: Vanderbilt University Press.
Elliott, Deni, and Judy E. Stern, eds. 1997. *Research ethics: A reader.* Hanover, NH: University Press of New England.
Elliot, Robert. 1997. *Faking nature: The ethics of environmental restoration.* London: Routledge.
Farnsworth, Elizabeth J., and Judy Rosovsky. 1993. The ethics of ecological field experimentation. *Conservation Biology* 7: 463–472.
Feffer, Andrew. 1993. *The Chicago pragmatists and American progressivism.* Ithaca, NY: Cornell University Press.
Festenstein, Matthew. 1997. *Pragmatism and political theory: From Dewey to Rorty.* Chicago: University of Chicago Press.
Fins, Joseph J., Matthew D. Bacchetta, and Franklin G. Miller. 1997. Clinical pragmatism: A method for moral problem solving. *Kennedy Institute of Ethics Journal* 7: 129–145.
Fish, Stanley. 1999. *The trouble with principle.* Cambridge, MA: Harvard University Press.
Fisher, Roger, and William L. Ury. 1991. *Getting to yes: Negotiating agreement without giving in.* New York: Penguin Books.
Fishkin, James S. 1991. *Democracy and deliberation: New directions in democratic reform.* New Haven, CT: Yale University Press.
———. 2009. *When the people speak: Deliberative democracy and public consultation.* Oxford, UK: Oxford University Press.
Flathman, Richard E. 1966. *The public interest: An essay concerning the normative discourse of politics.* New York: John Wiley and Sons.
Flourney, Alyson C. 2003. Building an environmental ethic from the ground up. *UC Davis Law Review* 37: 53–80.
Foot, Philippa. 2002. *Virtues and vices and other essays in moral philosophy.* Oxford, UK: Oxford University Press.
Fox, Douglas. 2007. Back to the no-analog future? *Science* 316: 823–825.
———. 2008. Solar energy trumps shade in California prosecution of tree owner. *Christian Science Monitor.* March 18.
Fox, Renee C., and Judith P. Swazey. 2008. *Observing bioethics.* Oxford, UK: Oxford University Press.
Fox, Stephen R. 1981. *John Muir and his legacy: The American conservation movement.* Boston: Little, Brown.
Freyfogle, Eric T. 2003. *The land we share: Private property and the common good.* Washington, DC: Island Press/Shearwater.
Frodeman, Robert. 2006. The policy turn in environmental philosophy. *Environmental Ethics* 28: 3–20.
Gavaghan, Helen. 2002. Life in the deep freeze. *Nature* 415: 828–830.
Geertz, Clifford. 1973. *The interpretation of cultures.* New York: Basic Books.
Gelbspan, Ross. 2005. *Boiling point: How politicians, big oil and coal, journalists, and activists have fueled a climate crisis—and what we can do to avert disaster.* New York: Basic Books.
Giles, Jim. 2004. Russian bid to drill Antarctic lake gets chilly response. *Nature* 430: 494.
Gobster, Paul H., and R. Bruce Hull, eds. 2000. *Restoring nature: Perspectives from the social sciences and the humanities.* Washington, DC: Island Press.

Goodin, Robert. E. 1995. *Utilitarianism as a public philosophy.* New York: Cambridge University Press.

———. 1996. Institutionalizing the public interest: The defense of deadlock and beyond. *American Political Science Review* 90: 331–343.

Goodpaster, Kenneth. 1978. On being morally considerable. *Journal of Philosophy* 75: 308–325.

Gottlieb, Robert. 1993. *Forcing the spring: The transformation of the American environmental movement.* Washington, DC: Island Press.

Gouinlock, James. 1990. What is the legacy of instrumentalism? Rorty's interpretation of Dewey. *Journal of the History of Philosophy* 28: 251–269.

Groombridge, Brian, and Martin D. Jenkins. 2002. *World atlas of biodiversity.* Berkeley: University of California Press.

Guber, Deborah Lynn. 2003. *The grassroots of a green revolution: Polling America on the environment.* Cambridge, MA: MIT Press.

Gundersen, Adolf G. 1995. *The environmental promise of democratic deliberation.* Madison: University of Wisconsin Press.

Gunderson, L. H., Craig R. Allen, and C. S. Holling, eds. 2009. *Foundations of ecological resilience.* Washington, DC: Island Press.

Gunderson, L. H., and C. S. Holling, eds. 2002. *Panarchy: Understanding transformations in human and natural systems.* Washington, DC: Island Press.

Gunderson, L. H., C. S. Holling, and Stephen S. Light, eds. 1995. *Barriers and bridges to the renewal of ecosystems and institutions.* New York: Columbia University Press.

Gunn, Giles. 1992. *Thinking across the American grain: Ideology, intellect, and the new pragmatism.* Chicago: University of Chicago Press.

———. 1998. Religion and the recent revival of pragmatism. In *The revival of pragmatism: New essays on social thought, law, and culture,* edited by Morris Dickstein, 404–417. Durham, NC: Duke University Press.

Gurung, K. K. 1983. *Heart of the jungle: The wildlife of Chitwan, Nepal.* London, UK: Andrew Deutsch.

Gutmann, Amy, and Dennis Thompson. 1996. *Democracy and disagreement.* Cambridge, MA: Harvard University Press.

Haack, Susan. 2004. Pragmatism, old and new. *Contemporary Pragmatism* 1: 3–41.

Halsey, Ashley, III. 2009. Deeply divided panel backs eradication of mute swans. *Washington Post.* May 16.

Hamner, M. Gail. 2002. *American pragmatism: A religious genealogy.* Oxford, UK: Oxford University Press.

Hannah, L. 2008. Protected areas and climate change. *Annals of the New York Academy of Sciences* 1134: 201–212.

Hannah, L., Guy Midgley, Sandy Andelman, Miguel Araújo, Greg Hughes, Enrique Martinez-Meyer, Richard Pearson, and Paul Williams. 2007. Protected area needs in a changing climate. *Frontiers in Ecology and the Environment* 5: 131–138.

Hannah, L., G. F. Midgley, T. Lovejoy, W. J. Bond, M. Bush, J. C. Lovett, D. Scott, and F. I. Woodward. 2002. Conservation of biodiversity in a changing climate. *Conservation Biology* 16: 264–268.

Hargrove, Eugene, ed. 1992. *The animal rights/environmental ethics debate: The environmental perspective.* Albany, NY: SUNY Press.

———. 2003. What's wrong? Who's to blame? *Environmental Ethics* 25: 3–4.

Hays, Samuel P. 2006. *Wars in the woods: The rise of ecological forestry in America.* Pittsburgh, PA: University of Pittsburgh Press.

Held, Virginia. 1970. *The public interest and individual interests.* New York: Basic Books.

Henson, A., D. Williams, J. Dupain, H. Gichohi, and P. Muruthi. 2009. The heartland conservation process: Enhancing biodiversity conservation and livelihoods through landscape-scale conservation planning in Africa. *Oryx* 43: 508–519.

Hickman, Larry. 2001. *Philosophical tools for technological culture: Putting pragmatism to work.* Bloomington: Indiana University Press.

Higgs, Eric S., and Richard J. Hobbs. 2010. Wild design: Principles to guide interventions in protected areas. In *Beyond naturalness: Rethinking park and wilderness stewardship in an era of rapid change,* edited by David N. Cole and Laurie Yung, 234–251. Washington, DC: Island Press.

Hill, Thomas E., Jr. 2000. *Respect, pluralism, and justice: Kantian perspectives.* Oxford, UK: Oxford University Press.

Hobbs, Richard J., Salvatore Arico, James Aronson, Jill S. Baron, Peter Bridgewater, Viki A. Cramer, Paul R. Epstein, John J. Ewel, Carlos A. Klink, Ariel E. Lugo, David Norton, Dennis Ojima, David M. Richardson, Eric W. Sanderson, Fernando Valladares, Montserrat Vilà, Regino Zamora, and Martin Zobel. 2006. Novel ecosystems: Theoretical and management aspects of the new ecological world order. *Global Ecology and Biogeography* 15: 1–7.

Hobbs, Richard J., David N. Cole, Laurie Yung, Erika S. Zavaleta, Gregory H. Aplet, F. Stuart Chapin, Peter B. Landres, David J. Parsons, Nathan L. Stephenson, Peter S. White, David M Graber, Eric S. Higgs, Constance I. Millar, John M. Randall, Kathy A. Tonnessen, and Stephen Woodley. 2010. Guiding concepts for park and wilderness stewardship in an era of global environmental change. *Frontiers in Ecology and the Environment* 8: 483–490.

Hobbs, Richard J., and Viki A. Cramer. 2008. Restoration ecology: Interventionist approaches for restoring and maintaining ecosystem function in the face of rapid environmental change. *Annual Review of Environment and Resources* 33: 39–61.

Hobbs, Richard J., Eric Higgs, and James A. Harris. 2009. Novel ecosystems: Implications for conservation and restoration. *Trends in Ecology and Evolution* 24: 599–605.

Hoddle, Mark S. 2004. Restoring balance: Using exotic species to control invasive exotic species. *Conservation Biology* 18: 38–49.

Hoegh-Guldberg, O., L. Hughes, S. McIntyre, D. B. Lindenmayer, C. Parmesan, H. P. Possingham, and C. D. Thomas. 2008. Assisted colonization and rapid climate change. *Science* 321: 345–346.

Hoegh-Guldberg, O., P. J. Mumby, A. J. Hooten, R. S. Steneck, P. Greenfield, E. Gomez, C. D. Harvell, P. F. Sale, A. J. Edwards, K. Caldeira, N. Knowlton C. M. Eakin, R. Iglesias-Prieto, N. Muthiga, R. H. Bradbury, A. Dubi, and M. E. Hatziolos. 2007. Coral reefs under rapid climate change and ocean acidification. *Science* 318: 1737–1742.

Hooker, Brad. 2000. *Ideal code, real world.* Oxford, UK: Clarendon Press.

Huang, Danwei. 2008. Assisted colonization won't help rare species. *Science* 322: 1049.

IPCC. 2007. *Climate change 2007: Synthesis report. Contribution of Working Groups I, II and III to the Fourth Assessment Report of the Intergovernmental Panel on Climate Change* [Core Writing Team, R. K. Pachauri and A. Reisinger (eds.)]. Geneva, Switzerland.

Jacobs, Lawrence R., Fay Lomax Cook, and Michael X. Delli Carpini. 2009. *Talking together: Public deliberation and political participation in America.* Chicago: University of Chicago Press.

James, Michael. 1981. Public interest and majority rule in Bentham's democratic theory. *Political Theory* 9: 49–64.

James, William. 1920. *A pluralistic universe.* New York: Longmans, Green.

Jamieson, Dale. 1998a. Animal liberation is an environmental ethic. *Environmental Values* 7: 41–57.

———. 1998b. Sustainability and beyond. *Ecological Economics* 24: 183–192.

———. 2001. Climate change and global environmental justice. In *Changing the atmosphere: Expert knowledge and global environmental governance,* edited by Clark A. Miller and Paul N. Edwards, 287–307. Cambridge, MA: MIT Press.

———. 2005. Adaptation, mitigation, and justice. In *Perspectives on climate change: Science, economics, politics, ethics,* edited by Walter Sinnott-Armstrong and Richard B. Howarth, 217–248. Amsterdam: Elsevier.

———. 2008. *Ethics and the environment: An introduction.* Cambridge, UK: Cambridge University Press.

Kant, Immanuel. 1998. *Groundwork of the metaphysics of morals.* Cambridge, UK: Cambridge University Press.

Katz, Eric. 1991. Defending the use of animals by business: Animal liberation and environmental ethics. In *Business, ethics and the environment: The public policy debate,* edited by W. M. Hoffman, R. Frederick, and E. S. Petry, Jr., 223–232. New York: Quorum Books.

———. 1997. *Nature as subject: Human obligation and natural community.* Lanham, MD: Rowman and Littlefield.

———. 2009. Convergence and ecological restoration: A counterexample. In *Nature in common? Environmental ethics and the contested foundations of environmental policy,* edited by Ben A. Minteer, 185–195. Philadelphia: Temple University Press.

Katz, Eric, and Lauren Oechsli. 1993. Moving beyond anthropocentrism: Environmental ethics, development, and the Amazon. *Environmental Ethics* 15: 49–59.

Keeley, Jon E. 2006. Fire management impacts on invasive plants in the western United States. *Conservation Biology* 20: 375–384.

Keiter, Robert B. 2001. The monument, the plan, and beyond. *Journal of Land, Resources, and Environmental Law* 21: 521–533.

———. 2003. *Keeping faith with nature: Ecosystems, democracy, and America's public lands.* New Haven, CT: Yale University Press.

Keller, Klaus, Gary Yohe, and Michael Schlesinger. 2008. Managing the risks of climate thresholds: Uncertainties and information needs. *Climatic Change* 91: 5–10.

Kellert, Stephen R. 1996. *The value of life: Biological diversity and human society.* Washington, DC: Island Press/Shearwater.

Kempton, W. M., J. S. Boster, and J. A. Hartley. 1995. *Environmental values in American culture.* Cambridge, MA: MIT Press.

Kloppenberg, James T. 1998. Pragmatism: An old name for some new ways of thinking? In *The revival of pragmatism: New essays on social thought, law, and culture,* edited by Morris Dickstein, 83–127. Durham, NC: Duke University Press.

Knight, Richard L., and Suzanne Riedel, eds. 2002. *Aldo Leopold and the ecological conscience.* Oxford, UK: Oxford University Press.

Krimsky, Sheldon. 2003. *Science in the private interest: Has the lure of profits corrupted biomedical research?* Lanham, MD: Rowman and Littlefield.

Lawler, Joshua J., Timothy T. Tear, Chris Pyke, M. Rebecca Shaw, Patrick Gonzalez, Peter Kareiva, Lara Hansen, Lee Hannah, Kirk Klausmeyer, Allison Aldous, Craig Bienz, and Sam Pearsall. 2010. Resource management in a changing and uncertain climate. *Frontiers in Ecology and the Environment* 8: 35–43.

Lee, J. J. 2005. Animal rights group sues over Steller sea lion research. *Seattle Times.* July 14.

Lee, Kai N. 1993. *Compass and gyroscope: Integrating science and politics for the environment.* Washington, DC: Island Press.

Leiserowitz, Anthony. 2006. Climate change risk perception and policy preferences: The role of affect, imagery, and values. *Climatic Change* 77: 45–72.

Leiserowitz, Anthony, Nicholas Smith, and Jennifer R. Marlon. 2010. *Americans' knowledge of climate change.* New Haven, CT: Yale Project on Climate Change Communication.

Available at http://environment.yale.edu/climate/files/ClimateChangeKnowledge2010.pdf.

Lélé, Sharachchandra, and Richard B. Norgaard. 1996. Sustainability and the scientist's burden. *Conservation Biology* 10: 354–365.

Lemons, John. 2007. Nature diminished or nature managed: Applying Rolston's environmental ethics in national parks. In *Nature, value, duty: Life on Earth with Holmes Rolston, III,* edited by Christopher J. Preston and Wayne Ouderkirk, 203–219. Dordrecht, Netherlands: Springer.

Lenton, Timothy M., Hermann Held, Elmar Kriegler, Jim W. Hall, Wolfgang Lucht, Stefan Rahmstorf, and Hans Joachim Schellnhuber. 2008. Tipping elements in the Earth's climate system. *Proceedings of the National Academy of Sciences* 105: 1786–1793.

Leopold, Aldo. 1949. *A Sand County almanac.* Oxford, UK: Oxford University Press.

———. 1991 (orig. 1923). Some fundamentals of conservation in the Southwest. In *The river of the mother of God: And other essays by Aldo Leopold,* edited by Susan L. Flader and J. Baird Callicott, 86–97. Madison: University of Wisconsin Press.

Light, Andrew. 2000. Ecological restoration and the culture of nature: A pragmatic perspective. In *Restoring nature: Perspectives from the social sciences and humanities,* edited by Paul Gobster and Bruce Hull, 49–70. Washington, DC: Island Press.

———. 2002. Contemporary environmental ethics: From metaethics to public philosophy. *Metaphilosophy* 33: 426–449.

———. 2004. Methodological pragmatism, animal welfare, and hunting. In *Animal pragmatism: Rethinking human-nonhuman relationships,* edited by E. McKenna and A. Light, 119–139. Bloomington: Indiana University Press.

Light, Andrew, and Eric Higgs. 1996. The politics of ecological restoration. *Environmental Ethics* 18: 227–247.

Light, Andrew, and Eric Katz, eds. 1996. *Environmental pragmatism.* London: Routledge.

Light, Andrew, and Holmes Rolston III. 2002. *Environmental ethics: An anthology.* Malden, MA: Blackwell.

Lippmann, Walter. 1955. *The public philosophy.* New York: New American Library.

Lips, Karen R., John D. Reeve, and Lani R. Witters. 2003. Ecological traits predicting amphibian population declines in Central America. *Conservation Biology* 17: 1078–1088.

List, Peter C., ed. 2000. *Environmental ethics and forestry: A reader.* Philadelphia: Temple University Press.

Lodge, David M., and Kristin Shrader-Frechette. 2003. Nonindigenous species: Ecological explanation, environmental ethics, and public policy. *Conservation Biology* 17: 31–37.

Loeb, Don. 1996. Generality and moral justification. *Philosophy and Phenomenological Research* 56: 79–96.

Lubchenco, Jane. 1998. Entering the century of the environment: A new social contract for science. *Science* 279: 491–497.

Lubick, Naomi. 2010. Emergency medicine for frogs. *Nature* 465: 680–681.

MacIntyre, Alasdair. 2007. *After virtue: A study in moral theory.* Third edition. Notre Dame, IN: University of Notre Dame Press.

Marris, Emma. 2008. Moving on assisted migration. *Nature Reports* 2: 112–113.

———. 2009. Ragamuffin Earth. *Nature* 460: 450–453.

Marsh, Helene, and Carole Eros. 1999. Ethics of field research: Do journals set the standard? *Science and Engineering Ethics* 5: 375–382.

Marsh, Helene, and Richard Kenchington. 2004. The role of ethics in experimental marine biology and ecology. *Journal of Experimental Marine Biology and Ecology* 300: 5–14.

May, Robert M. 2004. Ethics and amphibians. *Nature* 431: 403.

McCarthy, Michael A., and Kirsten M. Parris. 2004. Clarifying the effect of toe clipping on frogs with Bayesian statistics. *Journal of Applied Ecology* 41: 780–786.

McLachlan, Jason S., Jessica J. Hellmann, and Mark W. Schwartz. 2007. A framework for debate of assisted migration in an era of climate change. *Conservation Biology* 21: 297–302.

McLean, Joanne, and Steffen Straede. 2003. Conservation, relocation, and the paradigm of park and people management—a case study of Padampur villages and the Royal Chitwan National Park, Nepal. *Society and Natural Resources* 16: 509–526.

McShane, T. O., P. D. Hirsch, T. C. Trung, A. N. Songorwa, A. Kinzig, B. Monteferri, D. Mutekanga, H. Van Thang, J. L. Dammert, M. Pulgar-Vidal, M. Welch-Devine, J. P. Brosius, P. Coppolillo, and S. O'Connor. 2011. Hard choices: Making trade-offs between biodiversity conservation and human well-being. *Biological Conservation* 144: 966–972.

McShane, T. O., and Michael P. Wells, eds. 2004. *Getting biodiversity projects to work: Towards more effective conservation and development.* New York: Columbia University Press.

Mearns, Robin, and Andrew Norton, eds. 2009. *The social dimensions of climate change: Equity and vulnerability in a warming world.* Washington, DC: World Bank Publications.

Menand, Louis. 2001. *The metaphysical club: A story of ideas in America.* New York: Farrar, Straus, and Giroux.

Merriam, Kyle E., Tom W. McGinnis, and Jon E. Keeley. 2004. The role of fire and fire management in the invasion of nonnative plants in California. *Park Science* 22: 32–36, 52.

Milbrath, Lester W. 1984. *Environmentalists: Vanguard for a new society.* Albany, NY: SUNY Press.

Mill, John Stuart. 2002. *The basic writings of John Stuart Mill: On liberty, the subjection of women and utilitarianism.* Modern Library edition. New York: Random House.

Millennium Ecosystem Assessment. 2005. *Ecosystems and human well-being: Our human planet: Summary for decision makers.* Washington, DC: Island Press.

Miller, Franklin G., Joseph J. Fins, and Matthew D. Bacchetta. 1996. Clinical pragmatism: John Dewey and clinical ethics. *Journal of Contemporary Health Law and Policy* 13: 27–51.

Miller, Thaddeus R., Ben A. Minteer, and Leon-C. Malan. 2011. The new conservation debate: The view from practical ethics. *Biological Conservation* 144: 948–957.

Milly, P.C.D., Julio Betancourt, Malin Falkenmark, Robert M. Hirsch, Zbigniew W. Kundzewicz, Dennis P. Lettenmaier, and Ronald J. Stouffer. 2008. Stationarity is dead: Whither water management? *Science* 319: 573–574.

Minteer, Ben A. 1998. No experience necessary? Foundationalism and the retreat from culture in environmental ethics. *Environmental Values* 7: 333–348.

———. 2006. *The landscape of reform: Civic pragmatism and environmental thought in America.* Cambridge, MA: MIT Press.

———. 2008. Biocentric farming? Liberty Hyde Bailey and environmental ethics. *Environmental Ethics* 30: 341–359.

———, ed. 2009. *Nature in common? Environmental ethics and the contested foundations of environmental policy.* Philadelphia: Temple University Press.

Minteer, Ben A., and Robert E. Manning. 1999. Pragmatism in environmental ethics: Democracy, pluralism, and the management of nature. *Environmental Ethics* 21: 193–209.

———. 2000. Convergence in environmental values: An empirical and conceptual defense. *Ethics, Place, and Environment* 3: 47–60.

Monamy, Vaughan, and Miranda Gott. 2001. Practical and ethical considerations for students conducting ecological research involving wildlife. *Austral Ecology* 26: 293–300.

Murphy, Timothy F. 2004. *Case studies in biomedical research ethics.* Cambridge, MA: MIT Press.

Nash, Roderick F. 2001. *Wilderness and the American mind.* Fourth edition. New Haven, CT: Yale University Press.

National Oceanic and Atmospheric Association. 2007. *Steller sea lion and northern fur seal research: Final programmatic environmental impact statement.* Available at www.nmfs.noaa.gov/pr/permits/eis/steller.htm.

National Oceanic and Atmospheric Association–National Marine Fisheries Service. 2006. Newsletter: *Steller sea lion and northern fur seal research environmental impact statement.* Available at www.nmfs.noaa.gov/pr/pdfs/permits/steller_newsletter.pdf.

National Research Council. 2003. *Decline of the Steller sea lion in Alaskan Waters: Untangling food webs and fishing nets.* Washington, DC: National Academies Press.

Nature. 2004. Editorial: Precaution versus principles. *Nature* 429: 585.

———. 2006. News in Brief: Court settlement puts sea lions back under scrutiny. *Nature* 442: 121.

Nelson, Michael P., and J. Baird Callicott, eds. 2008. *The wilderness debate rages on: Continuing the great new wilderness debate.* Athens: University of Georgia Press.

Nepal, Sanjay K., and Karl E. Weber. 1995. The quandary of local people—park relations in Nepal's Royal Chitwan National Park. *Environmental Management* 19: 853–866.

Newton, Julianne Lutz, and Eric T. Freyfogle. 2005. Sustainability: A dissent. *Conservation Biology* 19: 23–32.

Nisbet, Matthew C., and Teresa Myers. 2007. The polls—trends: Twenty years of public opinion about global warming. *Public Opinion Quarterly* 71: 444–470.

Nordhaus, Ted, and Michael Shellenberger. 2007. *Break through: From the death of environmentalism to the politics of possibility.* Boston: Houghton Mifflin.

Norton, Bryan G. 1984. Environmental ethics and weak anthropocentrism. *Environmental Ethics* 6: 131–148.

———. 1986. Conservation and preservation: A conceptual rehabilitation. *Environmental Ethics* 8: 195–220.

———. 1987. *Why preserve natural variety?* Princeton, NJ: Princeton University Press.

———. 1991. *Toward unity among environmentalists.* Oxford, UK: Oxford University Press.

———. 1992. Epistemology and environmental values. *Monist* 75: 208–226.

———. 1995. Why I am not a nonanthropocentrist: Callicott and the failure of monistic inherentism. *Environmental Ethics* 17: 341–358.

———. 1996. Integration or reduction: Two approaches to environmental values. In *Environmental pragmatism,* edited by Andrew Light and Eric Katz, 105–138. London: Routledge.

———. 1998. Improving ecological communication: The role of ecologists in environmental policy formation. *Ecological Applications* 8: 350–364.

———. 2003. Which morals matter? Freeing moral reasoning from ideology. *UC Davis Law Review* 37: 81–94.

———. 2005. *Sustainability: A philosophy of adaptive ecosystem management.* Chicago: University of Chicago Press.

———. 2009. Convergence and divergence: The convergence hypothesis twenty years later. In *Nature in common? Environmental ethics and the contested foundations of environmental policy,* edited by Ben A. Minteer, 235–259. Philadelphia: Temple University Press.

Norton, Bryan G., Michael Hutchins, Elizabeth F. Stevens, and Terry L. Maple, eds. 1995. *Ethics on the Ark: Zoos, animal welfare, and wildlife conservation.* Washington, DC: Smithsonian Institution Press.

Norton, Bryan, and Ben Minteer. 2002. From environmental ethics to environmental public philosophy: Ethicists and economists, 1973–future. In *International yearbook of environ-*

mental and resource economics 2002/2003, edited by Tom Tietenberg and Henk Folmer, 373–407. Cheltenham, UK: Edward Elgar.

Norton, Bryan G., and Anne C. Steinemann. 2001. Environmental values and adaptive management. *Environmental Values* 10: 473–506.

Nozick, Robert. 1974. *Anarchy, state, and utopia.* New York: Basic Books.

Odenbaugh, Jay. 2003. Values, advocacy and conservation biology. *Environmental Values* 12: 55–69.

Oelschlaeger, Max. 1994. *Caring for creation: An ecumenical approach to the environmental crisis.* New Haven, CT: Yale University Press.

O'Leary, Rosemary, Robert F. Durant, Daniel J. Fiorino, and Paul S. Weiland. 1998. *Managing for the environment.* San Francisco: Jossey-Bass.

O'Leary, Rosemary, Tina Nabatchi, and Lisa B. Bingham. 2004. Environmental conflict resolution. In *Environmental governance reconsidered: Challenges, choices, and opportunities,* edited by Robert F. Durant, Daniel J. Fiorino, and Rosemary O'Leary, 323–354. Cambridge, MA: MIT Press.

O'Neil, Rick. 2000. Animal liberation versus environmentalism. *Environmental Ethics* 22: 183–190.

O'Neill, John. 2002. Deliberative democracy and environmental policy. In *Democracy and the claims of nature: Critical perspectives for a new century,* edited by Ben A. Minteer and Bob Pepperman Taylor, 257–275. Lanham, MD: Rowman and Littlefield.

O'Neill, John, Alan Holland, and Andrew Light. 2008. *Environmental values.* New York: Routledge.

O'Neill, Onora. 1989. *Constructions of reason.* New York: Cambridge University Press.

Oreskes, Naomi. 2004. The scientific consensus on climate change. *Science* 306: 1686.

Oreskes, Naomi, and Erik M. Conway. 2010. *Merchants of doubt: How a handful of scientists obscured the truth on issues from tobacco smoke to global warming.* New York: Bloomsbury Press.

Palmer, Margaret, Emily Bernhardt, Elizabeth Chornesky, Scott Collins, Andrew Dobson, Clifford Duke, Barry Gold, Robert Jacobson, Sharon Kingsland, Rhonda Kranz, Michael Mappin, M. Luisa Martinez, Fiorenza Micheli, Jennifer Morse, Michael Pace, Mercedes Pascual, Stephen Palumbi, O. J. Reichman, Ashley Simons, Alan Townsend, and Monica Turner. 2004. Ecology for a crowded planet. *Science* 304: 1251–1252.

Pappas, Gregory. 1998. Dewey's ethics: Morality as experience. In *Reading Dewey: Interpretations for a postmodern generation,* edited by Larry Hickman, 100–123. Bloomington: Indiana University Press.

Parmesan, Camille. 2006. Ecological and evolutionary responses to recent climate change. *Annual Review of Ecology, Evolution, and Systematics* 37: 637–669.

Parmesan, Camille, and Gary Yohe. 2003. A globally coherent fingerprint of climate change impacts across natural systems. *Nature* 421: 37–42.

Parris, Kirsten M., Sarah C. McCall, Michael A. McCarthy, Ben A. Minteer, Katie Steele, Sarah Bekessy, and Fabien Medvecky. 2010. Assessing ethical trade-offs in ecological field studies. *Journal of Applied Ecology* 47: 227–234.

Passmore, John. 1974. *Man's responsibility for nature: Ecological problems and Western traditions.* New York: Charles Scribner's Sons.

Pence, Gregory E. 2007. *Medical ethics: Accounts of the cases that shaped and define medical ethics.* Fifth edition. New York: McGraw-Hill.

Perry, Dan, and Gad Perry. 2008. Improving interactions between animal rights groups and conservation biologists. *Conservation Biology* 22: 27–35.

Pew Center for Global Climate Change. 2009. *Key scientific developments since the IPCC Fourth Assessment Report.* Available at www.pewclimate.org/brief/science-developments/June2009.

Pielke, Roger, Jr., Gwyn Prins, Steve Rayner, and Daniel Sarewitz. 2007. Climate change 2007: Lifting the taboo on adaptation. *Nature* 445: 597–598.

Pielke, Roger, Jr., and Daniel Sarewitz. 2002. Wanted: Scientific leadership on climate. *Issues in Science and Technology* Winter: 27–30.

Pojman, Louis P., and Paul Pojman, eds. 2007. *Environmental ethics: Readings in theory and application.* Fifth edition. Belmont, CA: Thomson/Wadsworth.

Posner, Richard A. 2003. *Law, pragmatism, and democracy.* Cambridge, MA: Harvard University Press.

Potvin, Catherine, Margaret Kraenzel, and Gilles Seutin, eds. 2001. *Protecting biological diversity: Roles and responsibilities.* Montreal: McGill–Queen's University Press.

Pounds, J. Alan, Martín R. Bustamante, Luis A. Coloma, Jamie A. Consuegra, Michael P. L. Fogden, Pru N. Foster, Enrique La Marca, Karen L. Masters, Andrés Merino-Viteri, Robert Puschendorf, Santiago R. Ron, G. Arturo Sánchez-Azofeifa, Christopher J. Still, and Bruce E. Young. 2006. Widespread amphibian extinctions from epidemic disease driven by global warming. *Nature* 439: 161–167.

Pressey, Robert L., Mar Cabeza, Matthew E. Watts, Richard M. Cowling, and Kerrie A. Wilson. 2007. Conservation planning in a changing world. *Trends in Ecology and Evolution* 22: 583–592.

Putnam, Hilary. 1992. *Renewing philosophy.* Cambridge, MA: Harvard University Press.

———. 1994. *Words and life.* Cambridge, MA: Harvard University Press.

Rawls, John. 1971. *A theory of justice.* Cambridge, MA: Belknap/Harvard University Press.

Reaser, J. K., and R. E. Dexter. 1996. *Rana pretiosa* (spotted frog). Toe clipping effects. *Herpetological Review* 27: 195–196.

Regan, Tom. 2004. *The case for animal rights.* Updated edition. Berkeley: University of California Press.

Rex, Erica. 2010. Skin fight: Could bacteria carried by amphibians save them from extinction? *Scientific American.* Available at www.scientificamerican.com/article.cfm?id=skin-fight-bacteria-frogs.

Ricciardi, Anthony, and Daniel Simberloff. 2009a. Assisted colonization: Good intentions and dubious risk assessment. *Trends in Ecology and Evolution* 24: 476–477.

———. 2009b. Assisted colonization is not a viable conservation strategy. *Trends in Ecology and Evolution* 24: 248–253.

Richardson, D. M., J. J. Hellmann, J. McLachlan, D. F. Sax, M. W. Schwartz, J. Brennan, P. Gonzalez, T. Root, O. Sala, S. H. Schneider, D. Ashe, A. Camacho, J. Rappaport Clark, R. Early, J. Etterson, D. Fielder, J. Gill, B. A. Minteer, S. Polasky, H. Safford, A. Thompson, and M. Vellend. 2009. Multidimensional evaluation of managed relocation. *Proceedings of the National Academy of Sciences* 106: 9721–9724.

Richardson, Henry S. 1990. Specifying norms as a way to resolve concrete ethical problems. *Philosophy and Public Affairs* 19: 279–310.

Rippe, Klaus P., and Peter Schaber. 1999. Democracy and environmental decision-making. *Environmental Values* 8: 75–88.

Robinson, Jackie, Beth Clouston, Jungho Suh, and Milani Chaloupka. 2008. Are citizens' juries a useful tool for assessing environmental value? *Environmental Conservation* 35: 351–360.

Robinson, John G. 1993. The limits to caring: Sustainable living and the loss of biodiversity. *Conservation Biology* 7: 20–28.

———. 2011. Ethical pluralism, pragmatism, and sustainability in conservation practice. *Biological Conservation* 144: 958–965.

Rockefeller, Steven C. 1991. *John Dewey: Religious faith and democratic humanism.* New York: Columbia University Press.

———. 1998. "Dewey's philosophy of religious experience." In *Reading Dewey: Interpretations for a postmodern generation,* edited by Larry A. Hickman, 124–148. Bloomington: Indiana University Press.

Roe, Dilys, and Joanna Elliot. 2004. Poverty reduction and biodiversity conservation: Rebuilding the bridges. *Oryx* 38: 137–139.

Rogers, Melvin L. 2008. *The undiscovered Dewey: Religion, morality, and the ethos of democracy.* New York: Columbia University Press.

Rolston, Holmes, III. 1975. Is there an ecological ethic? *Ethics* 85: 93–109.

———. 1986. *Philosophy gone wild: Environmental ethics.* Buffalo, NY: Prometheus Books.

———. 1988. *Environmental ethics: Duties to and values in the natural world.* Philadelphia: Temple University Press.

———. 1991. The wilderness idea reaffirmed. *Environmental Professional* 13: 370–377.

———. 1994. *Conserving natural value.* New York: Columbia University Press.

———. 1998. Saving nature, feeding people, and the foundations of ethics. *Environmental Values* 7: 349–357.

———. 1999. Respect for life: Counting what Singer finds of no account. In *Singer and his critics,* edited by Dale Jamieson, 247–268. Oxford, UK: Blackwell.

———. 2004. In situ and ex situ conservation: Philosophical and ethical concerns. In *Ex situ plant conservation: Supporting species in the wild,* edited by Edward O. Guerrant, Jr., Kayri Havens, and Mike Maunder, 21–39. Washington, DC: Island Press.

———. 2009. Converging versus reconstituting environmental ethics. In *Nature in common? Environmental ethics and the contested foundations of environmental policy,* edited by Ben A. Minteer, 97–117. Philadelphia: Temple University Press.

Root, Terry L., and Lesley Hughes. 2005. Present and future phenological changes in wild plants and animals. In *Climate change and biodiversity,* edited by T. E. Lovejoy and L. Hannah. New Haven, CT: Yale University Press.

Root, Terry L., Jeff T. Price, Kimberly R. Hall, Stephen H. Schneider, Cynthia Rosenzweig, and J. Alan Pounds. 2003. Fingerprints of global warming on wild animals and plants. *Nature* 421: 57–60.

Root, Terry L., and Stephen H. Schneider. 2006. Conservation and climate change: The challenges ahead. *Conservation Biology* 20: 706–708.

Rorty, Richard. 1991. *Objectivity, relativism, and truth.* New York: Cambridge University Press.

———. 1995. Response to James Gouinlock. In *Rorty and pragmatism: The philosopher responds to his critics,* edited by Herman Saatkamp, Jr., 91–99. Nashville, TN: Vanderbilt University Press.

———. 1999. *Philosophy and social hope.* London: Penguin Books.

Rosenzweig, C., G. Casassa, D. J. Karoly, A. Imeson, C. Liu, A. Menzel, S. Rawlins, T. L. Root, B. Seguin, and P. Tryjanowski. 2007. Assessment of observed changes and responses in natural and managed systems. In *Climate change 2007: Impacts, adaptation and vulnerability. Contribution of Working Group II to the Fourth Assessment Report of the Intergovernmental Panel on Climate Change,* edited by M. L. Parry, O. F. Canziani, J. P. Palutikof, P. J. van der Linden, and C. E. Hanson, 79–131. Cambridge, UK: Cambridge University Press.

Ross, W. D. 1930. *The right and the good.* Oxford, UK: Clarendon Press.

Routley, Richard. 1973. Is there a need for a new, an environmental ethic? *Proceedings of the XVth World Congress of Philosophy* 1: 205–210.

Runte, Alfred. 1997. *National parks: The American experience.* Third edition. Lincoln: University of Nebraska Press.

Sabatier, Paul A., Will Focht, Mark Lubell, Zev Trachtenberg, Arnold Vedlitz, and Marty Matlock, eds. 2005. *Swimming upstream: Collaborative approaches to watershed management.* Cambridge, MA: MIT Press.

Sachs, J. D., J.E.M. Baillie, W. J. Sutherland, P. R. Armsworth, N. Ash, J. Beddington, T. M. Blackburn, B. Collen, B. Gardiner, K. J. Gaston, H.C.J. Godfray, R. E. Green, P. H. Harvey, B. House, S. Knapp, N. F. Kümpel, D. W. Macdonald, G. M. Mace, J. Mallet, A. Matthews, R. M. May, O. Petchey, A. Purvis, D. Roe, K. Safi, K. Turner, M. Walpole, R. Watson, and K. E. Jones. 2009. Biodiversity conservation and the millennium development goals. *Science* 25: 1502–1503.

Sagoff, Mark. 1984. Animal liberation and environmental ethics: Bad marriage, quick divorce. *Osgoode Hall Law Journal* 22: 297–307.

———. 1998. Aggregation and deliberation in valuing environmental public goods: A look beyond contingent pricing. *Ecological Economics* 24: 213–230.

———. 2005. Do non-native species threaten the natural environment? *Journal of Agricultural and Environmental Ethics* 18: 215–236.

———. 2007. *The economy of the Earth: Philosophy, law, and the environment.* Second edition. New York: Cambridge University Press.

Sala, Osvaldo E., F. Stuart Chapin III, Juan J. Armesto, Eric Berlow, Janine Bloomfield, Rodolfo Dirzo, Elisabeth Huber-Sanwald, Laura F. Huenneke, Robert B. Jackson, Ann Kinzig, Rik Leemans, David M. Lodge, Harold A. Mooney, Martín Oesterheld, N. LeRoy Poff, Martin T. Sykes, Brian H. Walker, Marilyn Walker, and Diana H. Wall. 2000. Global biodiversity scenarios for the year 2100. *Science* 287: 1770–1774.

Sandel, Michael J. 1996. *Democracy's discontent: America in search of a public philosophy.* Cambridge, MA: Harvard University Press.

———. 2005. *Public philosophy: Essays on morality and politics.* Cambridge, MA: Harvard University Press.

Sanders, Lynn M. 1997. Against deliberation. *Political Theory* 25: 347–376.

Sandler, Ronald. 2010. The value of species and the ethical foundations of assisted colonization. *Conservation Biology* 24: 424–431.

Sandler, Ronald, and Phaedra C. Pezzullo, eds. 2007. *Environmental justice and environmentalism: The social justice challenge to the environmental movement.* Cambridge, MA: MIT Press.

Sarewitz, Daniel. 2009. Who is converging with whom? An open letter to Professor Bryan Norton from a policy wonk. In *Nature in common? Environmental ethics and the contested foundations of environmental policy,* edited by Ben A. Minteer, 228–232. Philadelphia: Temple University Press.

Sarkar, Sahotra. 2005. *Biodiversity and environmental philosophy.* Cambridge, UK: Cambridge University Press.

Sax, Dov F., Katherine F. Smith, and Andrew R. Thompson. 2009. Managed relocation: A nuanced evaluation is needed. *Trends in Ecology and Evolution* 24: 472–473.

Schiermeier, Quirin. 2010. Teams set for first taste of Antarctic lakes. *Scientific American.* Available at www.scientificamerican.com/article.cfm?id=lake-vostok-drilling-antarctica.

Schlaepfer Martin A., William D. Helenbrook, Katherina B. Searing, and Kevin T. Shoemaker. 2009. Assisted colonization: Evaluating contrasting management actions (and values) in the face of uncertainty. *Trends in Ecology and Evolution* 24: 471–472.

Schubert, Glendon A. 1960. *The public interest.* Glencoe, IL: Free Press.

Seddon, Philip J., Doug P. Armstrong, Pritpal Soorae, Frederic Launay, Sally Walker, Carlos R. Ruiz-Miranda, Sanjay Molur, Heather Koldewey, and Devra G. Kleiman. 2009. The risks of assisted colonization. *Conservation Biology* 23: 788–789.

Seelye, Katharine Q. 2010. Big wind farm off Cape Cod gets approval. *New York Times.* April 28.

Shamoo, Adil E., and David B. Resnik. 2009. *Responsible conduct of research.* Second edition. Oxford, UK: Oxford University Press.

Shindler, Bruce, Peter List, and Brent Steel. 1993. Managing federal forests: Public attitudes in Oregon and nationwide. *Journal of Forestry* 91: 36–42.

Shrader-Frechette, Kristin. 1994. *Ethics of scientific research.* Lanham, MD: Rowman and Littlefield.

———. 2002. *Environmental justice: Creating equality, reclaiming democracy.* Oxford, UK: Oxford University Press.

Shrader-Frechette, K. S., and Earl D. McCoy. 1993. *Method in ecology: Strategies for conservation.* Cambridge, UK: Cambridge University Press.

———. 1999. Molecular systematics, ethics, and biological decision making under uncertainty. *Conservation Biology* 13: 1008–1012.

Shutkin, William A. 2000. *The land that could be: Environmental and democracy in the twenty-first century.* Cambridge, MA: MIT Press.

Singer, Peter. 1975. *Animal liberation: A new ethics for our treatment of animals.* New York: New York Review/Random House.

———. 1979. *Practical ethics.* Cambridge, UK: Cambridge University Press.

———. 1993. *Practical ethics.* Second edition. Cambridge, UK: Cambridge University Press.

———. 1999. A response. In *Singer and his critics,* edited by Dale Jamieson. Oxford, UK: Blackwell.

———. 2002a. *Animal liberation.* Revised edition. New York: Harper Collins.

———. 2002b. *One world: The ethics of globalization.* New Haven, CT: Yale University Press.

Siurua, Hanna. 2006. Nature above people: Rolston and "fortress" conservation in the South. *Ethics and the Environment* 11: 71–96.

Smith, John E. 1963. *The spirit of American philosophy.* New York: Oxford University Press.

———. 1978. *Purpose and thought: The meaning of pragmatism.* Chicago: University of Chicago Press.

Smith, Kimberly K. 2003. *Wendell Berry and the agrarian tradition: A common grace.* Lawrence: University Press of Kansas.

Snow, C. P. 1959. *The two cultures and the scientific revolution.* New York: Cambridge University Press.

Soto, Cristina G. 2001. The potential impacts of global climate change on marine protected areas. *Reviews in Fish Biology and Fisheries* 11: 181–195.

Souraf, Frank J. 1957. The public interest reconsidered. *Journal of Politics* 19: 616–639.

Stern, Nicholas. 2007. *The economics of climate change: The Stern review.* Cambridge, UK: Cambridge University Press.

———. 2009. *The global deal: Climate change and the creation of a new era of progress and prosperity.* New York: Public Affairs.

Stone, Christopher D. 1972. Should trees have standing? Toward legal rights for natural objects. *Southern California Law Review* 45: 450–501.

———. 1987. *Earth and other ethics: The case for moral pluralism.* New York: Harper and Row.

———. 2003. Do morals matter? The influence of ethics on courts and congress in shaping U.S. environmental policies. *UC Davis Law Review* 37: 13–51.

Straede, Steffen, and Finn Helles. 2000. Park-people conflict resolution in Royal Chitwan National Park, Nepal: Buying time at high cost? *Environmental Conservation* 27: 368–381.

Stuart, Simon N., Janice S. Chanson, Neil A. Cox, Bruce E. Young, Ana S. L. Rodrigues, Debra L. Fischman, and Robert W. Waller. 2004. Status and trends of amphibian declines and extinctions worldwide. *Science* 306: 1783–1786.

Sunderland, T.C.H., C. Ehringhaus, and B. M. Campbell. 2008. Conservation and development in tropical forest landscapes: A time to face the trade-offs? *Environmental Conservation* 34: 276–279.

Susskind, Lawrence, and Jeffrey Cruikshank. 1987. *Breaking the impasse: Consensual approaches to resolving public disputes.* New York: Basic Books.

Swart, Jac. A. A. 2004. The wild animal as a research animal. *Journal of Agricultural and Environmental Ethics* 17: 181–197.

Taylor, Bob Pepperman. 1996. *America's bachelor uncle: Thoreau and the American polity.* Lawrence: University Press of Kansas.

———. 2004. *Citizenship and democratic doubt: The legacy of progressive thought.* Lawrence: University Press of Kansas.

Taylor, Paul W. 1986. *Respect for nature: A theory of environmental ethics.* Princeton, NJ: Princeton University Press.

Terborgh, John. 1999. *Requiem for nature.* Washington, DC: Island Press.

Thomas, Chris D., Alison Cameron, Rhys E. Green, Michel Bakkenes, Linda J. Beaumont, Yvonne C. Collingham, Barend F. N. Erasmus, Marinez Ferreira de Siqueira, Alan Grainger, Lee Hannah, Lesley Hughes, Brian Huntley, Albert S. van Jaarsveld, Guy F. Midgley, Lera Miles, Miguel A. Ortega-Huerta, A. Townsend Peterson, Oliver L. Phillips, and Stephen E. Williams. 2004. Extinction risk from climate change. *Nature* 427: 145–148.

Thomas, Craig W. 2003. *Bureaucratic landscapes: Interagency cooperation and the preservation of biodiversity.* Cambridge, MA: MIT Press.

Thompson, Paul B. 2010. *The agrarian vision: Sustainability and environmental ethics.* Lexington: University Press of Kentucky.

Thoreau, Henry David. 1985. *A week on the Concord and Merrimack rivers; Walden, or, Life in the woods; the Maine Woods; Cape Cod.* New York: Library of America.

Trainor, Sarah F. 2006. Realms of value: Conflicting natural resource values and incommensurability. *Environmental Values* 15: 3–29.

———. 2008. Finding common ground: Moral values and cultural identity in early conflict over the Grand Staircase–Escalante National Monument. *Journal of Land, Resources, and Environmental Law* 28: 331–359.

Tyndale-Biscoe, C. H. 1994. Virus-vectored immunocontraception of feral mammals. *Reproduction, Fertility and Development* 6: 281–287.

VanDeVeer, Donald, and Christine Pierce, eds. 2002. *The environmental ethics and policy book.* Third edition. Belmont, CA: Wadsworth.

Van Driesche, Jason, and Roy Van Driesche. 2004. *Nature out of place: Biological invasions in the global age.* Washington, DC: Island Press.

Varner, Gary E. 1991. No holism without pluralism. *Environmental Ethics* 13: 175–179.

———. 1998. *In nature's interests? Interests, animal rights, and environmental ethics.* Oxford, UK: Oxford University Press.

Veatch, Robert M., Amy M. Haddad, and Dan C. English. 2009. *Case studies in biomedical ethics.* New York: Oxford University Press.

Vucetich, John A., and Michael P. Nelson. 2007. What are 60 warblers worth? Killing in the name of conservation. *Oikos* 116: 1267–1278.

Wallace, James D. 1996. *Ethical norms, particular cases.* Ithaca, NY: Cornell University Press.

Walters, Carl J. 1986. *Adaptive management of renewable resources.* New York: Macmillan.

Walzer, Michael 1981. Philosophy and democracy. *Political Theory* 9: 379–399.

———. 2007. *Thinking politically: Essays in political theory.* New Haven, CT: Yale University Press.

Warren, Mark. 1992. Democratic theory and self-transformation. *American Political Science Review* 86: 8–23.

Weart, Spencer R. 2008. *The discovery of global warming.* Revised and expanded edition. Cambridge, MA: Harvard University Press.

Wenz, Peter S. 1993. Minimal, moderate, and extreme moral pluralism. *Environmental Ethics* 15: 61–74

Westbrook, Robert B. 1991. *John Dewey and American democracy.* Ithaca, NY: Cornell University Press.

———. 2005. *Democratic hope: Pragmatism and the politics of truth.* Ithaca, NY: Cornell University Press.

Weston, Anthony. 1985. Beyond intrinsic value: Pragmatism in environmental ethics. *Environmental Ethics* 7: 321–339.

Westra, Laura. 1994. *An environmental proposal for ethics: The principle of integrity.* Lanham, MD: Rowman and Littlefield.

———. 2009. Why Norton's approach is insufficient for environmental ethics. In *Nature in common? Environmental ethics and the contested foundations of environmental policy,* edited by Ben A. Minteer, 49–64. Philadelphia: Temple University Press.

White, Lynn, Jr. 1967. The historical roots of our ecologic crisis. *Science* 155: 1203–1207.

Wiens, John A. 2009. Landscape ecology as a foundation for sustainable conservation. *Landscape Ecology* 24: 1053–1065.

Williams, John W., and Stephen T. Jackson. 2007. Novel climates, no-analog plant communities, and ecological surprises: Past and future. *Frontiers in Ecology and Evolution* 5: 475–482.

Williams, Ted. 1997. The ugly swan. *Audubon* 99: 26–32.

Wilson, E. O. 2002. *The future of life.* New York: Alfred A. Knopf.

Wilson, P. Eddy. 1995. Emerson and Dewey on natural piety. *Journal of Religion* 75: 329–346.

Wise, Steven M. 2000. *Rattling the cage: Toward legal rights for animals.* New York: Perseus Books.

———. 2003. *Drawing the line: Science and the case for animal rights.* New York: Perseus Books.

Wondolleck, Julia M., and Steven L. Yaffee. 2000. *Making collaboration work: Lessons from innovation in natural resource management.* Washington, DC: Island Press.

Wu, Jianguo, and Orie L. Loucks. 1995. From balance of nature to hierarchical patch dynamics: A paradigm shift in ecology. *Quarterly Review of Biology* 70: 439–466.

Young, Iris. 1996. Communication and the other: Beyond deliberative democracy. In *Democracy and difference,* edited by Seyla Benhabib, 120–136. Princeton, NJ: Princeton University Press.

Zalasiewicz, Jan, Mark Williams, Will Steffen, and Paul Crutzen. 2010. The new world of the Anthropocene. *Environmental Science and Technology* 44: 2228–2231.

Zavaleta, Erika S., Richard J. Hobbs, and Harold A. Mooney. 2001. Viewing invasive species removal in a whole ecosystem context. *Trends in Ecology and Evolution* 16: 454–459.

Index

Ben A. Minteer is Associate Professor of Environmental Ethics and Policy in the School of Life Sciences and Senior Sustainability Scholar in the Global Institute of Sustainability at Arizona State University. He is the author of *The Landscape of Reform: Civic Pragmatism and Environmental Thought in America* and the editor of *Nature in Common? Environmental Ethics and the Contested Foundations of Environmental Policy* (Temple).